Palgrave Macmillan Studies in Banking and Financial Institutions
Series Editor: **Professor Philip Molyneux**

The Palgrave Macmillan Studies in Banking and Financial Institutions are international in orientation and include studies of banking within particular countries or regions, and studies of particular themes such as Corporate Banking, Risk Management, Mergers and Acquisitions, etc. The books' focus is on research and practice, and includes up-to-date and innovative studies on contemporary topics in banking that will have global impact and influence.

Titles include:

Yener Altunbaş, Blaise Gadanecz and Alper Kara
SYNDICATED LOANS
A Hybrid of Relationship Lending and Publicly Traded Debt

Yener Altunbaş, Alper Kara and Öslem Olgu
TURKISH BANKING
Banking under Political Instability and Chronic High Inflation

Elena Beccalli
IT AND EUROPEAN BANK PERFORMANCE

Paola Bongini, Stefano Chiarlone and Giovanni Ferri (*editors*)
EMERGING BANKING SYSTEMS

Vittorio Boscia, Alessandro Carretta and Paola Schwizer
COOPERATIVE BANKING: INNOVATIONS AND DEVELOPMENTS

Santiago Carbó, Edward P. M. Gardener and Philip Molyneux
FINANCIAL EXCLUSION

Allessandro Carretta, Franco Fiordelisi and Gianluca Mattarocci (*editors*)
NEW DRIVERS OF PERFORMANCE IN A CHANGING FINANCIAL WORLD

Violaine Cousin
BANKING IN CHINA

Franco Fiordelisi and Philip Molyneux
SHAREHOLDER VALUE IN BANKING

Hans Genberg and Cho-Hoi Hui
THE BANKING CENTRE IN HONG KONG
Competition, Efficiency, Performance and Risk

Carlo Gola and Alessandro Roselli
THE UK BANKING SYSTEM AND ITS REGULATORY AND SUPERVISORY
FRAMEWORK

Elisabetta Gualandri and Valeria Venturelli (*editors*)
BRIDGING THE EQUITY GAP FOR INNOVATIVE SMEs

Munawar Iqbal and Philip Molyneux
THIRTY YEARS OF ISLAMIC BANKING
History, Performance and Prospects

Kimio Kase and Tanguy Jacopin
CEOs AS LEADERS AND STRATEGY DESIGNERS
Explaining the Success of Spanish Banks

M. Mansoor Khan and M. Ishaq Bhatti
DEVELOPMENTS IN ISLAMIC BANKING
The Case of Pakistan

Mario La Torre and Gianfranco A. Vento
MICROFINANCE

Philip Molyneux and Munawar Iqbal
BANKING AND FINANCIAL SYSTEMS IN THE ARAB WORLD

Philip Molyneux and Eleuterio Vallelado (*editors*)
FRONTIERS OF BANKS IN A GLOBAL WORLD

Anastasia Nesvetailova
FRAGILE FINANCE
Debt, Speculation and Crisis in the Age of Global Credit

Dominique Rambure and Alec Nacamuli
PAYMENT SYSTEMS
From the Salt Mines to the Board Room

Catherine Schenk (*editor*)
HONG KONG SAR's MONETARY AND EXCHANGE RATE CHALLENGES
Historical Perspectives

Andrea Schertler
THE VENTURE CAPITAL INDUSTRY IN EUROPE

Alfred Slager
THE INTERNATIONALIZATION OF BANKS

Noël K. Tshiani
BUILDING CREDIBLE CENTRAL BANKS
Policy Lessons for Emerging Economies

Palgrave Macmillan Studies in Banking and Financial Institutions
Series Standing Order ISBN 978-1-4039-4872-4

You can receive future titles in this series as they are published by placing a standing order. Please contact your bookseller or, in case of difficulty, write to us at the address below with your name and address, the title of the series and the ISBN quoted above.

Customer Services Department, Macmillan Distribution Ltd, Houndmills, Basingstoke, Hampshire RG21 6XS, England

---

Cooperative Banking: Innovations and Developments

Edited by

Vittorio Boscia

Alessandro Carretta

Paola Schwizer

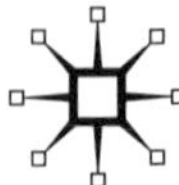

First published 2009 by
PALGRAVE MACMILLAN

Palgrave Macmillan in the UK is an imprint of Macmillan Publishers Limited, registered in England, company number 785998, of Houndmills, Basingstoke, Hampshire RG21 6XS.

Palgrave Macmillan in the US is a division of St Martin's Press LLC, 175 Fifth Avenue, New York, NY 10010.

Palgrave Macmillan is the global academic imprint of the above companies and has companies and representatives throughout the world.

Palgrave® and Macmillan® are registered trademarks in the United States, the United Kingdom, Europe and other countries.

ISBN-13: 978-1-4039-9669-5   hardback
ISBN-10: 1-4039-9669-5   hardback

This book is printed on paper suitable for recycling and made from fully managed and sustained forest sources. Logging, pulping and manufacturing processes are expected to conform to the environmental regulations of the country of origin.

A catalogue record for this book is available from the British Library.

Library of Congress Cataloging-in-Publication Data

Co-operative banking: innovations and developments/[edited by]
   Vittorio Boscia, Alessandro Carretta, Paola Schwizer.
      p. cm.—(Palgrave Macmillan studies in banking and financial
   institutions)
   Includes index.
   ISBN 978-1-4039-9669-5
   1. Banks and banking, Cooperative. I. Boscia, Vittorio. II.
   Carretta, Alessandro. III. Schwizer, Paola.
   HG2035.C6 2009
   334'.2—dc22   2008041042

10   9   8   7   6   5   4   3   2   1
18   17   16   15   14   13   12   11   10   09

Printed and bound in Great Britain by
CPI Antony Rowe, Chippenham and Eastbourne

Contents

Figures

Tables

Notes on Contributors

Simona Cosma is Lecturer in Banking and Finance at the University of Salento (Italy). She holds a Ph.D. in Banking and Finance from the University of Rome Tor Vergata. Her research interests and publications include risk management and bank organization and marketing. She has been also coordinator and lecturer in professional training courses for banks, and has acted as a consultant for the Italian Bankers' Association.
Email: s.cosma@economia.unile.it

Matteo Cotugno is a Postdoctoral Fellow in Banking and Finance in the Department of Management at University of Bologna. He holds a Ph.D. in Banking and Finance from the University of Rome Tor Vergata. His research interests and publications include corporate and investment banking, financial accounting, performance management and measurement in banking.
Email: m.cotugno@unibo.it

Roberto Di Salvo, economist, M.Phil. in Banking and Finance, is Deputy General Manager at Federcasse – Credito Cooperativo. He supervises several offices dealing with economic research, financial regulation analysis and implementation, international relations and strategic projects. He is also editor of the quarterly journal *Cooperazione di Credito* and frequently writes papers and essays on banking and cooperative issues.
Email: rdisalvo@federcasse.bcc.it

Franco Fiordelisi (MA, Ph.D.) is Professor in Banking and Finance at the Faculty of Economics 'Federico Caffè' of the University of Rome III, Italy. He is a member of the academic board for Ph.D.s in Banking and Finance at the University of Rome Tor Vergata. He is also Visiting Research Fellow at the University of Essex, UK. His main research interest is the economics of the banking and other financial institutions focusing on efficiency, productivity and shareholder value creation. His research has been published in the *Journal of Banking and Finance*, *Applied Economics*, OMEGA - The International Journal of Management Science

and other leading academic journals. He recently published *Shareholder Value in European Banking* (Palgrave Macmillan 2007) and *New Drivers of Performance in a Changing Financial World* (Palgrave Macmillan 2008). He has acted as a consultant to many banks and leasing and factoring companies.
Email: fiordeli@uniroma3.it

Claudio Giannotti is Associate Professor of Banking at the University LUM Jean Monnet of Casamassima, Bari. He is the Director of the Laboratory of Real Estate Finance with a Ph.D. in Banking and Finance from the University of Rome Tor Vergata. His research interests and publications include the relationship between banks and companies, credit and real estate securitization, the real estate market and portfolio management.
Email: giannotti@lum.it

Valeria Stefanelli is a Postdoctoral Fellow in Banking and Finance at University of Salento, Lecce, and Visiting Research Fellow, University of Wales, Bangor, UK. She holds a Ph.D. in Banking and Finance from the University of Rome Tor Vergata. Her research interests and publications include corporate governance and internal control systems in financial intermediaries, mergers and acquisitions, and bank management and organization.
Email: v.stefanelli@economia.unile.it

About the Editors

Vittorio Boscia (MA, Ph.D.) is full Professor in Banking in the Faculty of Economics 'Antonio de Viti de Marco' at University of Salento, Lecce, Italy. He holds a B.Sc. (Economics) degree from the University of Bari, Italy, and an MA and a Ph.D. from the University of Wales, Bangor, UK. He is a member of the academic board for Ph.D.s in Banking and Finance at the University of Rome Tor Vergata. He is Visiting Researcher at the School for Business and Regional Development, University of Wales, Bangor, UK. He is the author of a number of articles on several topics, including structure and efficiency of banking systems, small and cooperative banks, and regulation. At present he is researching in the areas of corporate banking, project financing and public finance.
Email: v.boscia@economia.unile.it

Alessandro Carretta is full Professor in Financial Markets and Institutions and Director of the Ph.D. Programme in Banking and Finance at the University of Rome Tor Vergata. He has been teaching banking and finance for more than 25 years, formerly at the universities of Urbino, Lecce and Milan Bocconi. His main research interest is banking management, focusing on banking groups and diversification, regulation and control, and corporate governance, culture and organizational change in banks. He has published in this area more than 100 books and articles in academic journals. Professor Carretta is a member of the committees and boards of several journals, research bodies and financial institutions.
Email: carretta@uniroma2.it

Paola Schwizer is full Professor of Banking at University of Parma and Professor at SDA Business School, Milan Bocconi University. She is the author of several publications in the fields of banking strategies and organization, corporate governance and internal control systems of financial institutions, regulation and competition in the financial system, corporate banking and financial services for SMEs, and value creation in banks and other financial institutions.
Email: paola.schwizer@unipr.it

Preface

Cooperative banks have traditionally played a central role in the economic and social development of their members and of the territories where they operate, while remaining stable, profitable and competitive economic entities. Many theoretical and empirical analyses on cooperative banks have been conducted by policymakers, academics and practitioners in order to investigate the reasons for this performance; but these studies have not produced unambiguous results and, in the meantime, have not exhausted all the arguments which dominate this issue. Moreover, while cooperative banks share specific common roots – that is, cooperation, mutuality, locality, member-ownership, ethics, solidarity, social cohesion, etc. – their business models have evolved differently over the centuries and within each country or continent.

These traditional arguments should be revised in the light of the recent trends in the economy and in financial sectors, such as globalization, innovation, deregulation, firm's size and shareholders value. These changes are dramatically and rapidly changing *inter alia* the structure and the playing field of cooperative banking systems around the world.

The attention of analysts is at present drawn to the 'modernity' of the traditional features of cooperation in banking, to the likely impact of the new trends – economic, social and legislative – on this kind of bank, and to how their competitive advantages evolve. The main goal of this book is to provide some insights into issues, basing the analysis on theoretical argument and empirical evidence.

The book is structured in two parts. The first part gives an account of the current role and rationale of cooperation in the economy and in the banking industry. It deals with some of the more significant characteristics of cooperative banks, such as regulation, institutional models, the role of member-customers, governance, capital and human resources, shareholder value and rating methodologies. The second part provides a more detailed account of cooperative banking, with an analysis of the supervisory regulations and rules that are likely to have a pervasive impact on the organizational and operational models of cooperative banks, especially in Europe.

The completion of this book is the result of the contributions and assistance of many people. First, we wish to express our gratitude to Professor Phil Molyneux, of the University of Wales, who encouraged us to embark on this study. We are also grateful to all the authors who contributed to the book. Finally, a special word of thanks goes to Lisa von Fircks, of Palgrave Macmillan, for her kind and professional support and understanding during the production of this study.

1
Introduction

V. Boscia, A. Carretta and P. Schwizer

Cooperative banks have been considered central players in economic and social development since the 19th century. Theoretical and empirical analyses identify their crucial role by reference to certain specific features, starting with their cooperative institutional form and their several forms of "proximity". The mission of cooperative banks is to promote the economic interests and the social and economic benefits of their members–customers–employees, within a not-for-profit framework. Their activity is founded on such crucial ideas as mutuality, locality, ethics, solidarity and social cohesion.

The importance of the specific role of cooperatives in banking activity has been recognized at both microeconomic and macroeconomic levels. Cooperative banks provide financial services to local markets, contributing to the economic growth of specific agents like small to medium-sized enterprises, but also individuals, farmers, professionals and residents in rural or outlying zones whose access to finance is often limited by their structural characteristic. Since their customers often coincide with their members, the main focus of cooperative banks – as distinct from commercial banks – is on the quality and the conditions of servicing or financing their customer–members, while profitability is no more than condition for survival.[1] Moreover, cooperative banks provide grants and other kinds of resources, contributing to employment, fostering social cohesion and developing regional and social economies. In this connection, the International Monetary Fund (IMF and World Bank, 2005) refers, at the macroeconomic level, to 'the role of microfinance, cooperative and community bank sectors in determining the degree of access to financial services by all parts of a population and to encourage conditions that would make such institutions sustainable'. Cooperative banks are also important for the stability of the financial system thanks to their sound capitalization, the low risk profile of their assets, the consistency of their performance, their intrinsic stability for peer and social monitoring, and their pioneering of corporate social responsibility among financial firms. Moreover, they provide incentives for competitiveness since they are among the major players in financial systems.

This role stems from the competitive power of cooperative banks, which is quite strong in their local markets. Cooperative banks generally operate in retail banking and have small dimensions. Their business model is a traditional commercial banking one that aims to offer high-quality, state-of-the-art products, at best (fair) prices to their member-customers and to a wider array of customers. They have traditionally been characterized by certain competitive advantages vis-à-vis other banks, such as: better delegated monitoring; proximity to, and stronger local relationships with, their customers; competitors restricted to other small banks; and more efficient control of management. At the same time they also suffer from certain structural and behavioural competitive disadvantages, such as: small dimensions; lower geographical and sectorial portfolio diversification; and fewer resources. Moreover, their flexible and simple procedures may allow decisions to become too informal and to be based excessively on personal factors, especially in lending activity.[2]

While these characteristics have allowed cooperative banks to survive so far, the current debate concerns the validity of the cooperative business model in the new banking environment. The pressures of international factors – namely, globalization, innovation, deregulation, disintermediation and shareholder value – are deeply modifying financial and banking markets.[3] These developments and related policies have generally enhanced the level of competition in banking markets, influencing banks' performance and the quality and price of financial services by squeezing profitability. In response to these changes, more efficient banks have initiated a process of deep restructuring and reorganization. An intensive process of consolidation has led to a reduction in the number of banks and to higher concentration in banking markets, and has reduced the traditional barriers commercial and retail banking, especially at the domestic level.

Cooperative banks face several challenges. Medium-sized and large banks are invading their 'niche' markets; strong competition is forcing them to extend or renew loans to risky customers; the new regulations imposing capital adequacy standards encourage less risk-averse borrowers to seek loans from less sophisticated banks which use simpler credit risk systems approaches; new and greater risks force commercial banks to acquire higher (and more expensive) professional competencies; the increasing quantity and quality of customers' demands requires them to provide a wide array of qualified services and an extensive branch network; technological advances require considerable investment in electronic systems; and 'near-banks' or 'quasi-banks' are increasing their weight in local markets.[4]

Cooperative banks have responded to these increasing competitive pressures. Networks, federations, other centralized organizations or more simple commercial agreements with larger 'producers' support their operations, increasing the efficiency of their back-offices and enabling them to offer a wider array of new products to more sophisticated customers. Moreover, cooperative banks try to increase their average dimension by exploiting economies of scale through consolidations, even if mergers and acquisitions are still made difficult by the banks' special status and culture.

This brief overview of the ongoing changes in the banking industry highlights the need to explore the 'modernity' of the traditional features of cooperative banks, the likely impact of new trends on this type of financial intermediary and the evolution of the cooperative banks' model. The main goal of this book is to provide some insights into, and to discuss specific issues arising from, innovation and development in cooperative banking. In light of this background, the book aims to answer several key questions, namely: what role or function do cooperative banks perform in the financial system? What explains their past and present success? What major challenges do they face? What is the future of cooperative banking?

In order to address these main research questions, the study is divided into two parts, which rely on different kinds of integrated methodologies.

Part One describes the current role and rationale of cooperation in the economy and in the banking industry, and deals with some of the more significant characteristics of cooperative banks, such as regulation, institutional models, the role of member-customers, kinds of governance, the role of capital and human resources, relationships with local communities and outsourcing strategies. Chapter 2 (by V. Boscia and R. Di Salvo) provides a comprehensive review of the relevant theoretical and empirical literature on cooperation in the banking sector, analysing its main characteristics and its current role in the economy in the context of the traditional theory of financial intermediation. The findings of the main literature on these topics are reported, and the past and current roles, both social and economic, of cooperative banks are assessed. Some fundamental ideas like mutuality, principles of democracy and solidarity, localism, adverse selection, information asymmetries and monitoring costs are also discussed. Chapter 3 (by P. Schwizer and V. Stefanelli) explores the corporate governance of cooperative banks. Indeed, in the new environment great emphasis has been placed on corporate governance, which is considered crucial to the safe and sound management of banks. The analysis moves from the theoretical analysis of shareholder and stakeholder views to synthesizing the main features of the governance model of European cooperative banks. Chapter 4 (by V. Stefanelli) discusses concentration in cooperative banking. Concentration is indeed one of the main strategies that the banking industry has adopted in order to meet the higher level of competition in the new environment and to gain a margin of economic efficiency. This chapter aims to investigate what the causes and effects of this kind of "external growth" strategy in the context of cooperative banking in order to assess whether it could be considered a strategic choice compatible with the traditional characteristics and competitive advantages of cooperative banking. Chapter 5 (by A. Carretta) focuses on outsourcing strategies that cooperative banks have adopted in order to overcome their disadvantages in terms of limited dimension, operativeness, geography and culture. The main aspects of outsourcing in the financial services industry are described. The goals of this strategy are also set out, such as simple cost reduction but also the efficiency and effectiveness of the core activities of banks. Thus, the chapter analyses the impact of outsourcing on the organizational, managerial and control dimensions of banks. Finally, it focuses on the special trend of 'outsourcing by category' that characterizes cooperative banking. Chapter 6 (by F. Fiordelisi) focuses on a specific aspect of cooperative banks' performance, namely, shareholder value and efficiency, drawing on a large sample from four European countries. This analysis highlights how the specific features of cooperative banks in the regulatory, governance and managerial fields may explain the differences in shareholder value and cost efficiency improvements in cooperative banking among the largest European banking industries. Finally, Chapter 7 (C. Giannotti) deals with the methodologies used by specialized rating agencies in evaluating default risks in cooperative banking. In this instance performance evaluation is based on an operational methodology. The chapter investigates whether rating methodologies developed for cooperative banks are different from those for other kinds of bank and, particularly, whether the specific features of cooperative banking may be seen as an advantage in terms of credit appraisal.

Part Two of the book paints a more detailed picture of cooperative banks. It provides a detailed analysis of certain supervisory regulations and schemes recently announced and implemented at the European level that will likely have an impact on the organizational and operational model of banks, particularly of cooperative banks in Europe. In particular, Chapter 8 (by S. Cosma) deals with the impact of the new capital requirements, named 'Basel 2', on cooperative banks. Indeed, among the new challenges for cooperative banking, the regulation of capital adequacy is absolutely central. The chapter investigates the likely impact of the new regulatory system on the cooperative banking sector in order to assess whether the New Basel Accord may lead to a competitive advantage or disadvantage for cooperative banks, notwithstanding the fact that the regulatory scheme does not discriminate on the basis of either legal category or organizational model. With reference to the supervisory regulation of internal controls, Chapter 9 (by V. Stefanelli) examines the distinctive features of the proposed framework for cooperative banks. The issue of internal controls is very important and immediate: international regulatory authorities consider internal controls, along with corporate governance, essential for the safe and sound management of each bank, and for the stability of the banking system as a whole. This is even more so in an environment in which the banking business and organizations are becoming more complex. General regulations set by the authorities should be adequately implemented at the bank level, so that they are compatible with the business and organization of each bank. The analysis also encompasses the internal control model developed at the system level. Chapter 10 (by M. Cotugno) describes the main effects of the introduction of the new IAS–IFRS accounting system on cooperative banking. In fact, IAS–IFRS not only affects the administrative sphere of banks, but also involves a cultural change on the part of management, since the delicate (and conflictual) relationship "earning management-accounting standards – incentive contracts" may have a strong impact on bank performance. Moreover, it may also affect the banks' organizational processes and internal controls.

Finally, Chapter 11 summarizes the main findings of the collection and discusses the prospects for cooperative banks in the light of the findings of the research.

Notes

1. See Meijer (1999).
2. See Nakamura (1994); Piot (1997).
3. See Schmidt (2000); ECB (1999; 2004;, 2005); Rybczynski (1988); Pavel and McElravey (1990); White (1998).
4. See Beland (1999).

References

Beland C. (1999), 'Co-operative Banks in a Financial World in Mutation: Challenges and Outlooks', International Co-operative Alliance, http://www.ica.coop

ECB (European Central Bank) (1999), Possible Effects of EMU on the EU Banking Systems in the Medium to Long Term, February.

ECB (European Central Bank) (2004), Report on EU Banking Structure, November.

ECB (European Central Bank) (2005), Report on EU Banking Sector Stability, October.

IMF (International Monetary Fund) and World Bank (2005), Financial Sector Assessment Program–Review, Lessons, and Issues Going Forward, http://www.imf.org/External/np/fsap/2005/022205.htm

Meijer W. (1999), The Future of Co-operative Banking in an Integrated Europe, Presented at ICA Congress and Generally Assembly, Quebec City, August.

Nakamura, L. I. (1994), Small Borrowers and the Survival of the Small Bank: Is Mouse Bank Mighty or Mickey?, *Federal Reserve Bank of Philadelphia*, Business Review, November–December: 3–15.

Pavel C. and J. N. McElravey (1990), Globalization in the Financial Services Industry, *Federal Bank of Chicago*, Economic Perspective, May/June: 3–18.

Piot B. (1997), Il sistema delle relazioni tra le banche cooperative e i soci: il quadro normativo europeo, Paper read at IRCEL Conference 'Motivations and Aims in the Local Cooperative Bank', Rome 27–8 February.

Rybczynski T. M. (1988), Financial Systems and Industrial Re-Structuring, *National Westminster Bank Review*, November.

Schmidt R. H. (2000), The Future of Banking in Europe, *Document de travail*, Centre d'Etudies Prospectives et d'Informations Internationales – CEPII – N, No. 00–22, December.

White W. R. (1998), The Coming Transformation of Continental European Banking?, *Bank of International Settlements*, Working Papers No. 54, Basle.

Part One Overview of Cooperative Banking

2
The Theory and Experience of Cooperative Banking

V. Boscia and R. Di Salvo

2.1 Introduction

Cooperative banks operate in a highly competitive environment. Indeed, a restructuring process is occurring in the banking industry under the pressures of financial market globalization and European integration.

The subsequent enhanced competition has emphasized 'size/dimension' and related features (such as business mix) as a competitive strategy. The outlook of investors, and consequently that of managers, is characterized by profit maximization and short-termism. This has sparked dynamic consolidation activity. This competitive environment and, more generally, financial innovation raise certain questions about the vitality of cooperative banks as financial intermediaries and certain concerns about the future of cooperative banks in terms of their modernity and consequently their survival and profitability. Academics, bankers and policymakers are currently questioning the validity of the cooperative bank model.

In order to study these issues, this chapter presents a brief overview of the evolution of the institutional and competitive environment in which cooperative banks operate, especially in connection with the European banking system. It then examines the main theoretical and empirical literature on the role and rationale of financial intermediaries, the speciality of banks, and the rationale of cooperative banks on the basis of their specific features and their competitive power, identifying both strengths and weaknesses. Finally, the chapter describes some of the main market, technological and regulatory threats to the future of cooperative banks, and cooperative banks main responses to them as they face the new environment.

2.2   The drivers of changes in the European banking system

European cooperative banks are threatened by the pressures of key social, legislative, economic, technological and other factors, both international and European.[1] Worldwide events generally include: globalization, innovation, deregulation, disintermediation, securitization consolidation, shareholders value and profit maximization.[2] Alongside these worldwide factors, the European financial system is involved in other, more specific processes, such as: the completion of the single market programme, with its extension to eastern countries; European monetary union; new policies on public debt; regulatory developments, like structural deregulation and the concomitant supervisory re-regulation; and the privatization process.[3]

These external and internal driving factors, with their interrelationships, deeply affect European financial systems, since these systems have long been controlled, restricted and protected by domestic regulatory frameworks. A first effect concerns the range and kinds of banking activities themselves. The new environment offers financial firms more opportunities to compete, with more freedom in new domestic and foreign markets. Securitization and disintermediation are provoking a generalized decrease in traditional lending and retail deposit banking activities. The introduction of the euro reduces (within the euro area) foreign exchange activities and shifts traditional lending activity from the public sector to the more risky private debtors, and also enhances banking activity in money and capital markets. Globalization and financial innovation are increasing the volume and types of risks managed by banks, deriving, inter alia, from the use of derivatives, international banking, securitization, and so on.[4]

These developments and related policies have generally enhanced the level of competition in European Union banking markets, influencing the quality and the price of financial services. In particular, the increased level of competition, both among financial institutions and among financial markets, is putting pressure on bank profitability. Banking, especially in the most bank-oriented systems, is increasingly threatened by, inter alia, other forms of 'non-bank' financial intermediaries, by asset and liability disintermediation, by new financial products and by new distributive channels. Some financial service prices have decreased, traditional interest margins are under pressure, non-interest income has generally increased, banks are under pressure to cut costs, risk taking has apparently increased, and capital has become a scarcer resource.[5] The deregulation process of lowering the traditional economic, physical and legislative barriers among European financial systems, and between the European countries and the rest of the world, has been accompanied by a number of structural changes in recent years. The number and types of new intermediaries, for example, have increased, and a process of consolidation is increasing the degree of concentration in European markets. This is leading to a reduction in excess banking capacity, which traditionally reflected imperfect competition in the era that preceded the single-market programme.[6] It would appear that competition in financial markets is presently taking the form of competition among national systems rather than among financial firms.

In response to these changes, more efficient banks have initiated a process of deep restructuring and reorganization. For example, an intensive process of consolidation aims to improve bank performance by combining financial, human and technical resources, by increasing banking productivity (i.e. volumes of financial products and services, expertise and skills) and by reducing their costs (exploiting scale economies, rationalizing distribution networks, introducing technology in banking processes), leading to a reduction in the number of banks and to higher concentration in banking markets.[7]

Several institutional, commercial and geographical segments of financial markets have been differently affected by the evolution of the competitive environment. For example, while wholesale and investment banking have long been subjected to these kinds of changes – since these business areas are already international and globalized, and comprise a contestable market – commercial and retail banking remain segmented and represents in many respects the 'last great barrier' to the full integration of European banking market.[8] Indeed, a large number of banks with different institutional forms (savings banks, cooperative banks, popular banks and private commercial banks) and with a geographically (regional or national) limited market have traditionally been protected from competition by domestic regulations,[9] by strong domestic–national peculiarities and by the language barrier.[10] Retail banking is rarely characterised by perfect competition, due to the presence of high entry barriers, such as investments in branch network, technologies, and human capital, and the time needed to form lasting relationships with customers.[11] On the other hand, a growing propensity of customers to demand a wider array of increasingly sophisticated financial products and services is forcing retail banks to update their offerings. Thus, retail banks are competing in the field of meeting the specific needs and expectations of their customers.

All of these structural and competitive changes have helped to shape a more complex and competitive arena, and have presented new corresponding challenges for European financial firms. Past limitations on competition may have protected inefficient managers, who presently have to adopt suitable strategies in order to survive in such a competitive environment.

2.3   The rationale and specialty of banks

The new competitive environment raises certain questions about the vitality of banks as financial intermediaries and certain concerns about the future of cooperative banks. To investigate these issues, this section examines the main theoretical and empirical literature on the role and rationale of financial intermediaries, the speciality of banks and the past rationale of cooperative banks in order to assess whether these factors are still relevant and also to defend a future rationale for cooperative banks.

2.3.1   An overview of financial intermediation theory

The main literature justifies theoretically the need for financial intermediation by reference to, inter alia, the presence in the financial markets of two kinds of friction: transaction costs and asymmetric information.[12] These frictions produce inefficiencies – such as restrictions on the amount of loans or penal conditions, like credit rationing or higher prices for loans[13] – which contribute to imperfect resource allocation and imperfect financial markets, thus preventing direct transfers between users and investors.[14]

In particular, *transaction costs* derive from the fundamental economic costs of financial transactions, like search costs, evaluating creditworthiness, monitoring and auditing borrowers, asset evaluation and trading.[15] Financial intermediaries may reduce these costs since they are able to exploit, inter alia, scale and scope economies which afford them a comparative advantage over direct fund exchange in markets. Although the presence of these forms of transaction cost is evident in financial markets, their magnitude alone is not sufficient to justify the existence of financial intermediaries. These costs have been significantly reduced by developments in financial markets (i.e. telecommunications, computer innovations, increases in financial information, and financial innovation). Consequently, this traditional rationale of financial intermediaries is no longer robust and sustainable in a world where transactions costs are apparently falling.[16]

The modern literature emphasizes the presence of another kind of friction, namely, asymmetric information. When borrowers ask lenders for funds to finance their projects, there is an asymmetric information problem between the two parties to the loan contract. In particular, entrepreneurs (borrowers) have an advantage since they hold more information about the inherent riskiness and returns of their own projects (and of themselves) than do the investors (lenders).[17] This unbalanced distribution of information generates market imperfections, which can also be seen as a specific form of transaction cost.[18] Theory identifies three types of problem deriving from this hidden information. The first is so-called *ex ante* adverse selection: information asymmetries (i.e. hidden characteristics of a project or of the entrepreneurs) prevent lenders from screening projects fully before they approve loans.[19] This problem may lead to the credit rationing phenomenon.[20] The second problem, 'interim moral hazard', concerns the behaviour of borrowers during the period of the contract: in this respect, problems (risks) for lenders stem from possible opportunistic behaviour on the part of borrowers after the approval of loans.[21] Opportunistic behaviour by agents may take the form of, inter alia, putting borrowed funds to alternative uses which are more risky; exerting little effort in fulfilling the agreed aims of projects; and attempting to renegotiate the terms of loan contracts.[22] The third and final information problem is '*ex post* state verification': a costly practice aimed at analysing the possible reasons for the failure of a project in order to punish or audit the failed borrower.[23] Another *ex post* problem of lending markets derives from the 'imperfect enforcement problem': that is, the possible difficulties in compelling borrowers to repay loans. This problem may arise from inefficient legal measures for recovering debts and associated costs, or from borrowers' lack of assets, or from the level of the debt being too low, which would render legal action cost-ineffective.[24]

In summary, these forms of inefficiency make the direct exchange of financial balances between surplus and deficit units difficult. Problems do not derive from the incapacity or inability of lenders to solve information asymmetries or transaction cost or imperfect enforcement problems. Indeed, lenders may adopt suitable *ex ante*, interim, and *ex post* instruments and methodologies to quantify the risk and consequently to assess the return that is consistent with that risk. The real problem derives rather from the cost of the resources (instruments, methodologies, professionals, and so on) which each lender has to bear in order to overcome these imperfections.[25]

2.3.2 Lending markets

In order to overcome these imperfections, lending markets have traditionally applied two concomitant practical solutions.[26] The first is the so-called direct methodology, which aims at solving information problems directly by screening and monitoring borrowers before and after the loan is granted. In particular, with *ex ante* information asymmetry problems it is possible to adopt signalling and screening procedures before drawing up the loan. As for the signalling procedure, according to Leland and Pyle (1977), asymmetric information may be overcome by entrepreneurs who send information about the quality of projects to investors. Borrowers may have the problem of the costs of sending information to investors (which may exceed the benefits), and rendering that information credible to investors. Other costs may derive from providing a 'true' signal to investors about the quality of projects. The signal is represented by the fraction of equity directly invested by entrepreneurs in projects. Whether or not the fraction is significant, it represents the borrower's confidence in the quality of the project, and is a sign of his or her willingness to repay the loan. This signal, too, has a cost, especially for risk-averse entrepreneurs, and it implies that the user has a larger fraction of funds to invest in his project.[27]

According to the 'signalling' approach, financial intermediaries are able to tackle information asymmetries and the problems deriving from signalling more efficiently than individual entrepreneurs can. Indeed, financial intermediaries, with their stable and professional organization, may gather, process and sell good-quality information better and at lower cost than individual firms can. Moreover, financial intermediaries can overcome credibility problems more effectively thanks to the higher quality of their information and of their investments, and as a result they can carry out their business with a greater degree of leverage.[28]

Information asymmetries may also be reduced by screening procedures. Following Boyd and Prescott (1986), a financial intermediary can be considered as a sort of coalition in which each component has a specific function, of which screening and monitoring are the most crucial. Financial intermediaries investigate the risk and return of proposed projects in order to compare projects with each other and with alternative forms of investment. In this respect, financial intermediaries as asset-transformers (dealers) are necessary in the lending market since they can reduce screening and monitoring costs more effectively than individual lenders can.[29]

As for *ex post* information asymmetries, financial intermediaries are necessary because they can minimize loans-contract monitoring and do so more efficiently than individuals can. According to the 'delegated monitoring theory' introduced by Diamond (1984), financial intermediaries (banks) are delegated by lenders (depositors) to reduce the costs of monitoring loan contracts. Intermediaries can minimize these costs since they are better able to exploit economies of scale in information collection and production. Moreover, they avoid free-rider problems[30] and the duplication of monitoring by individuals. Financial intermediaries sort out any incentive problems (delegation costs) by diversification, and can carry out the delegated monitoring with the advantage that no 'private' information is disclosed (thus protecting borrowers' privacy).[31]

Besides direct instruments, financial markets also use indirect practices and mechanisms to reduce enforcement problems. Lenders screen these problems by opportunely setting up the legal terms of loan contracts; that is, lenders provide users with incentives such as covenants to reduce opportunistic behaviour and to increase the probability of loans being repaid.[32] Traditionally, enforcement problems are tackled by structuring the loan in such a way that certain special conditions or covenants are included. For example, lenders request special collateral from borrowers, since collateral provides more *ex ante* information to investors (about the confidence of the borrower in the project, and about his or her intention to repay the loan), and limits moral hazard (preventing dangerous action by borrowers, and simplifying the repayment of loans in the event of the insolvency of borrowers). In addition, lenders request collateral from third persons, as well as additional information, peer monitoring and a larger borrower net worth as collateral.

To summarize, the frictions of financial markets may induce investors and users to favour an indirect (intermediated) circuit of funds, through financial intermediaries, rather than using direct finance in financial markets.[33] The modern rationale of financial intermediaries relies on the effectiveness and efficiency of these operators in reducing these elements of friction more effectively and at lower cost than individual borrowers or lenders can. Indeed, thanks to their structure, organization, and more generally their greater and dedicated resources, financial intermediaries can reduce the risks of investment and the costs of information,[34] allowing a better allocation of resources.[35] At the same time, they can improve the quality and the efficiency of their service.[36] Consequently, the more imperfections there are in financial markets, the more important the role of financial intermediaries is.

Despite the great variety of financial intermediaries currently in existence, the literature considers that banks occupy a special position.[37]

In the following sections, an overview is provided of the main theoretical literature that justifies the speciality of banks, and of some of the main specific features of cooperative banks.

2.4   The role and specialties of banks

It is widely agreed that, in a world with complete contracts and full information, there would be no need for financial institutions in order to achieve an efficient risk allocation.[38] Thus, the modern theory of financial intermediation explains the existence of banks and financial institutions by reference to the presence of certain forms of market imperfection. An extensive economic literature contains different but not mutually exclusive approaches that explain why banks exist. Gordon and Winton (2002) and Freixas and Santomero (2003) provide a wide survey on these approaches and also offer a deep insight into the rationale of bank regulation. Even though such a literature cannot be summarized for the purposes of this book, some parts of it should be singled out in order to better frame the role and position of cooperative financial institutions. Basically, the explanation of the existence of banks rests on three pillars:

(a) the need for the production and management of information about borrowers, which in turn arises from the existence of asymmetric information between lenders and borrowers and takes the form of screening and monitoring bank customers;
(b) the provision of liquidity risk insurance as economic agents are subject to uncertainty and may prefer a banking contract rather than financial securities in order to obtain some *ex ante* insurance; and
(c) the provision of diversified safe assets, which are generated by bank deposits.

These three main pillars can also be considered as the basis of bank regulation, since the peculiar role of banking intermediation calls for a compound set of incentives and controls aimed at reducing or even avoiding the cost of bank failures.

If the recent literature gives extensive answers to questions about the specific role of banks in the financial sector, further answers must be given about the reasons and rationale for the existence of different types of bank. Commercial banks (investor-owned and profit maximizing) are one of the most ancient forms of capitalistic organization, existing well before the Industrial Revolution. With the global expansion of market economies around the world, other organizational forms have emerged, competing, often successfully, mainly in retail banking and insurance. If the profit-maximizing firm is the most efficient organization in the typical neo-classical model, this variety of organizational forms may be explained by both government regulation and other forms of protection, or by specific market failures that are successfully addressed by these different organizational forms.

As analysed in the previous section, market failures in financial markets are due to imperfections which spring from asymmetric information problems. Furthermore, banking regulation stems from the need for a rational government response to these imperfections and, most definitely, to the risk of market failures. The recent economic literature has argued that ownership structures and organizational forms are indeed an endogenous result of rational choices made by agents facing market failures. According to Cuevas and Fischer (2006), at least three different and complementary approaches can be cited in order to understand how institutional features may deal more effectively with market failures.

The first approach has been developed within agency theory. Indeed, so-called agency problems arise because writing and enforcing contracts are not costless. Agency costs include the costs of structuring, monitoring and bonding a set of contracts among agents with conflicting interests, along with the residual loss incurred because the costs of the full enforcement of contracts exceed the benefits.[39] In financial institutions, contracts and agents are endowed with the peculiar nature of financial intermediation, in which the existence of asymmetric information between lenders and borrowers is agreed to be a key issue for evaluating how agency problems may be tackled and sorted out by banking contracts.

The second approach is related to transaction costs and hinges on the analysis of frictions and distortions in financial contracts and functions. Merton and Bodie (2005) state that, '… the particular institutions and organizational forms that arise within the financial system are an endogenous response to minimize the costs of transaction frictions and behavioural distortions in executing the financial functions common to every economy'. Within this approach, it is agreed that the firm's choice between issuing capital and issuing direct debt may basically depend on the degree of specificity of any investment, where significant firm-specific investments normally call for capital funds rather then debt issues. As long as lending covenants may be negotiable and adjustable over time, bank lending contracts may act as an intermediate form of contract between capital and direct debt.

The third approach is based on property right theory, in which a firm is first defined by its non-human assets; second, in the absence of comprehensive contracts, decisions need to be taken over how these assets are used. The theory argues that 'the authority to make such decisions ultimately rests with the owner(s) of the firm'.[40] The degree of separation between owners and managers, and the uniformity of interests and values among shareholders or members, may be two components relevant for assessing the viability and efficiency of different property right models.

2.5   A stylized model of cooperative banks

According to this framework and context, the role of cooperative banks can first be analysed by looking at their property rights structure and membership. In this regard, cooperative banks are distinct from other intermediaries in four senses:

(1) the owner-members are also clients of the bank, and the main objective of the bank is the fulfilment of members' well-being (mutuality);
(2) the borrower-members are largely represented by small business owners and small and medium-sized firms within the community (relationship-based conduct);
(3) the voting mechanism is based on the 'one member one vote' principle, with no possibility of unbundling voting and membership (economic democracy); and
(4) profit distribution is normally restrained since capitalization is basically fulfilled through retaining annual earnings (not-for-profit and mutuality).

Why do these features justify a specific role for cooperative banks, and why are they believed to reduce asymmetric information and the risk of market failure?

First, the capacity of a cooperative bank to reduce agency costs: a business organization, in order to survive, must supply goods and services at prices no higher than those of other forms of organization and still cover the costs. 'An organizational form survives in an activity when the costs and benefits of its residual claims and the approaches it provides to controlling agency problems combine with available production technology to allow the organization to deliver products at lower prices than other organizational forms.'[41] Thus, the presence of agency costs explains why different business organizations coexist, and cooperative banks may have a peculiar viable function. Indeed, it is widely agreed in the literature that a cooperative bank is able to lower agency costs between customer-members and the bank itself due to a 'peer monitoring' mechanism, which reduces asymmetric information on the part of customer-members.[42] On the one hand, the cost of screening and monitoring customer-members may be lower in a cooperative bank as information is more easily accessible, and soft information about the borrower is normally coupled with hard information, so enhancing the quality and scope of available data on his or her credit history. On the other hand, the peer monitoring acts also as a form of contract enforcement, since the risk of social and moral sanctions within the cooperative bank's community may be considered as a strong incentive to reduce free-riding or even fraudulent behaviours. According to the same conceptual tool, cooperative banks may be endowed with greater social interaction and mutual trust between bank loan officers and small business owners, which in turn can be converted into lower monitoring costs for the bank and better credit terms for the firm. Since small firms do not usually provide for good-quality data and structured, formalized information on business conduct, a thorough knowledge of the firm's economic and financial situation and of the quality of its investment projects necessarily implies the acquisition of private, unstructured information (soft information) and the use of relationship-lending technology. From this point of view, the key figure is the bank's loan officer, who is the repository of the soft information the bank has acquired about the firm and the local environment. However, the exploitation of this role involves a trade-off between the need to grant the loan officer considerable leeway in deciding which projects are to be financed and the minimization of agency costs. Thanks to their few hierarchical levels and their local nature, cooperative banks can have an advantage over other banks in managing this trade-off. This advantage may turn into greater incentives for bank staff to accumulate soft information and lower agency costs for the bank.[43]

Second, some more conceptual tools are offered by transaction cost economics: if small enterprises normally engage in firm-specific investments and demand capital rather than direct debt, the cooperative bank may efficiently offer bank debt as an intermediate negotiable form of financing, relying on a greater capability to negotiate covenants with the customer.[44] Thus, the proximity of the firm and the peculiar nature of the customer relationship give the cooperative bank some transaction-cost-specific advantages which may foster the placement of lending contracts at small enterprises. However, it can also be argued that this advantage is not unique to cooperative banks, since it does not necessarily stem from their cooperative nature but rather is related to the relationship-based approach to lending to businesses.

Third, property rights theory generally agrees with the hypothesis that the separation between owners and managers in a cooperative firm is rather severe, basically due to its wide and fragmented dispersed ownership, and hinders the efficient allocation of property rights. A high degree of separation between ownership and management may actually foster divergence of objectives among different stakeholders of a cooperative firm, reducing its efficiency,[45] and bring about expense-preference behaviours on the part of managers.

Nevertheless agency costs due the internal decision process may be lowered as the chain of decisions is usually shorter in a cooperative bank; in this respect, the separation between the ownership of the bank and its management may be reduced. Separation may also be reduced by appointing only members as managers of the firm and fostering members' participation at the annual general meeting and other social events. Moreover, new members are usually accepted if their 'personal value', together with other financial information, ensures credibility and consistency with the common cooperative principles and values.

2.6   Main features of the cooperative banking industry

The incentives and mechanisms described above depict a specific model of banking intermediation which is endowed with the basic principles of a cooperative bank. Nevertheless the essential features of this peculiar form of banking intermediation, as reported in the four points listed above, may differ significantly across the cooperative banks industry worldwide.[46] Moreover, cross-country diversification has also taken place in a long historical process, which cannot be properly analysed for the purposes of this chapter.

It may be useful to point out here features which may strengthen or weaken the rationale of the cooperative bank model. Thus, a classification of different forms of contemporary cooperative banking may be useful, even though it can never be considered exhaustive and definitive with respect to the different legal and regulatory frameworks that have been implemented in light of country-specific features.

The first cluster that may be singled out is that of cooperative banks with a large membership base, a wide business scope and an extensive operational area. Generally speaking, large cooperative banks take the form of a *banque populair* (*Volksbank* in German, *banca popolare* in Italian), which is based on the Schulze–Delitzsch model, named after its German promoter.[47] This model was developed in Germany during the second half of the 19th century and then spread over the rest of Europe and also to Canada.[48] The rationale of this model was the establishment of cooperative banks in urban areas as the expression of the emerging classes (traders, craftsmen, small and medium-sized firm owners, professionals) in that period, which needed more and more financially assistance and could not raise adequate resources from traditional commercial banks. Therefore, the development of cooperative banking was strictly related to the urbanization process and economic and the growth of the urban classes in most European countries. Nowadays, large urban cooperative banks turn out to be significantly endowed with both a highly dispersed membership base and a full retention of the one-member-one-vote principle, resembling the governance model of a non-contestable public company. Within this setting, most of the incentives and mechanisms that leave cooperative banks with significant advantages vis-à-vis commercial banks seem to be lessened. Indeed, the peer monitoring mechanism and the threat of social sanctions may be practically phased out by the urban dimension, while asymmetric information problems may arise with the enlargement of operational areas. Thus, the relationship-based approach of banking conduct, coupled with a strong customer base among small and medium-sized enterprises, can still be considered as one of the incentives which may give large cooperative banks a viable, competitive market position and ensure a specific role for them. Nevertheless property rights problems arising from a highly diversified membership may reduce the effectiveness of such a model, as the degree of separation between members and management increases with the fragmentation of membership, bringing about a higher risk of diverging interests among stakeholders.

A second cluster consists of small, local cooperative banks with strong mutual features. Indeed, they may be considered as those which retain most of the incentives and mechanisms justifying a specific function, with respect to other banks, in dealing with market failures and asymmetric information problems in local markets. This is basically the *Raiffeisen* model, which may be considered complementary to that of Schultze-Delitzsch as it was originally developed in rural areas to combat usury and to meet the basic financial needs of the rural population.

Peer monitoring due to the cooperative structure is made stronger and more effective by the focus on the local area and community, which also increases the efficacy of the threat of social and moral sanctions against fraudulent and opportunistic behaviours. Mutuality principles, which rest on the fulfilment of member-customers' well-being with significant limitations on profit distribution, provide further incentives for the functioning of the peer monitoring mechanism. Moreover, the relationship-based approach to banking business is strengthened by some degree of exclusivity of lending relations with small and very small local firms, which implies the enhancement of the cooperative-bank-specific information advantage. Finally, typical property rights problems may be eased in small mutual cooperatives as the degree of separation between members and managers can be significantly less, and the homogeneity of interests within the bank is likely to be higher, reducing the risk of inefficient conduct.

A third cluster may be identified comprising small, local cooperative banks which share certain core cooperative features of the other two clusters: basically, they maintain a local stance and are usually rooted in a well-defined community, which in turn foster relationship-based business conduct and facilitate both the peer monitoring function and the effectiveness of social and moral sanctions. At the same time, they may retain only a few principles of the cooperative model ('one member one vote'), having lost the mutuality constraint and limitations on profit distribution. On the one hand, the capacity to solve asymmetric information problems in local markets may be reduced as customers do not always need to be also members of the bank, and proximity can only marginally reduce information asymmetries between borrowers and the bank itself. On the other hand, more flexibility in profit distribution policy and the property rights structure may increase the degree of separation between owners and managers and reduce the homogeneity of interests among different types of stakeholder, bringing about governance inefficiencies. This type of cooperative bank may display the main features of both the *banque populair* model and the *Raiffeisen* model, mostly resembling the experience of the small-sized *banque populair* still rooted within a limited and defined local community.

2.7   An overview of the competitive power of cooperative banks

The above analyses have highlighted the main features which distinguish cooperative banks from other kinds of bank. This section aims to assess the competitive power of cooperative banks by identifying their strategic position, distinguishing between strengths and weaknesses.[49] This analysis is vital since, as with other economic actors, the competitive power of cooperative banks is founded on asserting and developing their strengths and on monitoring and controlling their weakness. Thus, they should always assess their strategic dimension in order to determine, for example, whether a specific feature which has been a strength in the past may have lost its positive effect or even been transformed into a weakness.

2.7.1 The strengths of cooperative banks

Generally, cooperative banks base their competitive position on specific features like cooperation, mutuality, ethics, solidarity, and social cohesion. Since cooperative banks usually operate in local retail banking and have small dimensions, they have to be able also to adapt these features to their traditional limited dimensions and market proximity, but also in line with the prevailing trends in banking markets. In this way, they may still play an important economic role in servicing local economies and certain marginal social groups, squarely confronting increased competition.

First, as described above, the specialty of cooperative banks derives from cooperation itself. Cooperation is a special kind of institutional 'philosophy' or set-up that is founded on a few simple principles: mutuality, democracy and not-for-profit. From these features the main competitive advantages of cooperative banks may be derived. A 'cooperative' is defined as 'an autonomous association of persons united voluntarily to meet their common economic, social, and cultural needs and aspirations through a jointly-owned and democratically-controlled enterprise'.[50] Cooperative banks act to promote the well-being of their members, who are also their main clients, as depositors and borrowers: this may lead to a greater loyalty of customers to 'their bank'. Members' 'sense of belonging' is enforced by the principle of 'one member one vote' that leads to a sort of economic democracy and equality that, may drive cooperatives' governance mechanism. Mutuality can also lower agency and delegating costs between banks and their member-customers.[51] In the case of cooperatives, member-shareholders may have more chances and incentives to control and monitor the management of cooperative banks, by reducing their opportunistic behaviour of managers and by acquiring more accessible information on their activity.[52] Another specific feature of cooperatives is their special schemes for profit distribution: they usually impose limitations on the distribution of profits, so that they usually are well capitalized (more retention of profits) and less risky (fewer pressures for profit exercised by their member-shareholders). Another advantage linked with their property rights structure derives from the peer-monitoring mechanism, that is, that specific monitoring or controlling activity performed by members–clients–employees on the possible opportunistic behaviour of other operators and customers.[53]

Second, another competitive advantage of cooperative banks may derive from their limited operational dimension, which implies proximity to their membership base and to their local territory. Geographical proximity to customers may bring a competitive advantage for many reasons. Local cooperative banks may have more and better-quality information about actual and potential customers, and about the socio-economic characteristics of the target market. Thus, they can efficiently and effectively reduce and manage information asymmetries on customers' risk profiles, which could lead to adverse selection and moral hazard problems. This higher level of information (reduced information asymmetry) may help 'proximity' banks to screen (so avoiding adverse selection), to monitor (so avoiding moral hazard), and also to manage insolvency (so avoiding bankruptcy, since the bank is able to investigate the overall wealth and income capacity of the debtor).[54] Moreover, proximity to customers allows banks to know more about not only the risk profile of their customers, but also their financial needs. The more long-standing the financial relationships with their customers, the lower are the information costs that banks bear.[55] Consequently, cooperative banks may better meet these financial needs, applying a customer-oriented approach. Thus, even the relationship with their customer will result strengthened. Such soft information allow banks to serve specific segments of the lending market about which only meagre and low-quality information is usually available and which, consequently, are not served by large banks, which are unable to capture that information. Moreover, proximity banks can exploit this advantage derived from their retail banking activities also to serve their customers who save with them, by both creating and enhancing opportunities to sell new finance and investment products. In summary, customer proximity starts a virtuous information circle, which involves the creation and the development of stronger, more durable, and closer financial relationships with small, local customers. Since proximity banks know their customers well, they are more able to finance them even when they are in financial difficulties, thus further strengthening their relationships with their client firms.[56] Moreover, this advantage is further enhanced by the continuity and the proximity of personnel, which enforces information efficiency and strengthens customer relationships.[57] Indeed, cooperative bank personnel often spend their entire careers in a small and defined market, knowing their customers personally and also their economic and financial characteristics and behaviour. A correlated advantage may, for example, flow from the involvement of local communities that may have a stronger interest in keeping 'their' cooperative banks profitable. Local banks may increase the level of information about local economies, and they may strengthen their relationships with their local customers thanks to their strong interdependence and integration vis-à-vis the local social and economic environment. Moreover, these features are further enhanced by the feature of mutuality, described above.[58] Small dimension and proximity are important for local communities imposing social (or non-economic) sanctions when the opportunistic behaviour of a borrower compromises the wealth of local cooperative banks.[59]

Finally, limited dimension also implies an advantage in terms of organization: a limited organizational form implies simple and less bureaucratized hierarchic structures, characterized by flexibility in decisions and in processes which are more tailored to local customers. Moreover, small, cooperative banks incur lower costs of internal delegation, such as the additional costs of bankers monitoring loan officers' activity.[60] The competitive advantages already mentioned are further enhanced by the specific characteristic of 'localism'.

2.7.2   The weaknesses of cooperative banks

Cooperative banks are also characterized by certain features that can be sources of weakness, influencing negatively their competitive power.

Initially, mutuality itself may turn out to be a disadvantage, for several reasons. Possible 'agency problems' between owners and management derive from the corporate governance of mutual-cooperative banks. In such entities, each shareholder holds just a small share of the bank equity and has few incentives to control the opportunistic behaviour of bank managers.[61] Another disadvantage of mutuality may derive from possible problems in financing banks' strategies to increase their capitalization, notwithstanding that cooperative banks usually run permanent programmes to retain their profits as a way to ensure the gradual, 'organic growth' of their capital. For example, an ordinary event for a cooperative is members cancelling their membership: in this circumstance, cooperative banks experience a natural reduction of their capital. But in some extreme cases, this can lead to a 'run on capital'.[62] Certainly, cooperatives banks encounter specific challenges in accessing financial markets when they need capital for regulatory reasons or to grow externally by acquisitions or to repair unexpected large losses. Cooperative banks may find that supplying their extraordinary demands for capital may be restricted or rendered more costly by their institutional form: indeed, for them it is not so easy to rapidly increase the number of their members, especially when they offer low returns on investments because of statutory limitations on profit distribution among members. The membership of large investors is even smaller. So these limitations discourage investors from choosing to invest in cooperative banks, which reduces these banks' ability to raise capital from markets.[63]

For the large number of small and local cooperative banks, another disadvantage flows from their limited dimensions. First, the portfolios of small cooperative banks are less diversified geographically and sectorially, and consequently have higher risk concentration: their investment activity is concentrated in restricted local markets and their loan portfolios are less diversified. This decreases the quality of their assets and increases the average level of risk.[64] Their limited size has negative implications also in terms of internal operational efficiency. For example, the limited volume of intermediation inhibits the exploitation of economies of scale and entails a heavier operative-cost structure. More generally, a small dimension potentially limits the effectiveness and the efficiency of investments which require a minimum portfolio size. This may lead to a lower investment capacity in technology and in branch networks. A small dimension may represent a market disadvantage as well. For example, small cooperative banks that offer a low diversification of supply to their customers may have less competitive power than larger banks that are able to offer a wider array of products to both local and more sophisticated customers. For example, in the case of clients that prefer to have a unique lending relationship with only one bank (i.e. the 'main bank'), small cooperative banks cannot maintain such a relationship with all their clients, since they do not have enough resources to allocate to all of them. With reference to organizational disadvantages, small cooperative banks have limited ability to recruit highly qualified management and to train their staff.[65] The possibly low level of staffing and the difficulty in training staff may limit small cooperative banks' capacity to respond to trends in financial and banking markets. In addition, flexibility and the low level of bureaucratization of bank decisions, which initially are competitive advantages, may become disadvantages when they allow loan decisions to become too 'informal' and based on 'personal' factors.[66]

Finally, other disadvantages are linked more specifically to localism. This may be a cause for concern because it can lead to a possibly abnormal involvement of banks in the socio-economic conditions of their local communities. For example, local pressure may persuade cooperative banks to finance customers and projects without considering the minimum requirement for the profitability of each investment. Another source of danger may flow from the possible role of political considerations or influential persons in the managements' loan decisions.[67] As a consequence of all these competitive disadvantages, small, local cooperative banks may have limited financial reputations.

2.8   Challenges to, and responses of, cooperative banks

The analyses above have highlighted the role of cooperative banks and their competitive position in banking markets. They are central economic agents that operate successfully in terms of benefiting their member-customers and developing their localities. The traditional conditions for their success comprise their special philosophy (that is, mutuality, solidarity, and so forth), their close and strong relationships with their member-customers, and on their market power in a given locality. Nevertheless since the 1980s cooperative banks have coped with a new competitive background, characterized by new challenges and threats. Thus, in order to continue to be healthy and to succeed in their existing environments, cooperative banks have to be active in developing their competitive power and in reorganizing their structure and their managerial conduct.[68] This section provides an overview of cooperative banks' main responses to the threats and challenges presented by the new environment. Obviously, there is no single scheme that is valid for all banks, since the various competitive advantages and disadvantages assume different weights for individual banks. Nevertheless it has been possible to identify some common strategies that these banks have adopted, based on their typical characteristics.

Although most cooperative banks operate at a local level and in a given territory, probably the greater challenge for them flows from globalization and its determinants, such as liberalization, free trade in goods and services, improvements in technology, and innovations. This process has led to a substantial liberalization of markets that has dismantled the traditional barriers that insulated economic, and particularly financial, actors from open competition. New international banking competitors have entered national markets. This has led to a generalized increase in the level of competition that has restricted the profit margins of banks. Moreover, it has pushed banks to increase their dimensions, to conduct their activities in new sectors and with new products, to diversify the sources of income, to find new sources of capital in financial markets, and to transfer risks by applying the 'originate-to-distribute' model of intermediation as opposed to the more traditional 'buy-and-hold' model. Finally, commercial banks have been stimulated to invade even the traditional local markets of cooperative banks, affecting the latter's power in their niche segment markets (i.e. small loans, sight deposits).

For cooperative banks, these changes are hardly compatible with mutuality principles, let alone with small dimension, with limited resources or with the local activity that characterize many cooperative banks. For example, globalization has directed the attention of banks to maximizing value for shareholders. In addition, the privatization that has occurred in some banking markets has highlighted the concept of 'value creation' for shareholders. In fact, this is not a surprising phenomenon: in open markets capital is allocated to where it brings more reward to initial investments in terms of cash flow. Thus, value maximization requires banks to remunerate their shareholders with 'adequate' returns. Cooperative banks, in contrast, offer low returns on investment (partly because of statutory restrictions on profit distribution) and weak incentives to hostile takeovers (because of the principle of 'one member one vote'). In such a context of low dividends and small potential for appreciation, value maximization for cooperatives' members should not be interpreted, as in commercial banks, in term of financial investment only. It has to be interpreted in terms of other benefits,[69] such as financial services for members at low cost, or the development of their locality. Evidently, not all economic actors are willing to accept these limitations.

In order to be competitive in the new environment and to meet the condition of 'value maximisation' for members, cooperative banks have founded their strategies on operational efficiency and on customer–member relationship management. Cooperative banks are aware of new forms of risks which require new models and techniques for their identification, measurement and management, and consequently they have reassessed their operational structure. For example, regarding lending activity, they have improved the quality of their assets (where they can) and of their overall lending products and procedures. Moreover, they have rationalized their operational costs as a crucial contribution to their overall profitability. This has not implied indiscriminate cost-cutting but rather a more productive use of inputs, aiming at obtaining a greater volume of production from the same level of input. This has been possible by reviewing and reorganizing production processes and attempting to obtain higher income from them – for example, by concentrating the most qualified resources in higher value-added sectors or by outsourcing policies.

Cooperative banks have looked particularly to their traditional roles, activities and areas of excellence in order to enhance their present positions. They have initially maintained strong and consolidated relationships with their customer-members, which is a source of one of their key competitive advantages.[70] Their future is linked to small-to-medium-size local firms, which while they continue to be vital still need finance for their projects, which large banks seldom provide. Cooperative banks have improved their ability to manage and enhance relationships with their traditional customers, who otherwise (because of the lowering of 'transfer costs') may be tempted to move to another bank.[71] Establishing new relationship models with customers helps cooperative banks to compete more effectively.[72] With this strategy, cooperative banks have increased customer loyalty and offset the competition of commercial banks. Moreover, increasing their knowledge of their customers allows cooperative banks to maintain their competitive advantages in traditional lending activities, where they can better screen and monitor customers in such typical 'information-intensive' services.[73] This strategy has been even more demanding to the extent that globalization has also led to a generalized increase in the sophistication of customers' needs. Many cooperative banks have redefined their business areas in terms of customers, market segments and products. In a context where many cooperative banks have limited dimensions and resources, they are unable to serve all customer segments or to produce all products internally. Thus they choose which customer segments to serve and which products to provide, and then which products to produce directly and which to acquire from outside. They also eventually need organizational divisions to serve their customers properly. In particular, they have focused their activity on traditional lending, since this provides a relatively stable intermediated volume on which to distribute their fixed costs, and strengthens customer relationships; but they have also integrated it with other products and services, meeting customers' needs for product innovation and diversification. They have strategically sought to maintain or enlarge their lending volumes, but they have also tried to enter less mature markets (such as securities, insurance, and pension funds especially for private individuals, and corporate finance services for firms), in order to help to preserve adequate profitability as well as income diversification. In future, for example, with reference to financing services, in an era of securitization local cooperative banks could provide information to financial markets about the quality of their customers. Because their services are based on better monitoring, cooperative banks can even guarantee the issues of their corporate customers who would otherwise not be eligible to access funds in securities markets.[74] Moreover, cooperative banks also have implemented instruments and methodologies developed in recent years by financial innovation (such as sharing and syndicate schemes, technology used for credit scoring, and asset-backed securities of their own loans), limiting the risks in term of sectorial and geographical concentration.[75]

The new relationship model applied with cooperative banks' member-customers has been confirmed, strengthened and enlarged even in their local territories and communities. Cooperative banks have enforced their role as reference entities in their targeted market as a whole by increasing their participation, support for and involvement in the social and economic initiatives of local communities. This kind of signalling behaviour can be viewed as part of their overall market segmentation, positioning and branding strategies.

Cooperative banks have also accompanied such strategies with a restructuring of their distribution design. Even though branches remain crucial for cooperative banks, for the special relationship with custom-ers is possible only in a physical place, distributional channels have been strongly influenced by technology, another feature of globaliza-tion. Technology becomes an even more crucial factor in banking activ-ity since it has affected the timing and location of the financial services supplied as well as product and process innovations. It has changed the relationships with customers, especially in retail banking services (ATM, POS, telephone banking, virtual banks, and so on). Moreover, technological advances have augmented the mobility of customers, many of whom now base their choice of bank on factors other than branch location alone, thus decreasing the 'loyalty' of customers. Then again, many cooperative banks have integrated more innovative chan-nels (automated and multimedia) into their traditional branches, so as to enhance efficiency (lower costs) and effectiveness (reducing the operational pressures in traditional branches). Obviously, these invest-ments are not always possible for cooperative banks, since they often lack the 'critical' size.

On this point, with the aim of restructuring and reorganizing, coop-erative banks have often coped with one of their main weakness, that is, their small size and the limited availability of capital and of other resources (human and technical). Like many others banks, even cooperative banks have experienced consolidation strategies to increase their size, in order to achieve a critical dimension to obtain operational efficiencies and adequate returns on investments. But consolidation has not always been a suitable strategy for cooperative banks, since it may have a negative impact. Increasing size generally tends to weaken some of cooperative banks' competitive advantages: that is, less information power; weaker customer relationships; less localism; less information for managers and loan officers; less peer monitoring; fewer social penalties; less social control from the local community on bank conduct; more agency problems; and more rigid organizational forms. Then again, consolidation is a powerful strategy, but at the same time, especially for cooperative banks, it may be dangerous. So they should be careful not to lose their local identity and the entire philosophy of mutuality.[76]

Another strategy for cooperative banks to overcome the limitations and the restrictions of limited dimension and resources is the development of trading agreements, alliances and networks with other financial intermediaries or with new entities (i.e. consortiums) set up with other cooperative banks. In particular, a positive experience has flowed from their joining regional and national structures, federations, other centralized organizations. These instruments support cooperative banks' management, activities and organization, allowing them to have more efficient back-offices and to offer a wider array of new sophisticated products to serve more sophisticated customers. In this way cooperative banks enhance their strong local roots with an expansion of and improvement in the supply of financial services (EACB, 2004b). In recent years, they have also created some associations at the supranational level, in order to create organisms for exchanging experiences and designing common strategies.

Finally, policy changes in European banking systems implied, besides deregulation, a need for re-regulation in order to ensure the safe and sound management of banks. Basel 2 and IAS, for example, are two of the main provisions designed by the authorities to set common criteria for banks' capitalization and transparency. Generally, these provisions have imposed on all forms of banks, without distinction, strict requirements in terms of the standardization of policies and operational forms, implying, inter alia, significant compliance costs. Then they could represent a regulatory threat to cooperative banks that may not have the resources to comply with them properly or to do so maintaining their initial equilibrium.

For example, Basel 2 is highly pervasive for all kind of banks. Its capital requirements create a strict correlation between the quantity of risks and the quality of risk management of a bank. An adequate level of capitalization has consequently become important and necessary, both for internal reasons (it can increase the operational capacity of banks) and for regulatory reasons (prudential regulation is founded on capital adequacy requirements). Thus, banks which operate in poor (and risky) markets and with few risk-management competences and skills have to increase their capital so as to be compliant with the new regulatory requirements. Moreover, the extensive disclosure introduced by the 'third pillar' will push cooperative banks to be more 'market-oriented' in terms of disclosure practices and requirements, since they are usually below the standards of commercial banks, especially the listed ones, in this respect.[77] Other prudential challenges flow from the provisions related to corporate governance and internal control procedures, in order to ensure safe and sound bank management and customer relationships. On the other hand, IAS-IFRS aims to increase the level of transparency by unifying the accounting standards also for banks, for example, by basing evaluation on new principles (such as fair value). Such a scheme also implies rapid strategic changes, mainly in terms of the higher level of transparency of risks measures, which is not always possible in cooperative banks. Thus, these examples of provisions show how difficult (and costly) is for a 'de-structured' entity like a cooperative bank to be compliant with the new regulations.

2.10 Conclusions

This chapter has provided an overview of the evolution that has occurred in cooperative banking. The restructuring process has occurred under the pressures of market globalization and, in Europe, of European integration. As a result, the level of competition has increased, and cooperative banks, which have existed for years in their niche of protected and controlled markets, are nowadays being forced to perform their activities in more open and competitive markets.

In order to assess the modernity and the validity of the cooperative bank model, this chapter has dealt with the main literature on the role and rationale of financial intermediaries and the speciality and the rationale of cooperative banks on the basis of their specific features. Their business model aims to offer high-quality, state-of-the-art products, at best (fair) prices to their member-customers. Their proximity with their customers allows and encourages cooperative banks to be rooted (and competitive) in their local markets and to establish long-term relationships with their clients. So cooperative banks can exploit sound and low-cost knowledge to select more accurately their financial position, to identify better their needs, and to monitor better their risks. It has emerged that this model of banking is still necessary for the development of the economy, particularly at the local level, and for the financing of specific segments of banking markets.

Nevertheless specific market, technological and regulatory threats are challenging cooperative banks, especially the more locally focused and those with limited dimension. The new environment forces them to modify their strategies in order to achieve efficiency and profitability. Cooperative banks consequently have to consider restructuring and redesigning their products and processes as well as setting up new operational and organizational structures. Their overall strategies are oriented towards strengthening their relationships with their customers' by enhancing traditional lending activity and reconciling this with more modern services in order to increase progressively their market share and to diversify their sources of income.

Notes

Although the chapter is the result of close cooperation between the authors, sections 2–3 and 7–9 should be attributed to V. Boscia and sections 4–6 to R. Di Salvo.

 1. See Boscia (2002).
 2. See Schmidt (2000); European Central Bank (1999; 2004; 2005); Rybczynski (1988); Pavel and McElravey (1990); Gardener (1995); Economic Research Europe (1997); White (1998).
 3. See Gardener (1995); Economic Research Europe (1997).
 4. See European Central Bank (1999).
 5. See Economic Research Europe (1997).
 6. See European Central Bank (1999).
 7. See Molyneux, Altunbas and Gardener (1996).
 8. See Economic Research Europe (1997).
 9. See Gardener, Howcroft and Williams (1996).
10. See Schmidt (2000).
11. See Vives (1991).
12. Those rationales of intermediaries are proposed by Boyd and Prescott (1986), Leland and Pyle (1977) and Diamond (1984).
13. See, for example, Stiglitz and Weiss (1981).
14. For a review of the literature on this topic see, for example, Allen and Santomero (1996) and Pittaluga (1991).
15. See Benston and Smith (1976).
16. See Freixas and Rochet (1997).
17. See Pagano and Panunzi (1998).

18. See Freixas and Rochet (1997).
19. See Guinnane (1997).
20. Credit rationing is a type of market failure. It emerges when badly informed lenders attribute an average unique and higher value (and price) to all projects, since they are unable to identify, measure and price the risk related to each project. In this way, lenders underestimate the risk of the most risky projects and overestimate the risk of the less risky ones. In this circumstance better firms avoid requesting loans, since they are charged higher prices than expected (based on the true quality of their projects). In this way, over time the average quality of loans in the market deteriorates, leading to market failure (Akerlof, 1970).
21. See Cenni and Corigliano (1996).
22. See Pagano and Panunzi (1998).
23. See Guinnane (1997); Freixas and Rochet (1997).
24. See Guinnane (1997).
25. See Guinnane (1997).
26. Borrowers have two main choices to finance their projects externally. First, they can issue their own debts directly on to financial markets in the form of bonds, commercial papers, and so on: this is called 'direct finance'. The success of any directly placed debt depends, inter alia, on the availability of public information. Usually, this kind of financing is used by firms with a consolidated reputation in financial markets, since a good and consolidated financial reputation helps lenders to judge the quality of the proposed project and the behaviour of the borrower (Pagano and Panunzi, 1998). But only by a few firms in the market enjoy this sort of advantage. Therefore, external financing most commonly takes the form of private debts, which are loan contracts drawn up privately between lenders and borrowers. In this case more asymmetric information problems arise; thus, debt contracts are characterised by a large number of clauses. The most common form of private debt issue is the bank loan: this comprises the second main kind of borrowing, namely, financial intermediation, or so-called indirect finance. With this form of financing, public information is mixed with private information deriving from the costly monitoring activity of financial intermediaries (Diamond, 1991).
27. See Diamond (1984).
28. See Leland and Pyle (1977); Dabrassi (1996).
29. Ramakrishnan and Thakor (1984) provide an explanation of the presence of financial intermediaries as 'pure brokers'. In this case, their rationale depends on the capacity of financial intermediaries to provide the market with reliable information. They avoid the duplication in information production which occurs when individual investors screen firms. For other related justifications of financial intermediaries with asymmetric information, see Freixas and Rochet (1997).
30. Free-rider problems arise when individuals who own a fraction of a loan have no incentive to monitor the loan because the benefits of doing so are not sufficient to cover the expenses, and so leave the monitoring to other lenders (Diamond, 1984).
31. See Diamond (1984).
32. See Hoff and Stiglitz (1990).

33. These problems have been opportunely solved only in a minority of cases, which reveals that financial markets are largely unable by themselves to favour the direct exchange of funds (Hoff and Stiglitz, 1990).
34. Financial intermediaries can share (and diversify) costs among a greater number of transactions, so exploiting returns to scale (Benston and Smith, 1976).
35. See Goodhart (1989).
36. See Dabrassi (1996).
37. Previous reviews of the vast literature on banking include those by Santomero (1984), Bhattacharya and Thakor (1993) and Swank (1996).
38. 'In neoclassical theory, institutions do not matter in the sense that equilibrium prices and the allocation of resources are unaffected by specific institutional structure. As long as markets are efficient and frictionless, one can use almost any convenient financial system in a model analysing asset demands and the derived equilibrium asset prices and risk allocations will be the same' (Merton and Bodie, 2005).
39. See Fama and Jensen (1983).
40. See Hart and Moore (1998).
41. See Fama and Jensen (1983).
42. See Stiglitz (1990).
43. A relevant stream of thought has been developed with respect to the relationship-lending issue. Many authors argue that it may have drawbacks under specified conditions. Thus, some incentives to reduce information asymmetries and the risk of market failures may be offset by drawbacks related to so-called information capture and 'soft budget constraint' problems. See in this regard Bhattacharya and Thakor (1993) and Farinha and Santos (2000).
44. See Pittaluga (1998).
45. See Hart and Moore (1998).
46. See Cuevas and Fischer (2006) at this regard.
47. Hermann Schultze-Delitzsch who worked together with Wilhelm Friedrich Raiffeisen for the establishment of urban cooperative banks and rural credit cooperatives all around Europe.
48. In Europe, they have kept their original naming, while in Canada have assumed that of their promoter Alphonse Desjardins and are still named as Caisses Desjardins, which indeed resemble both the Schultrze-Delitzch and Raiffeisen models.
49. See Fonteyne (2007).
50. See ICA (1995).
51. As discussed above, agency costs arise in any organisation when there are divergences of interest between managers and member-shareholders.
52. See Pagano and Panunzi (1998); Porta (1997).
53. See Kandel and Lazear (1992).
54. See Cannari and Signorini (1995).
55. See Pittaluga (1991).
56. See Arcangeli (1996).
57. See Borroni (1996).
58. Conversely, as the size of a bank increases, its link with its member-clients is loosened. In fact, big cooperatives may have fewer advantages in terms of reducing agency costs and of peer control than smaller ones.

59. See Pagano and Panunzi (1998).
60. See Cerasi and Daltung (1996).
61. See Pagano and Panunzi (1998).
62. See Fonteyne (2007).
63. See Nakamura (1994).
64. See Piot (1997).
65. See Piot (1997).
66. See Nakamura (1994).
67. See Piot (1997).
68. See Laszkiewicz (2004).
69. See Fonteyne (2007).
70. See Piot (1997).
71. The new relationship model is based on developing more personalized relationships with each customer, both on a personal level and by providing more tailor-made services – promoting, for example, those basic services which allow banks to strengthen their links with customers. Another way to enhance customer relationships is to become more transparent in the application of contracts, in pricing financial services, in offering 'tailor-made' financial advice and services, or in encouraging and helping small and medium-size firms to list their shares locally.
72. See Forestieri (1996); Cesarini and Gualtieri (1996); Angelini, Di Salvo and Ferri (1998).
73. See Pagano and Panunzi (1998).
74. See Pagano and Panunzi (1998).
75. See Cesarini and Gualtieri (1996).
76. For cooperative banks, consolidation is also hampered by other factors. Their special status protects them from hostile takeovers (EACB, 2004a). Their 'not-strictly-profit-oriented' nature allows cooperative banks to place less emphasis on the level of performance and then to take under control their risk-taking. Their peculiar ownership and governance protect the management from being subject to the 'take over threat' and to short-terminism (the excessive focus on short-term earnings). Thus, the long-term interests of cooperative banks and their managers coincide with those of their customers. Consolidation is also inhibited by dominant regional–national differences in their 'culture', even though the banks concerned might operate in the same area.
77. See Fonteyne (2007).

References

Akerlof G. A. (1970), The Market for 'Lemons': Quality Uncertainty and the Market Mechanism, *Quarterly Journal of Economics*, no. 84: 488–500.

Allen F. and A. M. Santomero (1996), The Theory of Financial Intermediation, Wharton Financial Institutions Center Working Paper, The Wharton School, University of Pennsylvania, no. 96–32.

Angelini P., Di Salvo R., and Ferri, G. (1998), 'Availability and Cost of Credit for Small Business: Customer Relationships and Credit Cooperatives', *Journal of Banking and Finance*, vol. 22(6), 925–54, 8.

Arcangeli S. (1996), Economia dell'impresa, informazione e banche popolari, Credito Popolare, no. 4: 551–89.

Benston G. J. and C. W. Smith (1976), A Transaction Cost Approach to the Theory of Financial Intermediation, *Journal of Finance*, vol. 31: 215–31.

Bhattacharya S. and A. V. Thakor (1993), Contemporary Banking Theory, *Journal of Financial Intermediation*, no. 3: 2–50.

Borroni M. (1996), Gli istituti centrali di categoria: situazione attuale e prospettive, *Credito popolare*, no. 2: 187–221.

Boscia V. (2002), *The Future of Small Banks in the New Competitive Environment. The Case of the Italian Banking Industry*, Bari: Cacucci Editore.

Boyd J. H. and E. Prescott (1986), Financial Intermediary-Coalitions, *Journal of Economic Theory*, no. 38, April.

Cenni S. and R. Corigliano (1996), I prestiti e la funzione allocativa della banca, in Onado (ed.), *La banca come impresa. Manuale di gestione bancaria* (Bologna: Il Mulino).

Cerasi V. and S. Daltung (1996), The Optimal Size of a Bank: Costs and Benefits of Diversification, Financial Markets Group Discussion Paper, no. 231, London School of Economics.

Cesarini F. and P. Gualtieri (1996), Globalità e localismo nei circuiti finanziari: il ruolo della banca, *Sinergie*, no. 39, January/April: 59–64.

Cuevas C. E. and Fisher K. P. (2006) 'Cooperative Financial Institutions!' World Bank Working Paper no. 82.

Dabrassi C. (1996), *Asimmetrie informative e mercati finanziari. Il ruolo degli enti creditizi* (Milan: Egea).

Diamond D. W. (1984), Financial Intermediation and Delegated Monitoring, *Review of Economic Studies*, vol. 51: 393–414.

Diamond D. W. (1991), Monitoring and Reputation: The Choice Between Bank Loans and Directly Placed Debt, *Journal of Political Economy* 99, 688–721.

EACB (European Association of Co-operative Banks) (2004a), Co-operative Banks in Europe: Values and Practices to Promote Development.

EACB (European Association of Co-operative Banks) (2004b), Vision of European Co-operative Banks: Committed to an Integrated Market.

ECB (European Central Bank) (1999), Possible Effects of EMU on the EU Banking Systems in the Medium to Long Term, February.

ECB (European Central Bank) (2004), Report on EU Banking Structure, November.

ECB (European Central Bank) (2005), EU Banking Sector Stability, October.

Economic Research Europe (1997), A Study of the Effectiveness and Impact of Internal Market Integration on the Banking and Credit Sector. A Summary Report.

Fama E. F. and Jensen M. C. (1983) 'Agency Problems and Residual Claims' *Journal of Law and Economics*, vol. 26, no. 2.

Farinha L. A. and Santos J. A. (2000). 'Switching from Single to Multiple Bank Lending Relationships: Determinants and Implications', in BIS Working Papers, no. 83.

Fonteyne W. (2007), Cooperative Banks in Europe – Policy Issues, IMF Working Paper, WP/07/159.

Forestieri G. (1996), I sistemi bancari tra ristrutturazione ed innovazione, Studi e Note di Economia, Monte dei Paschi di Siena, no. 3: 181–89.

Freixas X. and J. Rochet (1997), *Microeconomics of Banking* (Cambridge: MIT Press).

Freixas X. and Santomero A. M. (2003) 'An Overall Perspective on Banking Regulation'. UPF, Economics and Business Working Paper no. 664.

Gardener E. P. M. (1995), Banking Strategies in the European Union: Financial Services Firms After the Cecchini Report, Institute of European Finance, University of Wales, Research Paper, 95/7.

Gardener E. P. M., B. Howcroft and J. Williams (1996), The New Retail Banking Revolution, *Service Industries Journal*, vol. 19, no. 2.

Goodhart C. A. E. (1989), *Money, Information, and Uncertainty* (London: Macmillan).

Gordon G. and Winton A. (2002) 'Financial Intermediation', Wharton Financial Institution Center Working Paper no. 02–28.

Guinnane T. (1997), Motivazioni e ispirazione originaria delle cooperative di credito: il modello Raiffeisen, Paper read at IRCEL Conference 'Motivations and Aims in the Local Cooperative Bank', Rome 27–8 February.

Hoff K. and J. E. Stiglitz (1990), Introduction: Imperfect Information and Rural Credit Markets – Puzzles and Policy Perspectives, *World Bank Economic Review*, vol. 4, no. 3: 235–50.

Kandel E. and E. P. Lazear (1992), Peer Pressure and Partnerships, *Journal of Political Economy*, vol. 100, no. 4: 801–17.

Hart O. and Moore J. (1998) 'Cooperative vs. Outside Ownership', NBER Working Paper.

ICA (International Co-operative Alliance) (1995), 'Statement of Identity,' in: ICA News Issue 5&6.

Laszkiewicz E. (2004), *Mission of Cooperative Banks in the World. Experiences and Prospects*, International Co-operative Association, Seminar 2004.

Leland H. E. and D. H. Pyle (1977), Informational Asymmetries, Financial Structure, and Financial Intermediation, *Journal of Finance*, vol. 32, no. 2, May: 371–87.

Merton R. C. and Bodie Z. (2005) 'Design of Financial Systems: Toward a Synthesis of Function and Structure', *Journal of Investment Management*, vol. 3, no. 1.

Molyneux P., Y. Altunbas and E. P. G. Gardener (1996), *Efficiency in European Banking* (Chichester: Wiley).

Nakamura L. I. (1994), Small Borrowers and the Survival of the Small Bank: Is Mouse Bank Mighty or Mickey?, *Federal Reserve Bank of Philadelphia, Business Review*, November–December: 3–15.

Pagano M. and Panunzi F. (1998) 'Banche commerciali e banche cooperative: qual è la differenza?', *Cooperazione di Credito* no. 160–1.

Pavel C. and J. N. McElravey (1990), Globalization in the Financial Services Industry, Federal Bank of Chicago, Economic Perspective, May/June: 3–18.

Piot B. (1997), Il sistema delle relazioni tra le banche cooperative e i soci: il quadro normativo europeo, Paper read at IRCEL Conference 'Motivations and Aims in the Local Cooperative Bank', Rome 27–8 February.

Pittaluga G. B. (1991), *Il razionamento del credito: aspetti teorici e verifiche empiriche* (Milan: Franco Angeli).

Pittaluga G. B. (1998) 'La specificità della banca locale cooperativa e i connessi problemi di corporate governance', Cooperazione di Credito no. 160–1.

Porta A. (1997), Assetti proprietari dell'impresa bancaria: un confronto tra i diversi modelli, Paper read at IRCEL Conference 'Motivations and Aims in the Local Cooperative Bank', Rome 27–8 February.

Ramakrishnan R. T. S. and A. V. Thakor (1984), Information Reliability and a Theory of Financial Intermediation, *Review of Economic Studies*, vol. 51: 415–32.

Rybczynski T. M. (1988), Financial Systems and Industrial Re-Structuring, *National Westminster Bank Review*, November.

Santomero A. M. (1984), Modeling the Banking Firm, *Journal of Money, Credit, and Banking*, vol. 16, no. 4: 576–603.

Schmidt R. H. (2000), The Future of Banking in Europe, Document de travail, Centre d'Etudies Prospectives et d'Informations Internationales – CEPII – N. no. 00–22, December.

Stiglitz J. E. (1990), 'Peer Monitoring in Credit Markets', *World Bank Economic Review*, no. 4, 351–66.

Stiglitz J. E. and A. Weiss (1981), Credit Rationing in Markets with Imperfect Information, *American Economic Review* 71, 393–410.

Swank J. (1996), Theories of the Banking Firm: A Review of the Literature, *Bulletin of Economic Research*, vol. 48, no. 3: 173–207.

Vives X. (1991), Regulatory Reform in European Banking, *European Economic Review*, vol. 35: 505–15.

White W. R. (1998), The Coming Transformation of Continental European Banking?, Bank of International Settlements, Working Papers no. 54, Basle.

3
Institutional Models, Role of Shareholders (Member and Customers), Governance

P. Schwizer and V. Stefanelli

3.1 Introduction

In industrialized countries (OECD, 2004), financial globalization and stronger market competitiveness, as well as the large number of corporate malpractice cases which have occurred internationally (such as Enron and Worldcom in the USA, Ahold in the Netherlands, and Parmalat in Italy), have made the enforcement of corporate governance (CG)[1] control mechanisms a priority.

It is believed that effective administrative mechanisms within a company could in principle help increase the reliability, transparency and integrity of corporate behaviour by making bankruptcy less likely. This, in turn, would have the effect of increasing the value of the company, by lowering the cost of capital and increasing the competitiveness of the company on the market. As a result, in recent years a myriad of recommendations, reports, codes and guidelines have been issued by supranational bodies, regulatory authorities and category affiliates aiming to propagate and promote the correct principles of CG within companies. Internationally, 'OECD Principles on Corporate Governance', published in 1999 and revised in 2004, is a key document on banking regulation. It presents the criteria which are needed to define CG. These criteria, which are not binding in any particular country, are among the 12 standards which have been elaborated within the Financial Stability Forum to guarantee the soundness of financial systems, and are often referred to when national codes of self-regulation in the area of corporate governance are drafted.

In banking, the Basel Committee on Banking Supervision has acknowledged the utility of good CG principles even in surveying those banks and authorities which acknowledge OECD's information and adapt it so as to take into account the specificity that is intrinsic to banking (Basel Committee, 2006). In banking supervision, CG methods are considered crucial to ensuring the healthy and conservative management of a bank, which is essential to the banking industry correct running process and its overall economy.

The range of reinforcements, regulations and national codes presented by regulators added to existing laws are meant to make it easier both for intermediaries to improve governance systems – thus making them suitable for the company's size and complexity – and for regulators to evaluate qualitatively the same systems. In fact, the Basel Committee document shows that it is practically impossible to define and promote a governance model that is valid for all banks. Moreover, it acknowledges that in the international market governance structures differ according to the national, regulatory and market settings of any one bank as well as according to the microeconomic factors which are specific to the institutional structure of each individual case (ownership, extent of property concentration and contestability, organizational structure, and so on).

The move from the dominant *shareholder view* (Fama, 1980; Jensen and Meckling, 1976) to the supremacy of the *stakeholder view* (Freeman, 1984; Evan and Freeman, 1988) for the theoretical interpretation of CG models, and the acknowledgement of the relationship between banks and enterprises in banking surveillance schemes, show that the efficiency of such models depends on their ability to correlate long-term potential for success and the satisfaction of all of the bank's converging interests.

Therefore, the way in which governance works, according to an updated interpretation, widens the analytical perspective on the potential conflicts which arise during the bank's decision-making processes: as well as the traditional shareholder–management conflict, which is linked to agency problems, potential conflicts also exist between the bank and the broader profile of the stakeholders to which the bank has long-term commitments, and which must be considered as one of the decisive factors in corporate success.

For cooperative banks, the use of the two theoretical perspectives (shareholder and stakeholder) highlights how their governance model is distinct from that of commercial banks, which means that the shareholder–management and firm–stakeholder agency problems that are explained by the peculiar institutional structure are more complex.

The distinguishing features of the European cooperative bank model include enhanced capital fragmentation, the 'one member one vote' principle, the commitments which arise in the use of profits, and the principle of mutuality (EFMA, 2004; EACB, 2006). If they to some extent improve business relations with certain stakeholders, they also emphasize the areas of conflict that exist between shareholders and management. Similarly, the ownership structure, which is physically fragmented, creates role asymmetries among stakeholders (Schwizer, 1998), highlighting complex firm–stakeholder issues.

In similar situations, CG mechanisms must balance a wider variety of often diverging interests. They have to measure the achievement of objectives which are more ambitious than those of a bank (or of a firm) led by investors, and, in the absence of traditional external controls which are typical of commercial banks, there are far more means of control, including the informal sort. Moreover, this imperative for cooperative banking becomes more serious when certain regulatory changes introduced in most European countries are taken into account.

A falling away of governance issues can instead be identified if one considers the changes to the organization of assets, that is to say, the adoption of 'net' systems or networks, which have been defining the international division in recent times.

In this chapter an effort has been made to bring out the main problems and the complexity of the governance model of the European cooperative banks, with an emphasis on the changing profiles of the control mechanisms which emerge when the analysis of a single bank is compared with that of cooperative credit systems.

From a wider point of view, it is possible to show how recent innovations in banking regulation have affected the governance of cooperative banks, in terms of capital adequacy and the regulation of banks' organization and internal control systems (Basel Committee on Banking Supervision, 1998, 2001, 2002, 2005 and 2006). The compliance of cooperative banks with standards under such regulatory arrangements calls for an improvement in governance mechanisms, which can be carried out through higher participation levels and making top management responsible for the strategic and organizational choices made, which help reduce the risks of handling and control taken by the bank.

The following section provides a synthesis of theoretical analyses of governance found in the literature. The third section is on governance of banks with reference to their institutional and regulatory profile. The fourth section presents the particular models of governance in the European cooperative banking sector. The final section concludes.

3.2   A theoretical view of the problems of corporate governance

There are two perspectives[2] on the problems of CG in companies that were studied in the literature survey.

From a limited point of view, the *shareholder perspective* simplifies the dialectic of those interests which arise from the management of companies based only on the conflict between shareholders and management. CG becomes a way in which those who retain ownership rights rule the company to maximize their own profits. From this standpoint, CG models depend on the microeconomic factors which are specific to a given firm. They guarantee that the person chosen to control business choices works to maximize the value of the company. In current settings, on the basis of an efficient allocation of business resources, this situation, with respect to the aim of an efficient allocation of business resources, is difficult to honour because of the large number of shareholders who have lost interest in being involved in running a company and so hand over responsibility to management. This gives rise to a net separation between ownership and corporate control.

The agency problem which can arise under these circumstances – concurrent with the possibility that shareholders and managers promote conflicting interests when running their businesses – leads to information asymmetries, which weaken shareholders' control over the actions of management. This emphasizes the importance for CG mechanisms as a means to align the interests of managers and shareholders, thus minimizing the possibility of opportunistic behaviour on the part of the former (*expense preference*) to the detriment of the latter.

In the shareholder view, governance problems are associated with the agency problem, which could be moderated by internal mechanisms, such as the role of the board of directors, and by external factors, such as the presence of an efficient *market for corporate control* and the existence of an executive job market.

Evidence of the limitations of the efficient market hypotheses, which have arisen from company bankruptcies, as well as the general belief that the formula for successful company strategies must necessarily be coupled with the wishes of a larger category of stakeholders, is the basis of a more modern interpretation of CG systems, which arises from the *stakeholder perspective* (Freeman, 1984; Blair, 1995).

This viewpoint widens the profile of stakeholders. This means that, apart from shareholders, there would be the employees, the customers, the suppliers, the institutions, the category associations and the community in general, whose connection with the company, based on long-term contracts, must be considered as a contributory factor in its success.

In this case, governance systems also depend on macroeconomic factors which are associated with the environment and the area of production in which the company is involved. The aim is to achieve higher company value, an intricate result arising from the interests of each stakeholder.

This modern interpretation underlines the need for the diversified interests of the stakeholders to be aligned, so as to reach acceptable balanced levels before one could hope to coordinate the interests of the shareholders and management. It calls for a governance structure which is more complex than under the shareholder view, and where the ability to regulate relations among the various stakeholders requires the adoption of mechanisms which are predominantly internal to the company that can harmonize the variety of demands emanating from the categories of stakeholders.

The solutions to firm–stakeholder agency problems, which have arisen from this analysis, involve governance models with a greater range of internal mechanisms capable of maximizing the utility functions of the different stakeholder categories, at the same time creating value for the firm. The reference is, for example, to the establishment of organs capable of managing relations with the stakeholders and the representatives of the various categories. These organs should be able to mediate between the interests of all and the needs of the company, developing ways to allocate suitable resources to the requirements of the stakeholders. Moreover, the organs should adopt company information and communication systems which respond to the dialogue that arises from the interests of the various subjects and the marketing systems that are generalized to serve multiple stakeholder categories. Lastly, these organs should promote 'proactive' company behaviour aimed at anticipating and satisfying the demands of the stakeholders and influencing the external surroundings.

3.3   Corporate governance from the perspective of banking regulation

Similar CG issues apply to banking firms. The agency problems in shareholder–manager relations, which arise from the separation of ownership from control, and in firm–stakeholder relations, which arise from the need of management models to create value for a substantial share of stakeholder categories, afflict even financial intermediaries.[3]

The need to regulate the possible conflicts which subsist among economic agents is more urgent for banks than for other industries. In fact, a number of authors (La Porta et al., 2002; Adams and Mehran, 2003; Flannery et al., 2004; Levine, 2004; Masera, 2006) point out that the governance mechanisms become more important for intermediaries in light of the specialty of banks' activity. This can be summarized in the following points (Sang-Woo, 2004). First, banks are very vulnerable to shocks due to their highly leveraged balance-sheet structure and, more recently, financial deregulation and liberalization. Second, governments usually provide safety nets to banks and heavily regulate them because of the externality associated with banking sector stability, which reduces creditors' incentives to monitor banks. Third, information asymmetry is far more serious in banking than in non-financial industries due largely to the inter-temporal nature (involving a promise to pay in the future) of typical financial contracts and the increasing complexity of financial products. Lastly, banks can play an important monitoring and governance role for their corporate customers to safeguard their credit against corporate financial distress or bankruptcies. This role cannot be properly played without the sound governance of banks, which ensures that bank managers control risk and pursue profits.

The crucial importance of governance for the international banking system justifies the regulatory authorities' reliance on prudential regulation directives, aimed at promoting approval and respect for effective governing company rules on the part of banks of different countries (Basel Committee, 2006), based on certain features (size, complexity, corporate governance, economic significance, return and risk profile) that distinguish each bank.

From this viewpoint, the model put forward by the regulators usually seems to view corporate governance from the *stakeholder* perspective. This is confirmed by the belief that the objective of maximum agency performance must be pursued by means of a valid and careful administration that aims to protect the interests of the shareholders and the bank's stakeholders/investors, firms, regulatory authorities, and so forth.

The bank's top management is charged with using the governance principles set out in directives. Its mission is to define correct governance and organizational structures,[4] in order to carry out the following tasks:

- To allocate managerial, executive and control tasks within the organization based on criteria that support dialogue within the company and ensure a balance of power among the different social organs.

- To ensure the circulation of interactive mechanisms among the board of directors, top management and the internal and external auditors.
- To promote those qualities and appropriate skills that top management needs when making strategic choices that are consistent with market trends and with the desired risk–profit profile.
- To ensure the presence of people with authority and responsibility when it comes to controlling the organizational structure as a whole.
- To set up within the organizational structure a risk management unit and an internal auditing unit which are independent from the processes of operational management.
- To ensure that internal communication systems are capable of circulating the information and ensuring its diffusion among the various company units for the smooth administration and responsiveness of the different positions, including external ones, so that accurate and valid company information can be circulated into the market.

Other factors contribute to improving the effectiveness of CG, such as the use of corporate conduct codes, which are supported by systems guaranteeing that the company's personnel comply with them; the accurate definition of the business plan as a means to evaluate the bank's results and management's performance; adequate incentive mechanisms to ensure that management behaves correctly; the use of constant risk-monitoring tools, especially in those areas where there is the strongest corporate conflict.

Bank regulation includes, apart from internal mechanisms of CG, control mechanisms that are external to the banks. These promote the improvement of the governance model, even if indirectly, and guard against possible conflicts between banking economic agents. Such mechanisms comprise regulatory supervision and the discipline of market transparency as set out in the New Basel Capital Accord (Basel 2).

The second pillar of this New Accord gives regulators the authority to verify and monitor the actions of management. It is managers' responsibility to ensure that a bank has adequate capital coverage for the risk it takes on, leading to strong hierarchical control aimed at preventing managers pursuing their self-interest in such a way as to harm the bank's stakeholders. Similarly, market discipline is outlined in the third pillar of Basel 2. It sets out obligations to make certain kinds of information public and urges the banks' governing structures to always act in a constructive and efficient way to avoid possible penalties when seeking funds from investors and the market in general.[5]

In Europe the principles and mechanisms proposed by the regulators to strengthen CG are currently being implemented. The diffusion of a corporate culture which supports the use of governance mechanisms in listed banks is characterized by the implementation of the codes of conduct of the various European stock exchanges (the UK Combined Code, the Italian Corporate Governance Code, the French Vienot 2 Rapport, to name but a few).

In most European countries the injunctions contained in the codes are not compulsory but are based on self-discipline or *moral suasion*. Hence, even if observing the administrative and control modes described in these documents is voluntary, many banks have spontaneously complied with them due to market pressure or fear of damaging their reputation. In other countries, by contrast, the principles of national codes of conduct are even accepted by legislation, as in the USA, whose regulation seems much stricter. The main difference between these two regulatory approaches resides in the 'comply or explain' principle which informs European codes of conduct. The companies addressed by the code, usually listed banks, are urged to comply with its injunctions. Should they not do so, they are obliged to explain their refusal to the public. Hence, companies comply with the code even though it is not strictly a binding requirement.

The governance models set out by the various European codes seem to vary from the institutional and regulatory points of view. In fact, the ways in which the control mechanisms work range from a two-tier model (as in France and Germany), where the regulatory task of the board of directors is carried out by a separate entity exempt from executive functions, to a single-tiered model (as is in Britain) where the board of directors plays a wider-ranging role and, in certain models, is backed up by specific internal control units.[6]

3.4   European governance in cooperative credit banks: distinctive traits and effectiveness

The governance model of cooperative credit banks can be looked at from both the theoretical and the regulatory sides, as described in the preceding paragraphs.

The problems related to governance and identified in the above analysis of the two theoretical perspectives are present in the European cooperative banking sector, and their solution appears to be just as important when one considers the externalities of banking.

Cooperative banks have wanted to strengthen their own governance model, improving the internal control mechanisms of their organizational structure, also as a result of pressure from certain regulatory innovations which are specific to this division. However, when compared with that of commercial banks, the cooperative model still has a few distinct weak points of, mainly correlated with the institutional asset, which can threaten the industry competitiveness in the market.

In most European countries, since the 1980s important innovations have been introduced in cooperative credit so as to limit the restrictions imposed on this bank model and thus support its survival and growth in the financial markets.[7]

At first it could seem that certain measures conflict with co-operative principles, but it is definitely not true. However, the flexibility granted in this matter is limited. For example, the principle of one-member-one-vote, which is enshrined in the laws of all EU Member States, at least for first-degree cooperatives, is more flexible in some countries than in others. For the French, the statute on cooperative banks can announce that members hold multiple votes or, conversely, that the number of votes be directly proportional to the acceptance. Certain limits have been set to the maximum number of votes that a person, or a group of people, can hold to benefit from flexibility, and thus prevents the interests of investors becoming more important than the original purpose of the cooperative.

The same exclusion principle – whereby cooperatives can carry on their business only with their partners – is present and flexible in certain jurisdictions. In Italy, for example, certain activities are allowed with third parties who are not members of the cooperative as long as these are collateral operations that do not endanger the interests of members. In some countries, such as the Netherlands, commercial relations with non-members are not allowed. In other countries, the acceptance of capital from members who are external to the cooperative bank is endorsed, and it has no effect on the ownership structure since such investors cannot, in any case, dominate the decision-making process of the cooperative, which could be harmful to the cooperative's members.

Certain laws in individual European countries have reflected the administrative and control models of cooperative banks. The recent reform of Italian company law, for example, has also revolutionized the regulation of cooperatives in the area of corporate administration and control. For the companies involved, this has stimulated the reinforcement of company competitiveness and at the same time has incorporated the specific properties of the corporate model.[8] A similar goal can even be seen in the reform of the regulation of German cooperatives (Schraffl, 1999).

However, as a result of such modifications, the main difference between the present cooperative bank model and the commercial bank model remains the undisputed importance which is attributed to the individual member of the cooperative and the member's interests, as opposed to the bank's capital and the member's remuneration.

In fact, the significance of the individual member is enhanced by the principles of mutuality and locality observed applied by cooperative banks, which are reflected in the existing relations between the banks on the one side and their members, clients and territory on the other. Mutuality seeks to maximize the per capita remuneration of the members, while locality seeks the commitment of members to the bank's area of territorial competence.

Moreover, within the cooperative bank the position of the member is strengthened in a number of ways: by the democratic one-member-one-vote principle; by the time limit on holding shares with members' right to vote; by the way new members can be are admitted only with the agreement of existing members; and by certain bonds based on where the cooperative's annual profits are to be allocated. The analysis of the cooperative bank model which is set up in this way, based on the shareholder perspective which was examined above, allows one to understand how, within banks, agency problems between shareholders and management can become very intense.

The highly fragmented nature of the cooperative's social capital, which arises from the acknowledgement of one-member-one-vote, and the limit to the number of voting shares that a member can hold, can create a disincentive for those members to control management (free riding), thus exacerbating the agency's shareholder–management problem.

The literature suggests two ways to mitigate the problem. The first is monitoring those shareholders who are not involved in running the company; the second is an efficient capital market promoting takeovers (a 'bidder' buys a sufficient number of shares on the market to take control of the cooperative bank). However, the shareholder will be driven to exert effective control over management only by retaining a large enough share of the capital; but if ownership of the property is highly fragmented, and should there be a limit to the number of company shares one can own, it is very likely that, once again, a free-rider problem can arise, meaning that management would continue to have, in fact, a strong *expense preference*. In the same way, it is not possible for a takeover to occur since there is not a market of a right to vote.

Management's discretion in running the cooperative widens with restrictions on profit distribution, that is to say, legal reserve requirements retaining a significant number of amount of profit rather than distributing them as dividends to shareholders.

Moreover, limited attention to profitability as an aim of the cooperative bank justifies shareholders' intervention only when there is serious turmoil within the bank. Management is therefore aware that it is not assessed by reference to the profits flowing from investments; in the worse-case scenario, it will be dismissed in the event of bankruptcy. For this reason, management will want to safeguard itself from the risk of insolvency by setting aside a reserve of shares which is even greater than that allowed by the terms of the statute, thus invalidating the efficiency principle of the cooperative's allocation of financial assets.[9]

Opportunistic behaviour on the part of management can further impair the bank's competitiveness in the market, triggering 'inertial management' in which, depending of the maturity of the markets and the company's need to move towards diversified solutions and re-qualifying the commercial offer, management shows little motivation in change and in innovative company procedures (Baravelli, 1998). The lengthy stay of managers in certain cooperative banks (as in Italy, for example), promoting the interests of managers only, can even worsen the 'inertial management' problem.[10]

These considerations therefore highlight the weak points in the CG model, which does not seem to sufficiently safeguard the interests of the cooperative's members and owners, balancing and limiting the expense preferences of the management.

Certain authors have shown how such a limit can be attenuated by the cooperative model's peculiarities. Compared with commercial banks, the presence of a cooperative spirit as an ideological 'glue' on which the cooperative banking model relies can be an incentive to impose responsibility on management towards the members and to induce it to satisfy shareholders' financial expectations, since an increase in capital would be largely subscribed by existing members (Mottura and Drago, 1989; Baravelli, 1998).

To widen the analytical perspective, the conceptual schemes of the stakeholder perspective highlight further problems related to the cooperative bank governance model, but this time in the relation between the bank and the wider category of stakeholders.

The institutional structure of the bank model *in specie* does not in fact have an ownership structure of the composite sort, where different categories of economic subjects interact (administrators, debtors, creditors, employees). The one thing these subjects have in common is membership of the cooperative. Hence, there is a constant presence of multi-role members (administrator-members, employee-members, customer-members, financial members), whose objective functions can overlap only up to a point, and each assesses the company's management by using different parameters.[11] For example, the employee-member pays special attention to working conditions and the remuneration received; the financial member, rather, is responsive to the compensation for his or her financial investment in the cooperative.

Apart from the overlap of the roles of these members, conflicting elements can arise also from the asymmetric weight of each function carried out by members, which can influence the council in deciding which strategy the company should adopt.

In similar situations, it seems indispensable to have an effective governance body, whose aim is to formulate its own agency strategy based on the 'global' objective of the firm, integrating and monitoring the bank's interests. There are two reasons for this 'structural' integration of company interests. It ensures that economic return is not the only or the main guiding factor determining the bank's strategic decisions, and it also prevents a particular type of stakeholder 'capturing' the strategic decisions taken by the bank, so that integration can be achieved in an easier manner by means of a trade off between the delegation of the diversified interests of the multi-role members and CG set-up (Schwizer, 1998).

An improvement in the efficiency of governance mechanisms can also arise from the presence of an informative reporting system for the board of directors. The system must adequately cover the information needs of each individual role, and enable each to express the degree of satisfaction of the various interests which are present and therefore help guide the company's decisions (Carretta, 1998).

In the complexity of the conflict between bank and their stakeholders, there can instead be an attenuation of elements in the specific relation between the bank and its debtors, due to the presence of informal governance mechanisms triggered by the cooperative model and based on *peer monitoring* among members. While in commercial banks managers monitor debtors, in cooperative banks even member-clients have an interest in mutually controlling each other due to the cooperative nature of the institution.[12]

The local dimension, which is typical of European cooperative models, can still initiate informal governance mechanisms which are represented by extra-economic sanctions should the debtor go bankrupt, thus attenuating the conflicts which would arise with the bank. The local community in which the bank is rooted could impose social sanctions (which would be additional to the economic ones foreseen in these situations, like the rejection of loan applications by banks) to minimize possible opportunistic behaviour in the part of the debtor.

However, the growth strategies implemented by European cooperative banks and certain changes made to the legislation (for example, fewer business and commercial obligations to non-members) have increased cooperative banks' size and territorial efficiency, significantly eluding the informal control mechanisms which are based on peer monitoring among members and extra-economic sanctions on debtors – all of which weakens even further cooperative banks' governance.

In light of these considerations, it appears that the governance model for cooperative banks is, from the stakeholder perspective, particularly complex due to the presence of members with asymmetrical roles; but it is at least characterized by more efficient mechanisms than those of commercial banks for controlling the relation between the bank and its debtors.

If the object of the analysis of governance mechanisms is shifted to cooperative credit systems, then certain aspects become evident that distinguish it from the analysis of a single intermediary, which in some way seems to fill the gap presented by the weak spots identified above.

In fact, in the largest European countries (France, Italy, Spain, Germany), efforts expended in the search for organizational combinations which are more competitive have led most cooperative banks to evolve into pyramid-shaped national structures, with two or three levels of organizational decentralization (national, regional or local). These can be assimilated to 'integrated' systems or simply to a 'network'. A system with such a range allows lower levels wide margins of autonomy in managing customer relations and core-business activities and, at the same time, allocates policy direction and the control to the higher level, which allow it to rationalize the use of resources and the growth of investments.

However, in such a model the single cooperative, which is already a first-level governance unit, become a governance elements also at the system level. Therefore, the problem lies in a greater balance of the interests among the single cooperatives as members of central bodies and the recipients of the objects made by them. Such a balance seems more complex than that of a single bank if one considers that the central organisms lump together the various cooperatives, with peculiarities and needs which are more diversified (even territorially), that have to similarly converge on 'system' company objectives.

As the presence of multiple role-members increases, so do the problems, and they seem to become more complicated. It is a fact that the size of the 'system' of cooperative credit, by increasing the height of the hierarchical pyramid and further diversifying the profile of members, increases the costs of control or coordination (Williamson, 1967). This requires a governance model based on mechanisms that act on the entire network structure.

The central structures are particularly important in the system scenario. These are at the top of the various European systems and are absent from the governance model of the single intermediary. Apart from the strategic and managerial support to the single units, first-tier cooperative banks are increasingly taking on managerial control within cooperative systems. They also guard and develop the mutuality principle of the cooperatives, thus rectifying the weak points of its members when it comes to relating with management.

Based on the degree of cohesion attained by the cooperative system (Di Salvo, 2003), there are other governance mechanisms. These range from exclusively associative types of company integration to varieties of greater integration of the working type.

Among the former are those 'facilitating' organs of the institution which manage firm–stakeholder relations (*clubs for members or local committees*). These promote the requests of the various local network when preparing the strategy of the first-tier cooperative bank or achieve strategies and manage procedures at the system level connected with the approval of each bank according to the cooperative rules of internal management (*consent management*).

Among the latter, one can highlight the allocation of surveying and *internal auditing* to central organs that carry out instrumental and auxiliary services for local banks. In most systems, these organs also act as the institution's mechanisms of cross-guarantee and penalization of each single case guarding the credit exposure of the entire system (*crossguarantee system or joint liability*).

In spite of the efforts of European cooperative credit systems in defining a governance model capable of identifying the specific problems of the institutional asset, certain authors suggest further improvements to the internal mechanisms, focusing on member participation in the cooperative management of the 'system'. The lack of market indicators as a standard for evaluating the trend in management administration implies either that members must be highly active in monitoring and taking part in general meetings or that other research indices must be found (Presti, 1998; Di Salvo, 2003). Other authors have instead expressed their bafflement about the real ability of the cooperative banks' governance model to support competitiveness in the present market and, in view of its sometimes disappointing performance, they also suggest removing such a bank model for the sake of the efficiency of the European single market (Sironi, 2007).

3.5 Conclusions

The present chapter presents the main problems associated with, and the complexity of, the governance model of European cooperative banks, pointing out the changing profile of the control mechanisms which arise when the analysis moves from a single bank to cooperative credit systems.

In analysing problems related to the governance of a single cooperative bank, the use of the shareholder-perspective and stakeholder-perspective logics has identified certain weak points when compared with the way a commercial bank deals with shareholder–management and firm–stakeholders problems.

For shareholder–management transactions, the highly fragmented nature of the cooperatives' social capital and the restrictions in the destination of the earned profits could be a strong disincentive for those partners who control management behaviour, leading to greater shareholder–management problems within the agency. When traditional control mechanisms expected from theoretical schemes are absent, such as monitoring shareholders who are not involved in the operation of the cooperative bank and the efficiency of the market for corporate control, the discretion of management in overseeing the company widens, thus further exacerbating the agency's problems with shareholders, creating 'inertial management' situations which can, in the worst case, even compromise the survival of the bank on the market.

For firm–stakeholder dealings the overlap between the role of the partner and the presence of asymmetries can weaken the individual tasks carried out by any one partner with the firm–stakeholder. This can lead to strategic company decisions being taken which are of the 'captive' sort (attending mainly to the interests of a particular category of stakeholder) when there is no governing organism capable of defining an objective function of the 'global' sort that can balance and harmonize the interests of the different stakeholders within the bank.

The presence of informal governance mechanisms, typical of the cooperative model, are based on *peer monitoring* among partners and on extra-economic sanctions imposed on the debtor–partner. This tends to lead in the long term to a gradual decline and, if it continues, to increase the size of the territorial area where the cooperative bank operates, thus intensifying the conflict which arises in the firm–stakeholder relation in the bank model.

The change of perspective from single bank to cooperative bank system in the analysis of the governance model enables one to highlight the possible efficiency returns in the company's control mechanisms for each bank. Beside possible associative integrations and working to protect the relation between single banks – and the relation among these and their stakeholders – the presence of a central organism, which also has both the hierarchical control functions of local banks and the strategic and organizational support functions, can mitigate conflict between the management and the ownership of the cooperative bank.

Further solutions are, however, necessary to deal with the manifest weak spots of corporate governance mechanisms and offset the dangers which can arise from the disappearance of the cooperative banking model in the European scenario.

Notes

1. Corporate governance (CG) is defined by the OECD as 'a set of relationships between a company's management, its board, its shareholders, and other stakeholders. Corporate Governance also provides the structure through which the objectives of the company are set, and the means of attaining those objectives and monitoring performance are determined. Good CG should provide proper incentives for the board and management to pursue objectives that are in the interests of the company and its shareholders and should facilitate effective monitoring' (OECD, 2004).
2. In light of the aim of this chapter, it is appropriate to briefly recall the main theoretical approaches to CG by referring to some of the numerous publications on the subject: Berle and Means (1932); Shleifer and Vishny (1997); Denis (2001); Holmstrom and Kaplan (2003); Weir et al. (2003); Becht et al. (2005).
3. The debate on the role of corporate governance in banks was first presented by Fama (1985). For a more recent state-of-the-art analysis, see Polo (2007).
4. There is a vast literature on the relevance of the role of the board of directors in defining the bank's governance model. These publications focus on the effectiveness of the board in defining correct company control and, therefore,

better company performance. See Schwizer, Farina and Carretta (2005); Carretta, Regalli and Schwizer (2006).

5. For further reading see S. Cosma in this volume.

6. For an analysis of the different CG codes of conduct, see Costanzo, Priori and Sanguinetti (2007).

7. The large assortment of reforms ranges from the smaller minimum number of people necessary to constitute a cooperative to the possibility of giving certain members more than one vote, the cut-back on restrictions on activities and commerce with non-members, the possibility of issuing bonds representing equity risk or debt, the possibility of third parties taking part in the cooperative's capital issues, and lastly, the possibility of cooperative banks becoming stock companies. See European Commission (2003) and Regional (CE) no. 1435/2003 dated 22nd July, 2003 on the statute of the European Cooperative Company (ECC).

8. As is well known, the reform of Italian company law is in the D.Lgs. n. 6/2003. For a comment on the cooperative company set-up, see Cerioli, Costanzo and Sanguinetti (2004).

9. Evidence of this comes from a case study of Italian cooperative banks (Cardilli and Di Battista, 1997), which shows that the sector's level of capitalization is far higher than that of commercial banks and, in general, than that permitted by Italian banking law.

10. According to certain authors, however, the disadvantages arise in the long term as they are counterbalanced by the benefits of the commercial relation with the clients arising from managers' long duration; see Shleifer and Summer (1988). These considerations are strengthened given the benefits which are obtainable from a long-term relation between the bank and the debtor, which are connected to the advantages of screening, monitoring and enforcement on the debtor's behaviour and encouraged by relationship-banking logic; see De Bruyn and Ferri (2005). Other authors, in contrast, consider it damaging for managers remain in position extended periods of time, showing how long-duration commercial relations can lead to situations in which the cooperative bank cannot renew its line of credit with its debtor, even when *shock-absorber functions* are absent; see Pittaluga (1998).

11. A similar situation occurs for the fragmented ownership structure of financial intermediaries; see Schwizer (1998).

12. Peer monitoring is particularly evident in the Raiffesein and in the Grameen Cooperative Banks, where each member of the cooperative is interested in controlling that there be no opportunistic behaviour from the other members because, through a higher member share, it directly supports the consequences of a potential bankruptcy by one or more members, see Stiglitz (1990); Varian (1990).

References

Adams R. and Mehran H. (2003), Is Corporate Governance Different for Bank Holding Companies?, Economic Policy Review, April.

Baravelli M. (1998), Assetto proprietario, controlli esterni e interni e performance delle banche. Il caso italiano, in Airoldi, G. and Forestieri, G. (1998) (a cura di), Corporate Governance. Analisi e prospettive del caso italiano, EtasLibri, Milano.

Basel Committee on Banking Supervision (1998), Framework for Internal Control Systems in Banking Organisations, September.

——. (2001), Internal Audit in Banks and the Supervisor's Relationship with Auditors, August.

——. (2002), Internal Audit in Banks and the Supervisor's Relationship with Auditors: A Survey, August.

——. (2005), Basel II: International Convergence of Capital Measurement and Capital Standards: A Revised Framework, November.

——. (2006), Enhancing Corporate Governance for Banking Organisations, February.

Becht M. et al. (2005), Corporate Governance: An Assessment, *Oxford Review Economic Policy*, vol. 21, pp. 155–163.

Berle A. A. and Means G. C. (1932), *The Modern Corporation and Private Property*, Clearing House, Macmillan, New York.

Blair M. M. (1995), Ownership and Control: Rethinking Corporate Governance for the Twenty-First Century, Brookings, Washington DC.

Cardilli D. and Di Battista M. L. (1997), Il ruolo del patrimonio nel modello di proprietà e controllo delle banche di Credito Cooperativo italiane, *Cooperazione di Credito*, n. 156–7, aprile–settembre.

Carretta A. (1998), Modelli di corporate governance negli intermediari finanziari ad azionariato diffuso: il sistema informativo e gli indicatori di performance per il consiglio di amministrazione, in Airoldi, G. and Forestieri, G. (a cura di), *Corporate governance*, EtasLibri, Milano.

Carretta A., Farina V. and Schwizer P. (2005), Organizzazione e funzionamento dei consigli di amministrazione negli intermediari finanziari. Condizioni di efficacia, competenze e performance, Atti del Convegno ADEIMF, Parma, Novembre 2005.

Carretta A., Regalli, M. and Schwizer P. (2006), Indipendenza significa competenza? Un'analisi del funzionamento dei board dopo il SOA, Atti del Convegno AIDEA di Roma, Settembre.

Cerioli S. L., Costanzo P. and Sanguinetti A. (2004), *La riforma delle società cooperative. Disciplina civilistica e fiscale*. Adempimenti contabili, Egea.

Confederation of Finnish Co-operatives (2000), *Corporate Governance and Management Control in Co-operatives*, November.

Commissione Europea (2003), Le cooperative nell'Europa imprenditoriale, Documento di Lavoro dei Servizi della Commissione, Marzo.

——. Regolamento (CE) n. 1435/2003 relativo allo statuto della Società cooperativa europea (SCE), Luglio.

Costanzo P., Priori M. and Sanguinetti A. (2007), Governance e tutela del risparmio, Vita e Pensiero Università.

Denis D. K. (2001), Twenty-five Years of Corporate Governance Research and Counting, *Review of Financial Economics*, vol. 10/3, pp. 191–212.

De Bruyn R. and Ferri G. (2005), Le ragioni delle banche popolari: motivi teorici ed evidenze empiriche, Working Paper promosso dall'Associazione Nazionale delle Banche Popolari, Gennaio.

Di Salvo (2003), The Governance of Mutual and Cooperative Bank Systems in Europe, Cooperative Studies, BCC Federcasse, Maggio.

EFMA (European Financial Management and Marketing Association) (2004), Mutualist Banking Institutions in Europe. Cooperative Value in the Face of Market Globalization, no. 187, January–February.

European Association of Co-operative Banks (2006), Corporate Governance Principles in Co-operative Banks, June.

Evan W. M. and Freeman, R. E. (1988), A Stakeholder Theory of the Modern Corporation: Kantian Capitalism, in Beauchamp T. and Bowie N. (1988), Ethical Theory and Business, Prentice-Hall, Englewood Cliffs, 3rd ed., pp. 101–105.

Fama E. F. (1980), Agency Problems and the Theory of the Firm, *Journal of Political Economy*, vol. 88/2, pp. 288–307.

———. (1985), What's Different about Banks?, *Journal of Monetary Economics*, vol. 15/1, pp. 29–39.

Flannery M. J. et al. (2004), Market Evidence on the Opaqueness of Banking Firms' Assets, *Journal of Financial Economics*, no. 71.

Freeman R. E. (1984), Strategic Management: A Stakeholder Approach, Pitman, London.

Holmstrom B. and Kaplan S. N. (2003), The State of U.S. Corporate Governance: What's Right and What's Wrong?, Working Paper No. 9613, NBER.

Jensen M. C. and Meckling W. H. (1976), Theory of the Firm: Managerial Behaviour, Agency Costs and Ownership Structure, *Journal of Financial Economics*, vol. 13/3–4, pp. 305–60.

La Porta et al. (2002), Ownership Government of Banks, *Journal of Finance*, vol. 57, pp. 265–301.

Levine R. (2004), 'The Corporate Governance of Banks: A Concise Discussion of Concepts and Evidence', World Bank Policy Research Working Paper No. 3404 (http://econ.worldbank.org).

Masera R. (2006), *La corporate governance nelle banche*, Il Mulino, Bologna.

Mottura P. and Drago D. (1989), Assetti proprietari ed efficienza nelle banche, EGEA, Milano.

OECD (Organisation for Economic Co-operation and Development) (1999), Principi di Governo Societario dell'OCSE, Giugno.

———. (2004), Principi di Governo Societario, Aprile.

———. (2004), Principles of Corporate Governance.

Pittaluga G. B. (1998), La specificità della banca locale cooperative e i connessi problemi di corporate governance, in Cooperazione di credito, no. 160–61, Aprile–Settembre.

Polo A. (2007), Corporate Governance of Banks: The Current State of the Debate, MPRA Paper No. 2325 (http://mpra.ub.uni-muenchen.de).

Presti G. (1998), Il governo delle banche popolari e di credito cooperativo, Banca, impresa e società, Aprile.

Rebelo J. and Cabo P. (2005), Governance Control Mechanisms in Portuguese Agricultural Credit Cooperatives, Paper prepared for presentation at the 99th seminar of the European Association of Agricultural Economists, The Future of Rural Europe in the Global Agri-Food System, Copenhagen, Denmark, August 24–27, 2005.

Sang-Woo N. (2004), Corporate Governance of Banks: Review of Issues, Asian Development Bank Institute, June.

Schwizer P. (1998), I modelli di corporate governance ad azionariato diffuso, in Airoldi G. and Forestieri G. (1998) (a cura di), Corporate Governance. Analisi e prospettive del caso italiano, EtasLibri, Milano.

Schraffl I. (1999), Modelli di integrazione dei sistemi bancari cooperativi. I casi di Rabobank, del Credit Muuel e del Credito Agricola Mutuo, in Cooperazione di Credito, Ottobre/Dicembre.

Shleifer A. and Summer L. (1988), Breach of Trust in Hostile Takeovers, in Auerbach A. (1988) (a cura di), *Merger and Acquisitions*, NBER, University of Chicago Press.

Shleifer A. and Vishny R. W. (1997), A Survey of Corporate Governance, *Journal of Finance*, vol. 52/2, pp. 737–83.

Sironi A. (2007), Governance e Assetti proprietari nel mercato bancario europeo, in Economia e Management, no. 2.

Stiglitz J. (1990), Peer Monitoring in Credit Markets, *World Bank Economic Review*, no. 4, pp. 351–66.

Varian H. (1990), Monitoring Agents with Other Agents, *Journal of Institutional and Theoretical Economics*, vol. CXLVI, pp. 153–74.

Weir C. et al. (2003), An Empirical Analysis of the Impact of Corporate Governance Mechanisms on the Performance of UK Firms, Working Paper.

Williamson O. E. (1967), Hierarchical Control and Optimum Firm Size, *Journal of Political Economy*, April.

4
Merger and Acquisition in the Cooperative Banking Sector

V. Stefanelli

4.1 Introduction

Since the end of the 20th century a growing preoccupation has emerged with the forms of the cooperative company, whose survival seemed almost threatened by the deep changes that have occurred in the international economy (European Commission, 2001a).

As a consequence of an unquestioned acknowledgement of the role and the importance of these companies in the economic, social and cultural life of European Union – as also testified by the dimension that cooperatives have achieved in various economic contexts – a popular thesis maintains the need to restructure and reinforce the model, as individual cooperatives are unable to take complete advantage of their particular legal form in more competitive market contexts.

This is confirmed in the documents that the European Commission has recently produced about the diffusion and development of cooperative forms (European Commission, 2001a; 2001b; 2002; 2003; 2004), which contain some precise guidelines that define a specific model of the cooperative, based on cross-country aggregations, able to operate in global economic contexts like other joint-stock companies, and complying with the specificities of cooperative principles.

The reference is to the legal instrument represented by the Statute of the European Cooperative Society (ECS), defined by Directive 2003/72/EC and by Regulation EC N. 1435/2003, which regulates the cooperative company and whose main purpose is 'to allow the development of cross-country collaborations among European cooperative, mutualist and associative companies without renouncing their own specificities'.

In the spirit of the ECS Statute there is an attempt to promote the activity of the cooperative company by pointing out the necessity of operating in competitive conditions, thus developing an entrepreneurial culture that is functional to the achievement of the specific aim of mutuality, without losing sight of the requirements of efficiency and effectiveness of this form of company.

Further evidence of the development of cooperatives can be found also in national contexts. The recent reform of Italian company law, for example, has revolutionized the regulation of cooperatives with regard to statutory models of administration and company control, annual report, tax relief and the search for capital, and has thus provided an input into the consolidation and the entrepreneurial competitiveness of these companies, taking into consideration the specific characteristics of the company model.[1] A substantially similar purpose can be seen also in the recent reform of the regulation of cooperatives in Germany (Schraffl, 1999).

These considerations seem to be valid also for the particular cooperative credit bank sector, according to various transformations in the financial markets, to the specificity of these intermediaries and to their double economic role, as they are at the same time the source of and a support for the entrepreneurial fabric in which they are embedded.

The deep changes that have affected the European banking system in recent years (ECB, 2004a; 2004b) could in the long run weaken the competitive capacity of the cooperative bank model, requiring a broad process of restructuring, whose diffusion has also reached certain significant dimensions in all the European markets.

The recourse to merger and acquisition (M&A) seems, in general, to be the solution the banks and the financial intermediaries have for the most part adopted in present market contexts (ECB, 2000; 2005; Group of Ten, 2001). Although some national banking regulators envisage this alternative for cooperative banks, too, to formulate a truly adequate regime (as has happened in Italy) the search for the 'best dimension' has to be combined with a further element, namely, the territory, which represents both a limitation and at the same time a possible advantage for a cooperative bank that is able to interpret faithfully its own interests. This peculiarity raises questions about how far choices concerning concentration adopted by the rest of the banking system can be applied to the cooperative sector (EFMA, 2004).

If the realization of mergers and acquisitions seems to be a way to improve a company's efficiency, to strengthen its customer relationships and, ultimately, to ensure its survival in the market, the question to be answered is whether it is a suitable option for cooperative banks too, in view of the different features that this bank model has developed in various countries.

From the empirical point of view, concentration does not seem to be a universally shared strategic choice in the European cooperative sector: in the Italian case the evidence suggests the beginning of a wider restructuring process for the sector, which confirms, without any doubt, that the goal is to meet the competitive challenges the market has presented through company reinforcement and growth, but which also reveals the substantial diversity and variety of the operational solutions the intermediaries have adopted.

From a theoretical perspective, as a effect of a greater timeless – compared with internal growth – to exceed the limits connected with the cooperative bank model, concentration, could, according to some authors, almost threaten the sustainability of the model itself in the long run.

The present chapter is concerned with this debate and investigates the theoretical compatibility or coherence of the option of external growth that the cooperative banks have adopted with the peculiarities of this bank model.

Against the background of the changes in the context of European cooperative credit and of the characteristic features that the M&A phenomenon has assumed in different national contexts, the chapter aims to point out how the operations of concentration do not represent for cooperative banks, in the way they do for commercial banks, a strategic option that is compatible with the competitive advantages connected with the cooperative form in a long run. The arguments in support of this thesis stem from the peculiarities of the banking model.

Section 4.2 develops a descriptive analysis of the reorganization of the cooperative credit sector in Europe and aims to set out the diffusion, the purpose and the methods of fulfilment of concentration, also in light of the regulations in individual countries. Second 4.3 points out the possible advantages and disadvantages of concentration to the cooperative credit sector, in view of the distinctive characters of the cooperative model. Section 4.4 provides conclusions based on a synthesis of the considerations raised in the chapter.

4.2   M&A in European cooperative banks

The deep changes being witnessed in the present market contexts in Europe and the recent legislative modifications the regulators have introduced for small banks[2] represent an opportunity for the cooperative credit sector to reinforce its competitive model in the market.

As a consequence of the various changes, the perspectives of development in the market have seemed to be particularly complex for those banks that until now have enjoyed the benefits attached to a particular market niche and to the protection they are offered as a specific category of intermediary. On the one hand, the process of unification and globalization of bank markets has not (paradoxically) relegated to the shadows the local dimension of credit; on the contrary, it seems enhanced by the globalization–cum–localism combination that characterizes most European countries. On the other hand, the entrance of new operators in local credit markets, the growing overlap of banks' distributive networks, and the increase of the operations of foreign banks in retail financial services have all have increased the level of competition to which the cooperative banks are exposed, leading also to the disappearance of 'protected' markets in traditional geographic spaces of localization of small cooperative banks (monobranch/monocellular).

In such a market context, the tactic of some strategic levers has seemed – and not only to the operators – fundamental to generating an effective competitive response and to furnishing some adequate responses to member-customers' changeable demands from the point of view of the needs to undertake comparative evaluations of the services offered in terms of returns, access costs and quality.

The strategic options the European reality has defined in response to the market changes seem similar in terms of their purpose, but they prove to be different in terms of methods of realization, even if competitive pressures and the characteristics of the cooperative model are substantially similar in different countries.

In particular, the merger or acquisition's decision, which is carried out through operations of concentration, although it is frequent in different countries, does not seem to be the main one; exceeding the limitations of the cooperative bank in present market contexts, which are linked, as pointed out, to the poor availability of capital, to the need to widen the entrepreneurial base, and to the need to improve the level of company efficiency and management quality, is pursued through different strategic solutions.

As a consequence of an extreme concentration process, carried out through mergers and acquisitions whether voluntary or imposed by national legislators, as in the case of the German and Portuguese cooperative banks, in the market there is the definite choice of internal growth – through consolidation and the centralized group model – of the Dutch and Belgian cooperative banks; or, in a wider manner, the adoption of national pyramid structures, with two or three levels of organizational decentralization (national, regional and/or local) – comparable to 'integrated' or simply 'network' systems – that can allow single cooperative banks to exceed certain limits. This is the case with German, Spanish, French and Portuguese cooperative networks, whose structures are based on the centralization of functions at a national level, which can allow high level of efficiency and scale economies.[3]

An exception in the European context seems to be Britain, whose cooperative banks have often chosen to demutualize and, ultimately, to gradually disappear from the market (Llewellyn, 2000). With reference to the Italian case, recourse to the operations of concentration seems particularly extreme from the 1990s, that is, in the initial stages of the process of reorganizing cooperative credit. The regulators themselves also recognize the potential of Italian cooperative credit banks to have recourse to external growth solutions through merger operations.

The wide process of deregulation of the European bank sector, formalized in the First Community Directive n. 780/1977, has driven the banks to search for the 'best dimension' in order to protect creditors' interests and to keep the stability of the individual bank.[4]

In some countries, like Portugal and Italy, supervisors have the power to authorize the prosecution of mergers or acquisitions, the parliament has debated taking into consideration the majority shares the company's statute has defined. In this way, the supervisors give cooperative banks the possibility to carried out, respecting the geographical area of reference, concentration operations that may be either homogeneous, that is, within the same category, or heterogeneous, that is, among banks of different natures. In other words, they grant, although indirectly, the possibility changing the status of the cooperative in the case of heterogeneous M&As.

Since the 1980s, cooperative credit banks have without any doubt seized the opportunities to grow that the regulators have offered. For example, in the Italian case, from 1990 the cooperative credit sector displays a gradual but constant fall in the number of banks, from 701 in 1987 to 439 in 2005, and, consequently, the market share of the cooperative sector relative to that of commercial banks varies from 64 per cent in 1985 to 56 per cent in 2005, which is also a consequence of the fall in the number of commercial banks (IRCEL, 2005).

In the Portuguese case, since the late 1990s the structural problems faced by Caixas de Crédito Agricola Mutuo (CCAM) have made it increasingly difficult to attract equity capital and have obliged many banks to undertake economic and financial restructuring. The most visible aspect of that process was an intensive wave of mergers: between 1993 and 2002, 64 mergers involving 143 CCAM took place (almost 70 per cent of these in 1993 alone), with some banks being involved in more than one merger (Cabo and Rebelo, 2005). Successive horizontal mergers have further reduced the number of CCAM to the present 121 (Bank of Portugal, 2005).

In France, the concentration process has been particularly extreme and has as a direct consequence resulted in a sensible reduction in the global number of credit intermediaries: at the end of 1984 there were 2,001 *établissements de credit*, while at the end of 2005 there were 855, a reduction of 57.3 per cent (CECEI, 2005).

The concentration process in cooperative banks has allowed them rapidly to get over problems of unicellularity in cooperative credit – raising the medium size of the single intermediary – and to solve company problems arising from organizational deficiencies and financial imbalances.

The operations have been carried out mainly within the category, and for this reason they involve no extreme risk of survival for cooperative banks in the market. Cases of acquisition of cooperative banks by other banks have been usually restricted to the resolution of evident financial crisis.

Over recent years the trend towards concentrations in the European cooperative credit has almost slowed, which is probably due to the natural saturation of the market and to the preference for competitive strategies which are alternatives to internal growth.

In Europe, indeed, the whole cooperative credit sector has developed a new competitive strategy: together with the growth in size through concentration operations, there is the adoption of a network system based on principles of focalization, in the core business, in the reinforcement of distributive networks, and in the extreme recourse to outsourcing strategies (Carretta, 2005), able to offer both possible costs and benefits to individual banks.

This organizational structure looks like a coordinated system of autonomies – based on structures that act at different levels – with different but complementary functions and reinforced by common mechanisms of strategic trend, of coordination and of financial support.

Such an important system allows wide margins of autonomy at lower levels, in the management of customer relations and in core business activity; at the same time, it concedes to higher levels certain powers of direction and control that allow the rationalization of the use of resources and support the development of financial investments in order to improve the profits of the intermediaries.

The gradual reduction in the number of concentrations, which has been noted in recent years, can be interpreted as the result of an evaluation that operators themselves have carried out of the cost of the concentration option relative to the possible benefits obtainable from the network model.

Therefore, as far as the aims of the present analysis are concerned it seems reasonable, on the one hand, to speculate about the importance of external growth initiatives and, on the other hand, to search for further and deeper elements for an evaluation of the advantages of these solutions for the development of the cooperative sector.

4.3   An evaluation of the advantages and disadvantages of M&As for the development of European cooperative banks

Our evaluation of the advantages of concentration operations for cooperative banks has the purpose of assessing the theoretical compatibility or coherence of this strategic choice with the peculiarities and the sustainability of the cooperative bank model in the market in the long term.

As already mentioned in the introduction, our thesis argues that there is a potential incoherence, at a theoretical level, of concentrations as a solution for the development of the sector as they are incompatible with the competitive advantages connected with the cooperative bank model.

The analysis does not involve, of course, heterogeneous concentrations which, although not involved in turning round the cooperative banks acquired, seem not to be strategic choices with the purpose of developing cooperative banks, as they hasten their final disappearance from the market.

If one considers the competitive advantages of the cooperative bank model, the impact of an operation of homogeneous concentration allows us to identify several effects on the reality of the company involved in the operation. Table 4.1 shows the distinctive characteristics that are usually attributed to the cooperative bank model and describes the nature of the effect (negative or positive) that, in principle, a concentration operation could have on each of them.

As pointed out, the positive effects of concentration are expressed in the extension of the entrepreneurial base that facilitates growth in size and can allow an improvement in the availability of investment capital, a widening of the products portfolio and an improvement in the yield/risk profile in the credit portfolio, as a consequence of a greater geographical/sectorial diversification of the loans issued to customers. The growth in size enables the bank to achieve important scale economies,

Table 4.1 Effects of a concentration on the cooperative bank involved in the operation

Strong and weak points of the cooperative bank	Effects of the concentration on the cooperative bank	
	Nature	**Description**
– Strict relationship with its members and customers	Negative	– Weakening of the relationship with the members, because of the extension of the shareholders (passage from the socio-centric to the market-centric model).
– Reduced information asymmetries about the debtor (monitoring of the debtor)	Negative	– Reduction in the possibility of monitoring customers, as a consequence of greater distance from the market (reducing of credit quality).
– Inefficiency of the cooperative bank model (agency problem between members and management)	Negative	– Further fragmentation of the capital and disincentive of the members to exercise control over management.
– Limited commercial offer	Positive	– Extension of products portfolio (and of profits)
– Monitoring of customers (debtors)	Negative	– Weakening of extra-economic sanctioning mechanisms, as a consequence of information asymmetries and of distance from the market.
– High concentration of the portfolio's credit risk	Positive	– Improvement in the geographic/sectorial diversification of loans portfolio.

whose realization – it is important to specify – is not always verified in empirical studies. With regard to this fact, some authors maintain that the costs curve presents an 'L' progress, which allows capitalization of the cost synergies only within well-defined size thresholds of the bank (Di Salvo et al., 2002).

The negative effects, on the contrary, seem to threaten just those competitive advantages pointed out in the cooperative bank model.

The weakening of the cooperative spirit due to the increase in the number of shareholders and to the possible changeover from a member-centric model to a market-centric model, the widening of the bank–customer information asymmetries and the weakening of extra-economic ratifying mechanisms (peer monitoring and social control) produced by the greater distance among the bank, the debtors and the market, and the intensification of the agency problem between the members and the management as a consequence of the further fragmentation of the company base are considered, in theory, to be among the possible threats to the sustainability of the competitive advantages of the cooperative bank in the long term.

This range of negative effects ultimately impairs the quality of the credit of cooperative banks, which is their main strength in the market. It ultimately weakens the 'soft' mechanisms of credit management, typical of cooperative banks, and exposes them 'completely' to the risk connected with the segment of customers they traditionally serve, who are typically more risky than that (corporate and middle market) of commercial banks (IRCEL, Bollettino, 2005). A first sign of this can be seen, for example, in the greater growth of the unpaid debts of the cooperative banks compared with that of the commercial banks, as pointed out earlier.

The doubts about the external growth solution for cooperative banks can be confirmed by the empirical studies available in the literature concerning the effects of concentrations on cooperative banks.[5] Although these studies seem not to be particularly numerous, unlike those carried out for commercial banks, they point out, in particular, how fusion operations with strategic purposes do not offer significant advantages in terms of efficiency and profitability for the cooperative banks involved; furthermore, the attainment of the scale economies as a consequence of the widening of the productive structure is demonstrated in only a few cases, and it seems to be not particularly relevant (five per cent in the years following the operation).

The analysis of the advantages of concentration for cooperative banks is enriched by further possible negative effects, deriving from the nature and the complexity of the operation itself. M&As require a prior evaluation of the presence, within the companies involved, of the skills necessary to manage the post-merger and keep the target of the deal.

If the bank lacks such competences within itself, it will need to have recourse to heavy investments in generating and improving its own employees' management abilities. The absence of such investment, as an alternative, can result in weak and misleading plans of organizational integration, unable to promote the purposes of the operation, with possible repercussions on the retention levels of member-customers and, ultimately, on the income balances of the bank.

In the absence of any strong empirical tests, the theoretical analysis of the advantages of concentrations for cooperative banks suggests that such operations do not represent a valid or suitable option for the development of cooperative banks, as they do not allow the banks to overcome completely the limitations of the bank model (for example, the problem of company efficiency) and, furthermore, they ignore the importance of the physical component in relationships with customers, compromising the validity of territorial protection and increasing the risk borne by the company.

For these reasons, in order to develop the cooperative sector it is probably more advisable to reinforce the cooperative network, which seems, in contrast, to allow some important scale advantages without compromising the autonomy of single banks and, in the long run, the presence of cooperative banks themselves on the market.

4.4   Conclusions

Regulations on banking supervision and the economic literature single out specific features in the cooperative bank model and specific elements of fragility (reduced company size, poor availability of capital, company inefficiency).

The intensity of competitive pressures in the contexts of present markets and the recent legislative modifications European banking supervisors have introduced for small banks offer the cooperative credit sector the opportunity to restructure and reinforce its own competitive model in the market by overcoming of the limitations of the bank model.

The remarkable restructuring efforts that the cooperative credit sector has undergone in recent years have been founded also on a more or less extreme recourse to concentration operations of the homogeneous type, while respecting the banking regulations issued in individual countries on the issue of concentration among cooperatives.

In some countries, like Italy and Portugal, recourse to concentration operations has allowed the cooperative sector to achieve positive – but not significant – margins of profitability and an improvement in its competitiveness in the market (in terms of the growth of employees), without overcoming certain traditional limitations of cooperative banks, such as for example the level of company efficiency, and damaging, furthermore, the quality of the credit portfolio.

The comparison between the peculiarities of the cooperative model and the possible effects of concentration on individual banks has revealed, furthermore, how these operations ignore the importance of the physical component in customer relations, thus compromising the validity of territorial protection and the effectiveness of 'soft' mechanisms of credit management peculiar to the cooperative banks, so increasing the risk borne by cooperative banks. Further elements of perplexity regarding the external growth solution for cooperative banks derive from the efforts, not only of the economic kind, the cooperative banks are requested to make in view of the nature and the complexity of concentration operations.

In the absence of any strong empirical tests, the theoretical analysis of the advantages of the concentrations for cooperative shows that these operations do not represent a valid or suitable option for the development of cooperative banks

For these reasons, to develop the cooperative sector it seems probably more suitable to reinforce the cooperative network, which seems, in contrast to concentration, to allow some important scale advantages without compromising either the autonomy of individual banks or the long-term presence of cooperative banks themselves in the market.

Notes

1. As everybody knows, the reform of the Italian company law is contained in the D.Lgs. n. 6/2003; for a comment on the regulations concerning only the form of the cooperative company, see Cerioli, Costanzo and Sanguinetti (2004).
2. In the Italian case, for example, the reference is to the prudential regulations on internal controls and capital adequacy of banks; see Carretta, Schwizer and Stefanelli (2003).
3. For further details, see Cardoso (1999); Patarnello (2000); Palomo Zurdo and Valor (2001); Vandone (2003).
4. Previously, in some countries, such as for example Italy, the regulations imposed a freeze of new constitutions, ratified with the Comitato Interministeriale per il Credito ed il Risparmio's deliberation of the 23 June 1996, with the purpose of safeguarding the stability of the system.
5. See Clemente (1997), Di Salvo et al. (1998, 2002), Cingano and Schivardi (2003).

References

Bank of Italy, Relazione Annuale (various years).
——. (1999), Istruzioni di vigilanza per le banche, Aprile.
——. (2005), Bollettino di Vigilanza, Aprile.
Bank of Portugal (2005), Annual Report.
ECB (European Central Bank), Annual Reports, various years.
——. (2000), Mergers and Acquisitions Involving the EU Banking Industry – Facts and Implications.
——. (2004a), Report on EU Banking Structure, November.
——. (2004b), EU Banking Sector Stability, November.

Cabo P. and Rebelo J. (2005), Why Do Agricultural Credit Cooperatives Merge? The Portuguese Experience, *Annals of Public and Cooperative Economics*, vol. 76: 3, pp. 491–516.

Cardoso J. C. (President of FENACAM) (1999), The Background of the Portuguese Credito Agricola Mutuo and the Role of FENACAM in Defending the Cooperative System and the Rural Environment, dattiloscritto.

Carretta A. (2005), Politiche di outsourcing del Credito Cooperativo, intervento al 13 Convegno nazionale del Credito Cooperativo, Parma, 9–11 Dicembre 2005.

Carretta A., Schwizer P. and Stefanelli V. (2003), Oltre la regolamentazione: il sistema dei controlli interni degli intermediari finanziari. Cultura del controllo o controllo della cultura?, Ottavo Rapporto Fondazione Rosselli, Edibank, Milano.

Cerioli S. L., Costanzo P. and Sanguinetti A. (2004), La riforma delle società cooperative. Disciplina civilistica e fiscale. Adempimenti contabili, Egea.

Cingano F. and Schivardi F. (2003), Identifying the Sources of Local Productivity Growth, in *Temi di discussione Banca d'Italia*, no. 474, June.

Clemente C. (1997), Concentrazioni bancarie e mercati locali in Italia, in Cooperazione di Credito, intervento al XXII Convegno Regionale della Federazione delle Banche di Credito Cooperativo, 19–20 ottobre.

Comité des Etablissements de Crèdit et Des Entreprises d'Investissement (CECEI) (2005), Rapport Annuel, (available on http://www.banque-france.fr/fr/supervi/ telnomot/rapports/2005/integral.pdf).

Di Salvo R., La Torre M. and Maggiolini P. (1998), Le operazioni di concentrazione tra banche di credito cooperativo. Caratteri distintivi e fattori determinanti, in *Cooperazione di Credito*, no. 162.

Di Salvo R., Guidi A. and Mazzilis M. C. (2002), La riorganizzazione industriale del Credito Cooperativo: gli effetti delle concentrazioni sull'efficienza gestionale delle bcc e le implicazioni di policy, in Settimo Rapporto della Fondazione Rosselli, La banca senza confini. Mercati, concorrenti, tecnologie e strategie, Edibank.

EFMA (European Financial Management and Market Association) (2004), Mutualist Banking Institutions in Europe. Cooperative Value in the Face of Market Globalization, no. 187, January–February.

European Commission (2001a), Le cooperative nell'Europa Imprenditoriale, Documento di lavoro dei servizi della commissione.

——. (2001b), Libro Verde 'Promuovere un quadro europeo per la responsabilità sociale delle imprese'.

——. (2002), Report on Macroeconomics and Financial Sector Stability Development in candidate countries, Enlargement Paper, no. 8, April.

——. (2003), Regolamento CE no.143/03.

——. (2004), Comunicazione della Commissione al Consiglio, al Parlamento Europeo, al Comitato Economico e Sociale Europeo e al Comitato delle Regioni sulla promozione delle società cooperative in Europa.

Group of Ten, 2001, Report on Consolidation in the Financial Sector, January.

IRCEL, Bollettino Statistico, anni vari.

Llewellyn D. (2000), Il futuro del mutualismo nel Regno Unito. Il governo d'impresa nelle organizzazioni mutualistiche e nelle Plc, in *Cooperazione di Credito*, no. 169.

Palomo Zurdo R. J. and Valor C. (2001), Banca cooperativa. Entorno financiero y proyección social, Madrid: Unión Nacional de Cooperativas de Crédito y Ministerio de Trabajo y Asuntos Sociales (Dirección General de Fomento de la Economía Social y del Fondo Social Europeo).

Patarnello A. (2000), Il modello di riferimento delle strutture federative locali: verso una nuova configurazione, in *Cooperazione di credito*, no. 169.

Schraffl I. (1999), Modelli di integrazione dei sistemi bancari cooperativi. I casi di Rabobank, del Credit Muuel e del Credito Agricola Mutuo, in Cooperazione di Credito, Ottobre/Dicembre.

Vandone D. (2003), Le banche di credito cooperativo in Francia e in Spagna, in Cooperazione di Credito, no. 182.

5
Outsourcing Policies in Cooperative Banking

A. Carretta

5.1 Introduction

Outsourcing in cooperative banking can, for the most part, be analysed by way of responding to three significant questions. These questions are as follows:

(I) For what 'reasons', and in what areas, is outsourcing used by particular banks and financial intermediaries, according to the main literature on this subject and the most significant practices described therein?

(II) What are the guidelines for 'good' outsourcing, aimed at creating value according to safe and sound principles?

(III) What are the opportunities and risks of outsourcing policies followed by cooperative banks?

5.2 Trends in outsourcing policies

Global trends in outsourcing indicate that the demand for this type of external service provider in the financial service industry is increasing, with ever more complex and articulated procedures that meet diversified needs, not only complying with reductions in costs but also having to do with the externalization of core activities of the bank or in any case with a strong strategic impact on the development of banks.

There is a growing international trend within the financial service industry to apply outsourcing policies, that is, resorting to third parties to carry out activities (or aspects of them) that would traditionally be carried out within the organization.[1] According to estimates and forecasts given by the Basel Committee, the phenomenon of outsourcing involves, for example, more than a third of the financial system's entire expenditure in information technology (IT) and, from a more general perspective, it involves 15 per cent of the entire activity of the financial industry.[2] At least until 2008, the global rate of growth of outsourcing would be close to 11 per cent per year.[3]

Outsourcing as a solution is becoming more articulated and complex. There are different forms of outsourcing: within networks of cooperative banks, or with alliances with suppliers, or purely with 'contractual' action with third parties. It is linked to decisions on diversification and vertical and horizontal integration which characterize the external development of banks.

The literature on this theme highlights numerous motives for outsourcing. Schematically, they can be listed as follows:

- reduction of production costs
- focusing of bank resources mainly on core activities
- access to specialized know-how
- decision not to integrate different cultures within the bank
- need to reconfigure the cost structure from fixed to variable
- search for a quality, not reproducible within the bank
- aversion to risk.

Similarly, reasons for choosing not to use outsourcing include:

- reliance on services providers
- confidentiality of data and of production processes
- loss of distinctive know-how
- outsourcing agreements too long and inflexible
- excess of staff, not otherwise employable
- difficulty in assessing the price of outsourcing services
- lack of competence of services providers
- difficulties in controlling outsourced activities.

In any case, the choice of outsourcing seems to be governed by the attempt to maintain a satisfactory balance between vertical integration, which pushes towards centralizing all those activities related to businesses of a bank, and resorting to the external market in search of the 'best' acquisition opportunities of necessary inputs.[4]

In summary, the review of theoretical and empirical literature allows us to highlight two important conclusions that reconsider a number of commonplace issues on outsourcing, putting them into a correct perspective. These are:

(a) Cost reduction is only one of the incentives for outsourcing, and often it is not the most important. Other justifications include: the opportunity to redraw the boundaries of the bank's organization; access to technologies and expertise that are not easily reproducible; various types of risk mitigation; and a more timely and effective matching of the bank's strategies with the availability of inputs.[5]
(b) As a result, outsourcing policies often deal not only with marginal, low value added activities, but also with the bank's core activities or with activities with strong strategic impact on the bank's development.[6]

5.3   'Good' outsourcing

Outsourcing creates value if the bank has the ability to organize and manage its activities, including production, based on market logic (this is to say, to appeal to external third-party providers to find its inputs) rather than on a logic of internal organization. However, outsourced activities have to be organized, managed and controlled using a logic of integration, as applied to any bank.

The convenience of outsourcing depends on a complex mix of issues that are both internal and external to the bank, and difficult to evaluate on a general basis.

One approach is to look at the effects of outsourcing on production costs curves; at the capacity to manage and control, in an incorporated way, both internal processes and outsourced ones; and at how the 'freed' resources are used when outsourcing is used.[7] Another is to look at the effects of outsourcing on the bank's competitive strength, which depends, among other things, also on its production size and range, which are in turn influenced by outsourcing itself. Moreover, the choice of outsourcing depends also on likely restrictions and costs, such as forms of controls prescribed by regulators on the scale and nature of outsourcing strategies.[8]

In summary, outsourcing creates value if the bank that chooses it has the ability (and in many areas, certainly in the financial case, that is a 'distinct' ability) to organize and manage its own activities, including production, according to a market logic – using external providers, which are often very numerous[9] – to find production input, rather than a logic of internal organization.[10]

As far as safe and sound management of a bank is concerned, this implies:

(a) governing the balance between the search for excellent third-party service providers, able to ensure the 'best' possible outsourcing, and the ability to maintain medium- to long-term relations with them, which can reduce research costs and improve the experience curve of the bank;

(b) the ability to manage the always more common interdependencies between 'internal' and 'outsourced' activities, which become even more important when outsourcing occurs during specific phases of any process or with specific (core and support) activities;

(c) the effective and efficient ongoing monitoring and control of all outsourced activities;

(d) the maintenance of internal skills and cultural consistency on the outsourced activity. This would certainly facilitate the tasks referred to above by promoting continuous learning within the bank also in these activities; and

(e) an aptitude to anticipate trends and developments in the regulation of outsourcing, which will gradually tend to reinforce the attention of banks to this profile of external development. For example, it may require formalized outsourcing programmes, approved by the bank's corporate governance structures, with explicit analyses of outsourcing risks and effective risk-management programmes; or appropriate due diligence in choosing third-party service providers or internal control systems focused also on outsourced activities.[11]

Therefore, the 'safe and sound management' of outsourcing imposes explicit and implicit costs but, on the other hand, it is a necessary condition for the proper performance of this solution and, consequently, for its contribution to the creation of value for banks.

5.4   Risks and opportunities of outsourcing policies for cooperative banking

For cooperative banking, outsourcing is an option consistent with general trends in financial systems and essential for sustainable competition. 'Outsourcing by category' strengthens, rather than dispersing, the distinctive expertise and culture of cooperative banks. Moreover, it 'trains' banks to share (leading towards co-sourcing), which must, however, be balanced by a mechanism comparative to the 'external' market, which, in turn, may be a stimulus to the continuous search for the best outsourcing solutions.

In principle, the growth of outsourcing in cooperative banking is consistent with present general trends in financial systems and with the factors that enable outsourcing policies to create value. Specifically, the main opportunities offered by outsourcing policies may be summarized in the following considerations which, even if they are based mainly on the Italian case, can easily be extended to other instances.

Cooperative banks' use of outsourcing is, in different areas, an essential choice that allows them to compete using better cost structures, production range and specialized expertise.[12] The outsourcing developed within the cooperative bank category (a sort of *'outsourcing by category'*) retains and strengthens the specific know-how developed by outsourced activities. Therefore, this outsourcing model makes it possible to cultivate an adequate culture in areas where outsourcing would otherwise result in a progressive 'illiteracy' of the cooperative bank category, even of managerial profiles.[13]

For different activities, the choice of 'outsourcing by category' is a factor making for success. Indeed, it allows a better link to the specific features of cooperative banking that are often difficult to replicate in 'traditional' forms of outsourcing available on the market.

Outsourcing can be used as a training ground to share managerial practices and competencies and network logic, consistently with the tradition of cooperative banking; outsourcing can also be used in strategic areas, all being consistent with the overall trends of outsourcing.

In this respect, it is therefore advisable to use the expression 'co-sourcing' rather than 'outsourcing'. This because of the joint commitment of the category in this context and of the results one would wish to obtain from a 'strengthening' (and not just an 'externalization') of resources.

From this perspective, there is a strong probability that the category will incur a sort of self-referencing risk. This could jeopardize the ongoing search for optimal outsourcing conditions, which is necessary to give efficacy to such a solution. Moreover, it could, at least in principle, affect the autonomous decisions taken by the governing body of each bank.

In this respect, it might be useful to carry out an institutional and systematic comparison between the category as a whole and the external 'market'. This could be done by, for example setting up an advisory body made up of third-party consultants with the skills of the main activities subject to outsourcing. Such a body could provide an independent overview of the 'validity' of 'outsourcing by category' compared with systemic risk, which cannot be however neglected.[14]

5.5 Conclusions

The global trends of outsourcing indicate an increasing use by the financial service industry of this external development solution, with ever more complex and articulated forms, ready to meet the most diverse needs, not just simple cost reductions. It also concerns core activities of banks and has a strong strategic impact on banks' business development.

Outsourcing creates value if the bank has the ability to organize and manage its activities, including production, based on market logic (this is to say, to appeal to external third-party providers to find its inputs) rather than on a logic of internal organization. In the present situation in the financial service industry, this ability is probably a distinctive competence, particularly for smaller banks. However, outsourced activities must in any case be organized, managed and controlled by an integrated logic, within the bank as a whole.

For cooperative banking, outsourcing is a choice that is consistent with the general trends present in the financial system and essential for implementing sustainable competition. Outsourcing by category can strengthen, rather than disperse, the distinctive expertise and culture of cooperative banks. It also 'trains' towards sharing (from outsourcing to 'co-sourcing'), which must be balanced by mechanisms of comparison with the 'external' market. This may result in a continuous search for optimal outsourcing solutions.

Notes

Some ideas and preliminary assumptions concerning this matter have been discussed with some colleagues: Giorgio Di Giorgio, Marco Lamandini and Salvatore Maccarone, and friends Franco Caleffi e Roberto Di Salvo, presented at the 13th National Conference on cooperative credit (in Parma in 2005) and published in *Cooperazione di credito* (2005).
1. See European Central Bank (2004), p. 25 onwards.
2. See Basel Committee on Bank Supervision (2005).
3. See Beaumont and Khan (2005), p. 5.
4. See Beaumont and Khan (2005).
5. See Basel Committee on Bank Supervision (2005); Ang and Cummings (1997).
6. See Wood and Batiz-Lazo ; McLellan, Marcolin and Beamish (1995).
7. See Ang and Straub (1998).

8. See Lopez (2004).
9. According to a survey carried out by the European Central Bank (2004), more than half the banks in the sample engaged in excess of ten outsourced suppliers.
10. See Holzhauser, Lammers and Schwarze (2005).
11. See Basel Committee on Bank Supervision (2005), p. 14 onwards.
12. For a comparison between the cost levels of the banks that do and those that do not use outsourcing for IT, see for example, Associazione bancaria Italiana and Convenzione Interbancaria per i problemi di automazione (2005).
13. See Carretta (2001).
14. See European Central Bank (2004), p. 32.

References

Ang S. and Cummings L. L. (1997), Strategic Response to Institutional Influences on Information Systems Outsourcing, *Organizational Science*, May–June.

Ang S. and Straub D. W. (1998), Production and Transaction Economies and IS Outsourcing: A Study of the US Banking Industry, *MIS Quarterly*, December.

Associazione bancaria Italiana e Convenzione Interbancaria per i problemi dell'automazione (2005), Rilevazione dello stato dell'automazione del sistema creditizio, July.

Basel Committee on Bank Supervision (2005), *Outsourcing in Financial Services*, BIS, February.

Beaumont N. and Khan Z. (2005), A Taxonomy of Refereed Outsourcing Literature, Monash University, Working Paper, no. 22/05, May.

Carretta A. (2001), Il governo del cambiamento culturale in banca, Bancaria editrice, Rome.

Carretta A. (2005), Politiche di outsourcing del Credito Cooperativo, "Cooperazione di credito", July–December.

European Central Bank (2004), Report on EU Banking System, November.

Holzhauser M., Lammers M. and Schwarze F. (2005), Integrated Decision Model for Credit Product Outsourcing, *Wirtschaftsinformatik*, no. 2.

Lopez J. A. (2004), Outsourcing by Financial Services Firms: The Supervisory Response, *FRBSF Economic Letter*, November.

McLellan K., Marcolin B. L. and Beamish P. W. (1995), Financial and Strategic Motivations Behind is Outsourcing, *Journal of Information Technology*, no.10, pp. 299–321.

Wood D. and Batiz-Lazo D. (1997), Corporate Strategy, Centralization and Outsourcing in Banking, *International Association of Management Journal*, vol. 9(3), pp. 35–57.

6
Shareholder Value and Efficiency of Cooperative Banks in Europe

F. Fiordelisi

6.1   Introduction

This chapter aims to assess (a) the shareholder value created by cooperative banks and (b) their cost-efficiency levels, using a large sample of cooperative banks in France, Germany, Italy and the United Kingdom over the period 1995–2002.

While there is a substantial literature dealing with bank efficiency[1] and shareholder value,[2] only a few studies (e.g. Beccalli et al., 2006; Fernandez, 2002; Eisenbeis et al., 1999; Chu and Lim, 1998) have empirically analysed both issues in commercial banking; as far as we are aware, none focuses on cooperative banks. Beccalli et al. (2006) estimate the cost efficiency of a panel of European listed banks and find that changes in the prices of bank stocks reflect percentage changes in cost efficiency, particularly those derived from Data Envelopment Analysis (DEA) estimation. Fernandez (2002) analyse a panel of 142 banks operating in 18 countries between 1989 and 1998, and find that market returns have a strong positive relationship with pure efficiency change and technical change, but only a weak relationship with scale efficiency. Eisenbeis et al. (1999) estimate a negative relationship between cost inefficiency and stock returns and find that the stochastic frontier produces relatively more informative performance measures than does DEA. Chu and Lim (1998) analyse a panel of six Singapore-listed banks (over the period 1992–6) and find that variation in the price of bank stocks reflect change in profits rather than cost efficiency estimated using DEA. By contrast, various studies have empirically analysed the relationship between efficiency and profits (e.g. Spong et al., 1995; Berger and Mester, 1997; Beccalli et al. (2006) and, not surprisingly, usually find that there is a positive relationship (efficient banks are more profitable).

Our research presents new insights into how shareholder value and efficiency improvements are achieved in cooperative banking, focusing on the largest European industries. In this chapter we empirically assess the profitability and shareholder value created, and then estimate the cost efficiency levels.

6.2 The analysis of shareholder value

6.2.1 Framework

The concept of shareholder value is one of the oldest nostrums in business:[3] a company creates value for shareholders over a given time period when the return on invested capital is greater than its opportunity cost, or than the rate that investors could earn by investing in other securities with the same risk. As a consequence, the shareholder value (added) created over the period $t-1$, t ($SHV_{t-1,t}$) is obtained by multiplying this abnormal return, that is, Shareholder Total Return ($SHR_{t-1,t}$) minus the expected rate of return over the period $t-1$, t ($E(R)_{t-1,t}$), for the capital invested by shareholders, that is, expressed by the Market Value of the company's Equity capital (MVE) at the time $t-1$. In order to emphasize that this concept of 'value' implies a comparison of the shareholder return with the opportunity cost, the word 'added' is often used jointly with the term 'value' (e.g., market value added or economic value added). In detail:

$$SHV_{t-1,t} = \left[SHR_{t-1,t} - E(R)_{t-1,t}\right] \times MVE_{t-1} \tag{1}$$

Although this is straightforward, the problem of measuring created shareholder value is not solved since: (1) this calculation procedure can be adopted only for publicly traded companies. Since cooperative banks are usually not listed in capital markets, there is a strong need to find which performance indicators best capture created shareholder value; (2) this measurement procedure provides an accurate *ex post* assessment of the bank's ability to create shareholder value, but it has a limited use as an *ex ante* assessment since changes in stock prices, dividends, other payments to shareholders, outlays for capital increases and the conversion of convertible company's bonds are unknown; and (3) there are a number of competing bank performance measures, and it by no means clear which is preferred in terms of measuring value creation. For example, several performance measures were developed over the 1990s, and researchers and practitioners are grappling with different performance metrics. As a consequence, which method is best for assessing the value created by firms for their owners is a topic of current debate.[4]

6.2.2 Methodology and sample description

Since several studies have found that shareholder value can be measured for non-listed companies by the Economic Value Added (EVA) measure (e.g. Fiordelisi and Molyneux, 2006), we measure the shareholder value created by cooperative European banks using EVA. EVA expresses the surplus value created by a company in a given period, that is, the firm's profit net of the cost of all capital. This measure is computed as the product of the difference between the return on invested capital (ROIC) and its composite financing cost (i.e. cost of capital – CC) and the capital invested (CI) at the beginning of the period $(t-1)$.

$$EVA_{t-1,t} = NOPAT_{t-1,t} - \left(CI_{t-1} * CC_{t-1,t} \right)$$

(2)

In order to move book values closer to their economic values, various accounting adjustments are made. The first adjustment is standard for all kinds of companies, and concerns Research and Development (R&D) costs and training costs: these expenses are designed to generate future growth and, therefore, represent intangible investments. Current assets do not benefit from these expenses, and it would be incorrect to reduce operating income by the amount of these expenses. However, accounting standards require companies to treat all outlays for R&D as operating expenses in the income statement. As a consequence, this accounting distortion can be corrected by: (a) adding back these expenses in calculating NOPAT; (b) capitalizing all Research and Development (R&D) expenses and training costs in capital invested; (c) amortizing these capitalized expenses over an appropriate period: for example, according to Stern Stewart's statistics,[5] five years is the average useful life of R&D expenses. As such, investments in intangibles are treated in the same manner as investments in tangible assets.

The second adjustment, which concerns operating lease expenses, is also standard for all kind of companies. These costs are usually considered as operating costs in companies' cost–income statements. However, operating leases are disguised financial expenses since companies acquire a productive asset (and, therefore, finance their future production) by paying periodic rent (i.e. operating leases expenses). In order to face this conservative accounting practice, it is opportune to: (d) capitalize any operating lease expenses in calculating NOPAT; (e) treat the present value of expected lease commitments over time as capital invested in the firm; (f) amortize these capitalized expenses over an appropriate period.[6]

The other adjustments made account for banking peculiarities, and therefore these are specific to banks.[7] The third adjustment concerns loan loss provisions and loan loss reserves. The loan loss reserve aims to cover any future loan losses and for this reason it should be equal to the net present value of all future loan losses. In any single period, this reserve is reduced by net charge-offs (i.e. the current period losses due to credit risk) and replenished by loan loss provisions (i.e. the provision made in the current period to adjust the reserves both for pre-existing loans and for estimated future loan losses related to newly originated loans). This convention is certainly commendable from a management perspective since it implies that all loan losses are pre-funded out of current earnings. However, loan loss provisions are commonly used to manage earnings: if a bank achieves high operating returns, bank managers tend to overestimate this provision, while they are inclined to underestimate it if operating earnings are poor. This accounting practice introduces an important distortion in analysing bank performance since it smoothes earnings. Business is risky, and the volatility of profits is a manifestation of this risk: for purposes of economic performance evaluation, smoothing earnings is inappropriate. In order to face deal with this conservative accounting practice, it is opportune to: (g) add back loan loss provisions and deduct the net charge-offs in calculating NOPAT; (h) capitalize the net loan loss reserve as capital invested. These adjustments are intended to reduce the opportunities for management to smooth accounting profits.

The fourth adjustment regards taxes. Many banks show significant and persistent differences between book tax provisions and cash tax payments. Since these differences are quasi-permanent, deferred taxes should be considered as capital and, similarly to loan loss provisions, taxes need to be considered as current-period expenses for purposes of economic performance evaluation. This accounting conservatism can be dealt with by: (i) adding back loan book tax provisions and deducting the cash operating tax; (j) capitalizing the deferred tax credits (net of the deferred tax debits) as capital invested. Similarly to the adjustments for loan loss provisions, taxation adjustments are intended to reduce the opportunities for management to smooth accounting profits.

The fifth adjustment concerns restructuring charges. Since the late 1990s, many banks have carried out restructuring plans in order to improve their operating efficiency. To the extent that such restructuring charges represent disinvestments, these costs should be treated as a capital reduction rather than capital expenditure (and therefore reduce NOPAT). Limited data availability prevents us from evaluating the extent of real disinvestments due to restructuring charges; these costs are omitted when adjusting NOPAT and capital invested.

The sixth adjustment aims to correct for distortions derived from the 'general risk reserve', a standard feature in Italian banking. This provision is a reserve that covers a bank's future generic loan losses: in any single period, this reserve is reduced by net charge-offs (i.e. the current period losses) and replenished by general risk provisions (i.e. the provision made in the current period to adjust the reserve according to the bank's risks). Similarly to the loan loss reserve, this convention is certainly commendable from a management prospective, but it is used in an opportunistic manner. This accounting practice introduces an important distortion in analysing banks' performance since it smoothes earnings. In order to deal with this conservative accounting practice, it is opportune to: (k) add back general risk provisions and deduct the net charge-offs in calculating NOPAT; (l) capitalize the general risk reserve as capital invested. These adjustments aim to reduce the opportunities for management to smooth accounting profits.

Regarding the definition of capital invested, this cannot be measured using total assets (as for a non-financial company) and, consequently, the cost of invested capital is not estimated as Weighted Average Cost of Capital (WACC). While this solution is certainly accurate for non-banking companies, this procedure would be misleading for commercial banks. Since financial intermediation is the core business of banks, debts should be considered as a productive input in banking rather than a financing source (as for other companies). As such, interest expenses represent the cost of acquiring this input and, consequently, should be considered as an operating cost rather than a financial cost (as for other companies). As a consequence, if the capital charge is calculated following a standard procedure (i.e. applying WACC on total assets), EVA will be biased since it will double count the charge on debt. As such, the charge on debt should be first subtracted from NOPAT (the capital charge is calculated on the overall capital – that is, equity and debt – invested in the bank and, consequently, it includes the charge on debt) and, second, it would be subtracted from operating proceeds in calculating NOPAT: interest expenses (i.e. the charge on debt capital) are in fact subtracted from operating revenues. In the case of banks, it seems reasonable to calculate the capital invested (and, consequently, the capital charge) focusing on equity capital[8] and to measure the capital invested in the bank as the book value of shareholder equity. Regarding the cost of capital, the capital charge cannot be obtained applying the bank's WACC on the capital invested because the latter is given by the equity capital and not by the overall capital (debt and equity). Consequently, a commercial bank's cost of capital invested should be measured by the cost of equity.[9] To support this view, Sironi (1999) identifies four differences (labelled as 'the separation principle', 'banks as providers of liquidity services', 'capital ratios', 'off-balance sheet pro') between a bank's cost of capital and that of a non-financial company, and observes 'with a capital structure exogenously determined by regulators, a marginal cost of debt close to that obtainable from the interbank market, and relatively similar to that of all other major banks, and an array of products that do not need any debt financing, banks should look at their cost of equity capital as a key variable'.[10] The cost of equity (k^e) is estimated using the Capital Asset Pricing Model (CAPM), looking at investors' expected return. In this framework, there are three inputs for estimating the cost of equity: (1) Risk Free Rate: following a standard procedure,[11] this has been estimated taking the annual rate of return of a long-term government bond; (2) Equity Risk Premium: the modified historical approach proposed by Damodaran (2005) has been applied.[12] Equity Risk Premium is obtained by adding a country premium to the case premium for mature equity markets, such us the United States[13] The country premium is obtained by adjusting[14] the country bond spreads: this latter spread has been obtained by comparing European government bond rates[15] with the US MORGAN Government Bond return indices over the period analysed (January 1995–June 2003); (3) Beta: these coefficients have been estimated using daily data on an annual basis by regressing the bank's share returns against stock market returns.[16] These regression Betas have been successively adjusted following the Bloomberg procedure.[17] Figure 6.1 summarize our EVA calculation procedure.

Our sample consists of unlisted banks from France, Germany, and Italy between 1995 and 2002 with financial information obtained form Bankscope database.[18] Table 6.1 provides the number of banks considered for estimating each frontier.

6.2.3 Results

Tables 6.2–6.4 report our profitability and shareholder value estimates for the European banking markets analysed. In France, we found that banks appear to generate substantially superior mean profits to those in Italy and Germany. If we consider all bank categories (Table 6.2), French banks generated increasing annual mean profit from euro

$$EVA_{t-1,t} = NOPAT_{t-1,t} - (IC_{t-1} * K^e_{t-1,t})$$

Where: $NOPAT_{t-1,t}$ = EBIT (1–tax rate) +

        + R&D Expenses

        + Training expenses

        + Operating Lease Expenses

        + Loan loss provisions – Net charge-off

        + Book tax provisions – Cash operating tax

        + General risk provisions – Net charge-off

    IC_{t-1} = Book value of equity

        + Capitalized R&D expenses

        + Training expenses

        – Proxy for amortized R&D expenses

        –Proxy for amortized training expenses

        + Proxy for the present value of expected lease commitments over time

        – Proxy for amortized operating lease commitments

        + Net loan loss reserve

        + Deferred tax credits

        – Deferred tax debits

        + General Risk Reserve

Figure 6.1   Economic Value Added (EVA) for banks: Our calculation procedure.

17.61 million in 1995 to euro 60.70 million in 2002, and the mean value over the period 1995–2002 is 33.94% euro million. French banks registered constantly positive mean levels of returns on equity (ROE) and returns on assets (ROA) in this period. ROE ranged between 3.3% in 1996 and 6.59% in 2000 and ROA is constantly around 0.4%

Table 6.1 The number of banks in samples used for estimating efficiency with SFA and DEA, 1995–2002

Panel (A) SFA		1995	1996	1997	1998	1999	2000	2001	2002
France	Commercial banks	166	179	190	198	198	201	211	201
	Cooperative & savings banks*	102	102	120	122	126	129	142	136
		(80;22)	(80;22)	(95;25)	(97;25)	(101;25)	(100;29)	(111;31)	(98;28)
Germany	Commercial banks	123	125	140	149	151	167	170	170
	Cooperative & savings banks*	1,097	1,263	1,400	1,517	1,702	1,829	1,987	1,985
		(585;512)	(714;549)	(832;568)	(930;587)	(1,102;600)	(1,220;609)	(1,371;616)	(1,381;604)
Italy	Commercial banks	72	78	84	105	115	124	128	139
	Cooperative & savings banks*	157	164	195	326	450	530	569	586
		(86;71)	(102;62)	(132;63)	(262;64)	(386;64)	(464;66)	(505;64)	(520;66)
United Kingdom	Commercial banks	58	62	68	76	84	85	88	85
	Cooperative & savings banks*	0	0	0	0	0	0	0	0

(Continued)

Table 6.1   (Continued)

Panel (B) DEA		1995	1996	1997	1998	1999	2000	2001	2002
France	Commercial banks	175	191	199	208	213	218	235	227
France	Cooperative & savings banks*	103	112	120	122	126	131	147	139
France		(81;22)	(90;22)	(95;25)	(97;25)	(101;25)	(102;29)	(116;31)	(110;29)
Germany	Commercial banks	123	125	140	149	151	167	170	170
Germany	Cooperative & savings banks*	1,099 (587;512)	1,260 (715;549)	1,402 (835;567)	1,522 (937;585)	1,710 (1,112;598)	1,842 (1,234;608)	2,002 (1,389;613)	2,013 (1,403;610)
Italy	Commercial banks	79	82	87	106	117	127	132	144
Italy	Cooperative & savings banks*	150 (88;62)	171 (109;62)	198 (135;63)	333 (269;64)	458 (393;65)	544 (478;66)	584 (518;66)	598 (532;66)
United Kingdom	Commercial banks	58	62	68	76	84	85	88	85
United Kingdom	Cooperative & savings banks*	0	0	0	0	0	0	0	0

* The first number in the brackets refers to the number of cooperative banks and the second to the number of savings banks.
Source: Bankscope.

Table 6.2 Profitability and shareholder value created in French banking systems, 1995–2002

Panel (A) EVA	1995			1996			1997			1998		
	Mean*	St. dev*	% Positive[+]	Mean*	St. dev*	% Positive[+]	Mean*	St. dev*	% Positive[+]	Mean*	St. dev*	% Positive[+]
Commercial banks	−18.36	149.32	45.61	−14.08	105.38	44.50	−16.57	219.46	52.53	−12.27	157.61	49.66
Cooperative banks	−8.97	37.28	46.25	−11.45	65.60	43.82	0.51	38.94	52.17	3.86	64.94	50.00
Savings banks	−17.85	49.18	4.55	−14.80	64.87	36.36	−13.92	48.50	12.00	−8.25	10.85	12.00
Total	−14.43	100.66	39.36	−13.43	91.67	43.72	−11.47	154.41	49.27	−7.44	120.66	46.95

	1999			2000			2001			2002		
	Mean*	St. dev*	% Positive[+]	Mean*	St. dev*	% Positive[+]	Mean*	St. dev*	% Positive[+]	Mean*	St. dev*	% Positive[+]
Commercial Bank	−0.82	90.41	52.53	−3.80	187.99	53.67	7.28	228.73	59.74	16.92	372.48	60.27
Cooperative Bank	−0.68	90.84	48.98	−100.92	614.55	61.00	−115.22	691.90	52.68	−126.28	854.01	67.92
Savings Bank	−7.69	30.27	28.00	−4.19	8.62	34.48	19.91	90.67	58.06	29.74	102.60	72.41
Total	−1.23	83.04	46.94	−30.96	292.61	54.16	−26.98	351.08	57.57	−22.78	488.34	63.39

(Continued)

Table 6.2   (Continued)

Panel (B)	1995			1996			1997			1998		
EVA on capital invested	Mean[+]	St. dev[+]	% Positive[+]	Mean[+]	St. dev[+]	% Positive[+]	Mean[+]	St. dev[+]	% Positive[+]	Mean[+]	St. dev[+]	% Positive[+]
Commercial banks	−0.39	16.58	45.61	−1.80	17.51	44.50	1.63	16.43	52.53	−0.55	13.02	49.66
Cooperative banks	−0.81	5.28	46.25	−0.68	3.64	43.82	−0.43	4.00	52.17	−0.59	4.80	50.00
Savings banks	−3.23	2.43	4.55	−0.40	1.93	36.36	−1.19	2.13	12.00	−2.22	2.46	12.00
Total	−0.68	11.26	39.36	−1.40	12.62	43.72	0.82	11.76	49.27	−0.69	9.93	46.95

	1999			2000			2001			2002		
	Mean[+]	St. dev[+]	% Positive[+]	Mean[+]	St. dev[+]	% Positive[+]	Mean[+]	St. dev[+]	% Positive[+]	Mean[+]	St. dev[+]	% Positive[+]
Commercial banks	0.86	19.83	52.53	0.67	20.33	53.67	0.98	24.97	59.74	1.01	19.00	60.27
Cooperative banks	−1.32	9.12	48.98	−0.14	5.93	61.00	0.68	4.80	52.68	3.67	5.62	67.92
Savings banks	−0.79	2.06	28.00	−0.33	3.41	34.48	0.48	6.90	58.06	2.07	6.80	72.41
Total	0.12	14.94	47.94	0.36	14.94	54.16	0.85	17.72	57.57	1.85	14.25	63.39

Panel (C) Net income*	1995			1996			1997			1998		
	Mean*	St. dev*	% Positive[+]	Mean*	St. dev*	% Positive[+]	Mean*	St. dev*	% Positive[+]	Mean*	St. dev*	% Positive[+]
Commercial banks	16.34	62.65	80.70	15.48	72.82	81.15	8.74	177.07	78.79	25.25	142.79	84.51
Cooperative banks	29.43	122.33	96.25	35.11	155.80	97.75	39.27	181.55	96.74	45.47	204.20	97.87
Savings bank	18.25	52.96	100.00	20.17	59.76	95.45	20.44	61.33	100.00	22.25	71.94	100.00
Total	18.80	73.37	80.34	21.12	94.21	86.68	18.40	169.34	85.58	30.70	154.74	89.42

	1999			2000			2001			2002		
	Mean*	St. dev*	% Positive[+]	Mean*	St. dev*	% Positive[+]	Mean*	St. dev*	% Positive[+]	Mean*	St. dev*	% Positive[+]
Commercial banks	20.34	139.37	76.04	40.01	202.02	79.45	53.60	294.79	82.76	52.47	382.26	83.93
Cooperative banks	54.17	265.03	96.94	64.27	308.39	97.00	56.86	186.97	98.21	72.17	253.64	99.06
Savings banks	33.64	120.03	100.00	37.69	137.37	100.00	59.76	181.57	100.00	74.15	214.49	96.55
Total	29.79	167.36	80.67	46.60	226.50	86.02	55.03	254.72	88.58	59.75	332.66	89.21

(Continued)

Table 6.2 (Continued)

Panel (D) Return on equity	1995			1996			1997			1998		
	Mean[+]	St. dev[+]	% Positive[+]	Mean[+]	St. dev[+]	% Positive[+]	Mean[+]	St. dev[+]	% Positive[+]	Mean[+]	St. dev[+]	% Positive[+]
Commercial banks	4.81	24.03	80.70	2.23	26.75	81.15	4.75	18.39	78.79	4.66	17.72	84.51
Cooperative banks	5.77	11.48	96.25	6.39	4.99	97.75	4.31	16.78	96.74	6.45	4.23	97.87
Savings banks	3.15	2.47	100.00	3.24	1.92	95.45	3.45	1.61	100.00	3.37	1.64	100.00
Total	4.59	17.27	80.34	3.43	19.05	86.68	4.52	16.62	85.58	5.07	12.73	89.42

Panel (D) Return on equity	1999			2000			2001			2002		
	Mean[+]	St. dev[+]	% Positive[+]	Mean[+]	St. dev[+]	% Positive[+]	Mean[+]	St. dev[+]	% Positive[+]	Mean[+]	St. dev[+]	% Positive[+]
Commercial banks	2.39	32.92	76.04	6.42	29.29	79.45	5.32	28.21	82.76	4.70	32.76	83.93
Cooperative banks	7.55	8.12	96.94	7.50	4.84	97.00	7.17	4.77	98.21	6.68	8.45	99.06
Savings banks	4.31	1.66	100.00	4.79	1.62	100.00	5.91	5.42	100.00	6.31	6.30	96.55
Total	3.85	22.75	80.67	6.59	20.22	86.02	5.90	19.64	88.58	5.39	23.80	89.21

Panel (E) Return on Assets	1995			1996			1997			1998		
	Mean[+]	St. dev[+]	% Positive[+]	Mean[+]	St. dev[+]	% Positive[+]	Mean[+]	St. dev[+]	% Positive[+]	Mean[+]	St. dev[+]	% Positive[+]
Commercial banks	0.40	1.39	80.70	0.37	1.74	81.15	0.51	1.30	78.79	0.47	1.09	84.51
Cooperative banks	0.39	0.38	96.25	0.40	0.26	97.75	0.38	0.43	96.74	0.40	0.43	97.87
Savings banks	0.14	0.10	100.00	0.14	0.09	95.45	0.15	0.08	100.00	0.14	0.08	100.00
Total	0.35	0.92	80.34	0.36	1.22	86.68	0.45	0.95	85.58	0.43	0.83	89.42

	1999			2000			2001			2002		
	Mean[+]	St. dev[+]	% Positive[+]	Mean[+]	St. dev[+]	% Positive[+]	Mean[+]	St. dev[+]	% Positive[+]	Mean[+]	St. dev[+]	% Positive[+]
Commercial banks	0.35	1.65	76.04	0.50	1.67	79.45	0.58	1.71	82.76	0.72	2.46	83.93
Cooperative banks	0.40	0.44	96.94	0.43	0.45	97.00	0.51	0.25	98.21	0.60	0.29	99.06
Savings banks	0.16	0.08	100.00	0.20	0.10	100.00	1.09	4.89	100.00	0.25	0.16	96.55
Total	0.34	1.15	80.67	0.45	1.20	86.02	0.60	1.54	88.58	0.65	1.66	89.21

* [+] Values in millions of Euro and in percentage, respectively.

Table 6.3   Profitability and shareholder value created in German banking systems, 1995–2002

Panel (A) EVA*	1995			1996			1997			1998		
	Mean*	St. dev*	% Positive[+]	Mean*	St. dev*	% Positive[+]	Mean*	St. dev*	% Positive[+]	Mean*	St. dev*	% Positive[+]
Commercial banks	−1.54	19.73	46.03	−5.54	32.32	38.85	−4.33	38.50	45.39	6.02	178.47	37.42
Cooperative banks	−1.00	15.38	35.41	−0.06	2.83	62.14	0.03	4.92	62.63	−0.20	2.46	42.54
Savings banks	−0.88	3.80	25.68	0.00	2.41	55.19	−0.12	2.79	54.31	−1.25	4.79	31.46
Total	−1.00	11.00	32.45	−0.58	5.60	57.12	−0.45	7.43	57.92	−0.58	20.28	38.21

	1999			2000			2001			2002		
	Mean*	St. dev*	% Positive[+]	Mean*	St. dev*	% Positive[+]	Mean*	St. dev*	% Positive[+]	Mean*	St. dev*	% Positive[+]
Commercial banks	−0.41	174.67	32.76	−28.43	211.07	35.00	−7.49	239.59	32.43	−43.99	338.52	32.97
Cooperative banks	−0.46	7.27	36.76	1.28	40.24	32.88	−1.44	28.20	21.85	−0.13	29.57	46.61
Savings banks	−1.68	6.36	26.29	−2.10	6.22	19.70	−3.14	9.74	13.66	−1.55	23.55	25.37
Total	−0.84	22.59	33.05	−2.40	45.42	29.13	−2.43	41.06	20.47	−4.27	54.30	39.57

Panel (B) EVA on capital invested	1995			1996			1997			1998		
	Mean[+]	St. dev[+]	% Positive[+]	Mean[+]	St. dev[+]	% Positive[+]	Mean[+]	St. dev[+]	% Positive[+]	Mean[+]	St. dev[+]	% Positive[+]
Commercial banks	1.54	7.55	46.03	0.56	7.26	38.85	0.92	6.40	45.39	−0.06	12.56	37.42
Cooperative banks	−0.86	3.12	35.41	1.04	4.83	62.14	0.98	3.43	62.63	0.18	5.44	42.54
Savings banks	−0.92	5.15	25.68	0.39	2.34	55.19	0.39	2.39	54.31	−0.78	2.25	31.46
Total	−0.64	4.42	32.45	0.74	4.10	57.12	0.76	3.34	57.92	−0.17	5.02	38.21

	1999			2000			2001			2002		
	Mean+	St. dev+	% Positive+	Mean+	St. dev+	% Positive+	Mean+	St. dev+	% Positive+	Mean+	St. dev+	% Positive+
Commercial banks	−0.84	7.88	32.76	−1.01	8.57	35.0 0	−2.03	8.12	32.43	−2.02	13.25	32.97
Cooperative banks	−0.34	4.51	36.76	−0.63	4.45	32.88	−2.03	6.46	21.85	0.54	6.23	46.61
Savings banks	−1.19	2.74	26.29	−1.65	2.40	19.70	−2.39	2.67	13.66	−1.56	3.91	25.37
Total	−0.66	4.26	33.05	−0.97	4.21	29.13	−2.13	5.55	20.47	−0.26	6.19	39.57

Panel (C) Net income*	1995			1996			1997			1998		
	Mean*	St. dev*	% Positive+	Mean*	St. dev*	% Positive+	Mean*	St. dev*	% Positive+	Mean*	St. dev*	% Positive+
Commercial banks	20.87	82.26	84.13	19.61	84.95	78.42	21.32	92.30	82.89	31.57	149.73	79.75
Cooperative banks	1.32	2.93	99.49	1.43	4.80	99.45	1.41	5.78	99.05	1.24	4.64	98.52
Savings banks	3.68	5.90	99.42	3.74	5.55	99.45	3.83	5.76	99.47	4.21	13.11	99.83
Total	4.31	12.33	97.88	4.13	13.05	97.36	4.24	14.23	97.62	5.20	21.60	97.16

	1999			2000			2001			2002		
	Mean*	St. dev*	% Positive+	Mean*	St. dev*	% Positive+	Mean*	St. dev*	% Positive+	Mean*	St. dev*	% Positive+
Commercial banks	25.13	196.36	73.71	13.66	165.23	78.02	−20.01	886.36	78.07	−21.54	346.36	74.60
Cooperative banks	1.08	3.96	97.59	1.08	4.90	97.99	0.99	5.05	93.38	0.98	3.87	95.42
Savings banks	4.12	16.19	99.33	4.41	17.36	99.51	4.32	18.52	99.35	4.37	23.02	97.24
Total	4.29	25.80	95.92	3.21	23.05	96.65	0.13	83.84	93.74	−0.01	38.42	94.14

(Continued)

Table 6.3   (Continued)

Panel (D) Return on equity	1995			1996			1997			1998		
	Mean[+]	St. dev[+]	% Positive[+]	Mean[+]	St. dev[+]	% Positive[+]	Mean[+]	St. dev[+]	% Positive[+]	Mean[+]	St. dev[+]	% Positive[+]
Commercial banks	6.47	6.47	84.13	6.19	7.79	78.42	6.66	6.74	82.89	6.40	12.15	79.75
Cooperative banks	7.12	2.61	99.49	7.02	2.80	99.45	6.66	3.23	99.05	5.93	3.16	98.52
Savings banks	7.24	4.52	99.42	7.30	3.38	99.45	7.14	3.03	99.47	6.48	2.77	99.83
Total	7.10	3.80	97.88	7.05	3.52	97.36	6.84	3.50	97.62	6.17	3.90	97.16

	1999			2000			2001			2002		
	Mean[+]	St. dev[+]	% Positive[+]	Mean[+]	St. dev[+]	% Positive[+]	Mean[+]	St. dev[+]	% Positive[+]	Mean[+]	St. dev[+]	% Positive[+]
Commercial banks	5.57	9.50	73.71	3.60	27.91	78.02	13.87	109.93	78.07	−8.29	132.18	74.60
Cooperative banks	5.43	3.68	97.59	5.05	2.85	97.99	4.08	5.32	93.38	4.22	5.27	95.42
Savings banks	5.95	4.51	99.33	5.55	3.32	99.51	4.93	4.20	99.35	1.77	53.04	97.24
Total	5.61	4.49	95.92	5.07	5.25	96.65	5.15	13.91	93.74	2.47	29.32	94.14

Panel (E) Return on assets	1995			1996			1997			1998		
	Mean[+]	St. dev[+]	% Positive[+]	Mean[+]	St. dev[+]	% Positive[+]	Mean[+]	St. dev[+]	% Positive[+]	Mean[+]	St. dev[+]	% Positive[+]
Commercial banks	0.47	0.68	84.13	0.48	0.83	78.42	0.51	0.67	82.89	1.06	7.92	79.75
Cooperative banks	0.32	0.14	99.49	0.32	0.15	99.45	0.31	0.16	99.05	0.29	0.15	98.52
Savings banks	0.30	0.19	99.42	0.30	0.15	99.45	0.30	0.14	99.47	0.27	0.13	99.83
Total	0.33	0.21	97.88	0.33	0.22	97.36	0.33	0.20	97.62	0.36	0.89	97.16

	1999			2000			2001			2002		
	Mean[+]	St. dev[+]	% Positive[+]	Mean[+]	St. dev[+]	% Positive[+]	Mean[+]	St. dev[+]	% Positive[+]	Mean[+]	St. dev[+]	% Positive[+]
Commercial banks	0.46	1.23	73.71	0.41	2.07	78.02	0.14	7.82	78.07	-0.30	6.38	74.60
Cooperative banks	0.27	0.20	97.59	0.26	0.16	97.99	0.22	0.28	93.38	0.24	0.25	95.42
Savings banks	0.25	0.23	99.33	0.24	0.14	99.51	0.24	0.36	99.35	0.20	0.43	97.24
Total	0.28	0.30	95.92	0.27	0.33	96.65	0.22	0.94	93.74	0.18	0.82	94.14

*[+] Values in millions of Euro and in percentage, respectively.

in the period 1995–2000, while this sharply increased up to 0.65% in 2002. We found that the percentage of banks with positive net income is around 80–90%. The analysis of profitability ratios exhibit that French cooperative banks are, on average, more able than commercial banks to remunerate equity capital with profits, while cooperative and commercial banks have similar ROA mean levels between 1995 and 2002. In addition, the percentage of banks with positive net income is constantly and substantially larger for cooperative and savings banks than for commercial banks. It is interesting to note that, although savings banks seems to be (on average) less profitable than cooperative banks, almost all savings banks analysed generate profits in the period analysed.

In terms of shareholder value created, we found that mean levels of EVA_{bkg} are usually negative in every year and for all bank categories, with few exceptions (e.g. commercial banks in 2001 and 2002). The analysis of the ratio between EVA_{bkg} and capital invested enables us to quantify the size of shareholder value destroyed by French banks over the period analysed. We found that French banks substantially destroyed value for their shareholders in 1995, 1996 and 1998, while generating value in 1997 and from 1999 to 2002. We found substantial differences between commercial, cooperative and savings banks. French commercial banks appear to generate higher mean ratio between EVA_{bkg} and capital invested than the savings and cooperative banks from 1996 up to 2001. We found that French cooperative and savings banks achieve positive mean levels only in 2001 and 2002, while (on average) these banks seem to have destroyed a small part of shareholder value (around 1% of capital invested). If we look at the number of banks with a positive EVA_{bkg}, this percentage increased over the period analysed from 39.36% in 1995 to 63.39% in 2002, showing a greater ability of French banks to create value for their shareholders.

In Italy, banks appear to generate substantially lower mean profits than in France. Italian banks of all categories achieved annual mean profit between of euro 14.32 million over the period 1995–2002 (ranging from 3.02 euro million in 1997 to 19.19 euro million in 2001). Italian banks registered constantly positive ROE and ROA over the period 1995–2002, which are, surprisingly, higher than those of French banks. The percentage of banks with positive net income is similar to that in France (around 90–95%). By distinguishing according to bank categories, commercial banks achieved lower mean income than cooperative and savings banks between 1995 and 1997. However, the analysis of profitability ratios (both ROE and ROA) enables us to quantify the profit generation. We found that all banks in Italy achieved positive mean values and that cooperative and savings banks are, on average, more profitable than commercial banks. In addition, the percentage of banks with positive net income was constantly and substantially larger for cooperative and savings banks than for commercial banks. In terms of shareholder value created, we found that mean levels of EVA_{bkg} are usually negative in every year and for all bank categories (with few exceptions). The analysis of the ratio between EVA_{bkg} and capital invested enables us to quantify the amount of shareholder value destroyed by Italian banks over the period analysed. We found that Italian banks destroyed value for their shareholders in 1995, generated value annually from 1996 to 2000 and slightly destroyed value in both 2001 and 2002. We found substantial differences between commercial, cooperative and savings banks. Italian savings banks registered a lower mean ratio between EVA_{bkg} and capital invested than the commercial and cooperative banks from 1995 to 1999 and a higher mean ratio from 2000 to 2002. Italian cooperative banks are usually found to have destroyed value, except in 1999 and 2000. Commercial banks seem to have destroyed value annually between 1995 and 1998 and since then have created value for their shareholders. Looking at the number of banks with a positive EVA_{bkg}, we found that Italian banks broadly (around 90%) generate profits, but only a portion of these banks also create value for their shareholders. In detail, the percentage of banks with a positive EVA_{bkg} was very low in 1995 and 1996 (around 13%) and, since then, substantially increased.

German banks are found to generate lower profits and shareholder value than those in the other two countries. German banks in all categories achieved annual mean profits of around euro 4 million from 1995 to 1999 and close to zero in 2000 and 2001. As result, German banks generated a mean annual net income of euro 2.91 million. Although net inc=ome is lower than in the other countries, we found in Germany the highest percentage of banks generating profits (96.06%). In addition, German banks registered constantly positive ROE and ROA over the period 1995–2002. These mean levels are, however, strongly affected by the high number of German cooperative banks (around four times that of commercial banks). By distinguishing according to bank categories, we found that commercial German banks (similarly to Italian banks) achieved higher mean income than cooperative and savings banks annually between 1995 and 2000, while registered substantial mean net losses in 2001 and 2000. However, the analysis of profitability ratios (both ROE and ROA) enables us to note that German cooperative and savings banks are on average more profitable than commercial banks and that these banks achieved positive profits also in 2001 and 2002. In addition, the percentage of banks with positive net income is constantly and substantially larger for cooperative and savings banks than for commercial banks.

The lower profitability of German banks seems to be confirmed also in terms of shareholder value created. We found that the mean levels of EVA_{bkg} are usually negative in every year and for all bank categories (with few exceptions). The analysis of the ratio between EVA_{bkg} and capital invested enables us to quantify the size of shareholder value destroyed by German banks over the period analysed. We found that German banks annually destroyed value for their shareholders of around 1% of capital invested, except in 1996 and 1997, when they created value for shareholders. We did not find substantial differences between commercial, cooperative and savings banks. Looking at the number of banks with a positive EVA_{bkg}, we found that while 90% of German banks generate profits, only a small portion of these banks also create value for their shareholders. Only in 1996 and 1997 was the percentage of banks with a positive EVA_{bkg} more than 50%, while this percentage ranges between 20% and 40% in the other years.

6.3   The analysis of cost efficiency

6.3.1   Framework

Improving productive efficiency is one of the main endogenous channels for creating shareholder value in a bank. Productive efficiency is a broad concept, and it can be better defined by focusing on different aspects: technical efficiency, allocative efficiency, overall efficiency and scale efficiency. Technical Efficiency (TE) expresses the ability of a firm to obtain maximal outputs from a given set of inputs or to minimize inputs for a given target of outputs: this component focuses only on physical quantities and technical relationships. Allocative Efficiencies (AE) refer to the ability of using inputs in optimal proportions, given their respective prices and production technology. Overall Efficiency (OE), also called 'X-efficiency' (or Economic Efficiency), expresses the ability of a firm to choose its input and/or output levels and mix them to optimize its economic goals.

This section deals with the empirical investigation of efficiency, and is organized in three subsections concerning respectively the methodology, the sample description and the results.

6.3.2   Methodology

We measure banking cost efficiency using two different methods: Stochastic Frontier Analysis (SFA) and Data Envelopment Analysis (DEA). We adopt two frontier methods of efficiency measurement so as to be able to test the robustness of our estimates. First, we used Stochastic Frontier Analysis (SFA) to estimate cost X-efficiency for a sample of European banks over the period 1995–2002. Specifically, we use Battese and Coelli's (1995) stochastic frontier model, where:

$$\ln TC_{it} = x_{it}\beta + \left(V_{it} + U_{it}\right) \tag{3}$$

TC_i is the logarithm of the cost of production of the i-th bank, x_i is a $kx1$ vector of standardized input prices and output of the i-th bank, β is a vector of unknown parameters, V_i are random variables which are assumed to be i.i.d $N(0,\sigma_v^2)$ and independent of U_i, U_i are non-negative random variables which are assumed to account for the cost inefficiency in production and are assumed to be i.i.d $N(m_{it}\sigma^2 u)$, m_{it} is defined as $m_{it} = Z_{it}$, δ, Z_{it}, is a $px1$ vector of variables which may influence the efficiency of a bank, and δ is an $px1$ vector of parameters to be estimated. Since our sample is composed of different type of banks (namely, commercial, cooperative and savings banks) and data from an eight-year period, the Battese and Coelli (1992) model enables us to control whether a particular time period influences bank efficiency.

We use the standard translog functional form and our cost function is the following:[19]

$$\ln TC = \alpha_0 + \sum_{i=1}^{3}\alpha_i \; \ln y_i + \sum_{j=1}^{3}\beta_j \; \ln w_j +$$

$$+ \frac{1}{2}\left[\sum_{i=1}^{3}\sum_{j=1}^{3}\delta_{ij} \; \ln y_i \ln y_j + \sum_{i=1}^{3}\sum_{j=1}^{3}\gamma_{ij} \; \ln w_i \ln w_j\right] + \tag{4}$$

$$+ \sum_{i=1}^{3}\sum_{j=1}^{3}\rho_{ij} \; \ln y_i \ln w_j + \ln u_c + \ln \varepsilon_c$$

where TC is the logarithm of the cost of production, y_i is the output quantities for the i-th output, and w_i is the input prices for the i-th input. In order guarantee the linear homogeneity in factor prices (i.e., $\sum_{j=1}^{3}\beta_j=1, \sum_{i=1}^{3}\gamma_{ij}=0$ and $\sum_{i=1}^{3}\rho_{ij}=0$ it is necessary (and sufficient) to apply the follow ing restrictions: (1) the standard symmetry: according with this restriction, it is assumed that $\delta_{ij}=\delta_{ji}$ and $\gamma_{ij}=\gamma_{ji}$; (2) linear restriction of the cost function. In addition, the factor share equations (embodying restrictions imposed by Shephard's Lemma or Hotelling's Lemma) are excluded since these would impose the undesirable assumption of no allocative inefficiencies (see, for example, Berger and Mester, 1997).

To define bank inputs and outputs, we have adopted the value-added approach, originally proposed by Berger and Humphrey (1992), to identify bank outputs, and we posit that labour (price of labour is measured as personnel expenses over total assets), physical capital (price of physical capital is expressed as total capital equipment expenses over total fixed assets) and financial capital (price of financial capital is measured as interest costs on borrowed funds) are inputs, whereas demand deposits, total loans and other earning assets are outputs, as illustrated in Figure 6.2 The value-added approach identifies bank inputs and outputs depending on the contribution of bank items (on both sides of the balance sheet) to the creation of bank value added. In the value-added context, deposits are considered to have certain output features, and various previous studies have used deposits as outputs (i.e. the sum of demand deposits). We consider only demand deposits as a bank output, since banks usually pay low interest rates on these funds and charge fees on depositors for all services provided with demand deposits. One might claim that off-balance sheet (OBS) items may play a role in generating bank value added, and some studies have included these items as bank outputs. However, we omit consideration of OBS items since our sample includes many small banks (especially mutual banks and savings banks) that do not have OBS items or data are not available in the Bankscope database.

In addition, we measure cost efficiency using a non-parametric approach, that is, Data Envelopment Analysis (DEA). We use DEA to estimate the economic efficiency for our sample of banks so that we can distinguish between technical, allocative and scale efficiency. We can also use these estimates to cross-check the consistency of the parametric estimates. DEA is a linear programming methodology which uses data on the input and output quantities of a group of firms to construct a piece-wise linear surface over the data points. Companies on the frontier surface are called 'technically efficient', while other companies are labelled as 'technically inefficient': efficiency scores are determined by comparing their performance to the envelopment surface. DEA was developed by Charnes et al. (1978), which generalized the piece-wise-linear conical hull approach to estimate the efficient frontier and radial inefficiencies scores (proposed by Farrell, 1957) to multiple outputs and reformulated the optimization process as a mathematical programming problem.

*Panel (a) SFA**

Total Costs (TC) – Total costs of production (comprizing operating costs and interest paid on deposits);

Input 1 (w_1) – average cost of labour (personnel expenses/total assets);

Input 2 (w_2) – average cost of physical capital (total equipment capital expenses/total fixed-tangible assets);

Input 3 (w_3) – average cost of financial capital deposits (interest costs on borrowed funds on the average amount of borrowed funds);

Output 1 (Y_1) – demand deposits;

Output 2 (Y_2) – total loans;

Output 3 (Y_3) – other earning assets;

Panel (b) DEA

Input 1 (X_1) – labour (measured as average number of employees);

Input 2 (X_2) – physical capital (expressed as the average value of fixed-tangible assets);

Input 3 (X_3) – financial capital (measured as loanable funds);

Output 1 (Y_1) – demand deposits;

Output 2 (Y_2) – total loans;

Output 3 (Y_3) – other earning assets;

Price Input 1 – Average Labour costs (Total labour costs on number of employees);

Price Input 2 – Total equipment capital expenses/total fixed-tangible assets;

Price Input 3 – Interest costs on borrowed funds on the average amount of borrowed funds.

** Since it is assumed a constraint of linear homogeneity in process, TC, w_1 and w_2 are standardized by the price of capital w_3.*

Figure 6.2 Input and outputs used in estimating cost efficiency in European banking

Successively, Banker et al. (1984) improved the model by removing the assumption of Constant Returns to Scale (CRS). The Variable returns to Scale (VRS) model proposed by Banker et al. (1984) is often solved in two stages:[20] as suggested in Ali and Seiford (1993), the first involves a proportional contraction in inputs, while the second stage proposes a maximization of the sum of (any remaining) slacks. This second-stage linear programming problem (which must be solved for each of the N Decision Making Units (DMU's) involved) may be defined by:

$$\text{Max}_{\lambda,OS,IS} - \left(M1'OS + k1'IS\right),$$
$$\text{St} - y_i + Y\lambda - OS \geq 0$$
$$\theta x_i - X\lambda - IS \geq 0 \tag{5}$$
$$\lambda \geq 0, OS \geq 0, IS \geq 0$$

where x_i is a $Kx1$ vector of inputs for the i-th banks, y_i is a $Mx1$vector of outputs for the i-th banks, X is an input matrix KxN, Y is an output matrix MxN, $M1$ is a $Mx1$ vector of ones, $K1$ is a $Kx1$ vector of ones, OS is an $Mx1$ vector of output slacks, OS is an $Kx1$ vector of input slacks (note that in this second stage θ is not a variable, but its value is taken from the first stage results).

However, because the second stage implies the maximization rather than a minimization of the sums of slacks, and the projected point obtained is not invariant to the unit of measurement, the specification of the peers and targets (necessary for the calculations of the efficiency scores) obtained in the second stage may be unsatisfactory. To address this problem, DEA is solved using the multi-stage DEA methodology proposed by Coelli (1998) in our empirical analysis. This method involves a sequence of DEA models to identify the projected efficient points and is therefore more computationally demanding than other methods:[21] however, it avoids the necessity to maximize the sum of slacks and the efficient projected points identified are invariant to units of measurement. In detail, the multi-stage DEA approach involves six steps:

(1) Run the multiplier form of the following DEA model, originally proposed by Charnes et al. (1978);

$$\text{Max } \mu,v\left(\mu'y_i\right)$$
$$\text{St. } v'x_i = 1$$
$$\mu'y_{j,} - v'x_j < 0, j = 1,2,...,N \tag{6}$$
$$\mu, v \geq 0$$

where x_i is a $KX1$ vector of inputs for the i-th bank, y_i is a $MX1$vector of outputs for the i-th DMU, the notation change from u is an MX1 vector of output weights and v is an KX1 vector of input weights.
(2) Identify the efficient set in a Koopmans (1951) sense (i.e. all firms without slacks and with a technical efficiency score of $\theta = 1$). This

result is achieved by running the following linear programming (LP) model, where any remaining slacks are maximized;[22]

$$\text{Max}_{\lambda, os, Is} - (M1'OS + k1'IS),$$
$$\text{St.} - y_i + Y\lambda - OS \geq 0$$
$$cx_i - X\lambda - IS \geq 0 \tag{7}$$
$$\lambda \geq 0, OS \geq 0, IS \geq 0$$

where cx_i refers to the input vector of the i-th bank which has been contracted by being multiplied by the θ obtained in step 1, x_i is a $Kx1$ vector of inputs for the i-th bank, y_i is a $Mx1$ vector of outputs for the i-th bank, X is an input matrix KxN, Y is an output matrix MxN, $M1$ is a $Mx1$ vector of ones, $K1$ is a $Kx1$ vector of ones, OS is an $Mx1$ vector of output slacks, OS is an $Kx1$ vector of input slacks.

(3) Identify (for the i-th firm in the 'slack' set) all input dimensions in which some slack may exist. This result is achieved by running a sequence of K LP's, where in each LP only one of the inputs[23] is allowed to contract. The LP model for the j-th input of the i-th firm is specified as follows:

$$\text{Min}_{\theta \lambda, } \theta,$$
$$\text{St.} - y_i + Y_e \lambda \geq 0$$
$$\theta cx_i^j - X_e^j \lambda \geq 0$$
$$cx_i^{1j} - X_i^{1j} \lambda \geq 0 \tag{8}$$
$$\lambda \geq 0$$

where cx_i^j refers to the i-th input of the i-th bank which has been contracted by being multiplied by the θ obtained in step 1, X_e^j is an input matrix $1xN_e$ vector of the j-*th* inputs of all efficient firms, $cx_i^{\neq j}$ is the $(K-1)x1$ vector of inputs of the i-th firm (excluding the j-th input) which has been contracted by being multiplied by the θ obtained in step 1, X_e^j is the $(K-1)xN_e$ matrix of inputs of all efficient firms (excluding the j-th input), N_e is the number of efficient firms (identified in step 2), Y_e is the number of outputs of these efficient firms, y_i is a $Mx1$ vector of outputs for the i-th bank (it is important to note that this LP model breaks down when some inputs are zero).

(4) Seek a radial reduction in all inputs identified as having potential slack by running the following LP model:

$$\text{Min}_{\theta\lambda,}\,\theta$$
$$\text{st.} -y_i + Y_e\lambda \geq 0$$
$$\theta cx_i^s - X_e^s\lambda \geq 0 \tag{9}$$
$$cx_i^{ns} - X_e^{ns}\lambda \geq 0$$
$$\lambda \geq 0$$

where cx_i refers to the input vector of the i-th bank which has been contracted by being multiplied by the θ obtained in step 1, X_e^j is the $(K$-$1)xN_e$ matrix of inputs of all efficient firms (excluding the j-th input), N_e is the number of efficient firms (identified in step 2), Y_e is the number of outputs of these efficient firms, y_i is a $Mx1$vector of outputs for the i-th bank, θ is a scalar (note that the superscript 's' refers to the subset of inputs having potential slack and 'ns' identifies the remainder of the inputs).

(5) Look for the input slack remaining in any dimension by repeating steps 3 and 4 on the projected point identified in step 4 until no slack remains in any input; and

(6) Conduct a radial expansion in output slack dimensions by repeating steps 3–5 on the project point from step 5 until no slack remains in any output. These final projected points will be on the efficient surface. It is interesting to note that these projected points will be unit invariant to the units of measurement adopted.[24]

After technical and scale efficiencies are measured, cost efficiency and allocative efficiency are estimated since price information is available and cost minimization is a reasonable behavioural objective for European banks. As such, the following DEA model enables us to measure cost efficiency under VRS and cost minimization[25] assumptions:

$$\min_{\lambda,xi^*}\,w_i'x_i^*$$
$$\text{st:} -y_i + Y\lambda \geq 0,$$
$$x_i^* - X\lambda \geq 0 \tag{10}$$
$$N1'\lambda = 1$$
$$\lambda \geq 0$$

where w_i is a vector of input prices for the i-th bank, x_i^* (which is calculated by LP) is the cost minimizing vector of input for the i-th DMU, given w_i and y_i.

The total cost, the allocative and the scale efficiency of the i-th firm are calculated as follows:

- Cost Efficiency is CE $= w_i'x_i^*/w_i'x_i$, which represents the ratio of minimum cost to be observed;
- Allocative Efficiency[26] AE $= \frac{CE}{TE}$ is.
- Scale efficiency is obtained by solving for both the CRS model (proposed by Charnes et al., 1978) and the multi-stage DEA VRS model and comparing the results as follows: $TE_{CRS} = TE_{VRS} \times SE$. In order to analyse whether returns to scale are increasing or decreasing, this can be determined by solving for 'non-increasing returns to scale' in the input orientation.

Following the value-added approach for defining bank inputs and outputs (as in the SFA estimates), we posit[27] that labour (measured as personnel expenses), physical capital (expressed as the average value of fixed tangible assets) and financial capital (measured as loanable funds) are inputs, whereas demand deposits, total loans and other earning assets are outputs.

The sample consists of unlisted banks from France, Germany and Italy between 1995 and 2002, with financial information obtained form Bankscope database,[28] as the same sample of banks was used to investigate shareholder value in banking. We use a cross-section sample by year, by country and by bank category as this is preferred to a panel data set or an international sample. We use a cross-section sample by year since many bank observations would have been lost in the selection of a balanced panel data set. We prefer to use a sample of domestic banks for estimating the cost efficiency frontier since banks in the same country are more homogeneous (and comparable) than banks working in different countries. Similarly, we include various specific banks according to ownership type (namely, commercial banks and, jointly, cooperative and savings banks[29]) since this seems to guarantee a greater homogeneity in the sample. As such, we have estimated 56 frontiers using both DEA and SFA.[30]

6.3.3 Results

Table 6.4 reports descriptive statistics of the cost X-efficiency measures derived from SFA. Overall, European banks display analysed inefficiency scores ranging from 7.3% (UK commercial banks in 1995) to 38.9% (German cooperative banks in 2001), and the level of dispersion of average efficiency scores varies substantially from 4.2% (German savings

Table 6.4 Profitability and shareholder value created in Italian banking systems, 1995–2002.

Panel (A) EVA*	1995			1996			1997			1998		
	Mean*	St. dev*	% Positive[+]	Mean*	St. dev*	% Positive[+]	Mean*	St. dev*	% Positive[+]	Mean*	St. dev*	% Positive[+]
Commercial banks	−68.20	162.80	13.75	−59.90	151.11	20.48	−43.51	195.06	31.87	−13.63	148.63	40.00
Cooperative banks	−8.58	15.73	14.61	−5.54	16.94	12.80	−2.87	11.61	45.95	−1.52	17.73	47.59
Savings banks	−29.68	102.23	6.45	−23.61	75.85	4.76	−19.47	82.03	25.40	−13.34	57.23	24.62
Total	−34.89	89.88	12.12	−26.39	71.73	13.28	−18.58	81.58	37.42	−6.03	54.21	42.58

Panel (A) EVA*	1999			2000			2001			2002		
	Mean*	St. dev*	% Positive[+]	Mean*	St. dev*	% Positive[+]	Mean*	St. dev*	% Positive[+]	Mean*	St. dev*	% Positive[+]
Commercial banks	21.41	109.56	65.00	38.22	145.27	56.92	−9.35	242.04	45.32	−5.17	257.36	52.78
Cooperative banks	0.34	10.78	63.13	−0.48	15.84	39.24	−1.02	18.53	26.92	0.16	17.03	32.84
Savings banks	−11.87	136.90	59.09	5.95	50.46	75.76	−5.40	52.88	42.42	9.91	41.78	63.64
Total	3.21	44.35	63.06	7.39	43.41	46.03	−2.98	63.81	31.78	−0.01	65.16	39.34

Panel (B) EVA on capital investe d	1995			1996			1997			1998		
	Mean[+]	St. dev[+]	% Positive[+]	Mean[+]	St. dev[+]	% Positive[+]	Mean[+]	St. dev[+]	% Positive[+]	Mean[+]	St. dev[+]	% Positive[+]
Commercial banks	−8.11	8.46	13.75	−5.16	9.01	20.48	−2.30	9.71	31.87	−0.87	8.20	40.00
Cooperative banks	−5.40	5.54	14.61	−3.83	4.60	12.80	−0.22	4.05	45.95	0.69	5.72	47.59
Savings banks	−8.79	4.11	6.45	−6.55	4.56	4.76	−3.21	4.75	25.40	−2.54	4.36	24.62
Total	−7.25	6.17	12.12	−4.87	5.94	13.28	−1.47	5.90	37.42	−0.13	6.12	42.58

	1999			2000			2001			2002		
	Mean[+]	St. dev[+]	% Positive[+]	Mean[+]	St. dev[+]	% Positive[+]	Mean[+]	St. dev[+]	% Positive[+]	Mean[+]	St. dev[+]	% Positive[+]
Commercial banks	2.72	9.18	65.00	1.76	14.22	56.92	0.06	13.09	45.32	0.67	14.27	52.78
Cooperative banks	2.00	5.09	63.13	−0.74	5.32	39.24	−2.36	5.23	26.92	−1.80	6.67	32.84
Savings banks	1.17	4.92	59.09	4.30	6.81	75.76	−0.91	5.71	42.42	2.71	10.10	63.64
Total	2.05	5.89	63.06	0.21	7.13	46.03	−1.77	6.76	31.78	−0.93	8.43	39.34

(Continued)

Table 6.4   (Continued)

Panel (C) Net income*	1995			1996			1997			1998		
	Mean*	St. dev*	% Positive[+]	Mean*	St. dev*	% Positive[+]	Mean*	St. dev*	% Positive[+]	Mean*	St. dev*	% Positive[+]
Commercial banks	5.09	87.55	83.75	−2.42	185.01	89.16	−9.58	262.15	89.01	41.48	112.80	84.55
Cooperative banks	8.10	15.50	97.75	6.43	24.68	98.40	7.15	15.91	98.65	4.67	13.94	98.28
Savings banks	8.87	27.36	93.55	11.48	29.39	96.83	11.50	18.29	98.41	12.29	26.95	96.92
Total	7.26	43.64	91.77	4.89	74.88	95.20	3.02	90.61	95.70	14.45	39.14	94.84

	1999			2000			2001			2002		
	Mean*	St. dev*	% Positive[+]	Mean*	St. dev*	% Positive[+]	Mean*	St. dev*	% Positive[+]	Mean*	St. dev*	% Positive[+]
Commercial banks	47.47	131.49	89.17	65.06	195.23	86.92	74.66	201.19	90.65	63.79	186.50	86.11
Cooperative banks	3.81	13.54	97.35	3.85	15.23	94.97	4.40	20.83	95.14	5.03	26.28	94.86
Savings banks	12.88	25.33	95.45	17.89	46.14	95.45	21.36	48.90	93.94	25.20	69.47	96.97
Total	13.52	38.38	95.51	16.67	51.94	93.51	19.19	57.40	94.18	18.02	60.69	93.37

Panel (D) Return on Equity	1995			1996			1997			1998		
	Mean[+]	St.dev[+]	%Positive[+]	Mean[+]	St.dev[+]	%Positive[+]	Mean[+]	St.dev[+]	%Positive[+]	Mean[+]	St.dev[+]	%Positive[+]
Commercial banks	1.53	15.33	83.75	4.26	6.44	89.16	4.13	11.88	89.01	3.62	10.17	84.55
Cooperative banks	7.83	6.40	97.75	8.77	6.67	98.40	9.87	4.73	98.65	9.71	4.80	98.28
Savings banks	2.07	6.75	93.55	3.95	2.27	96.83	4.34	2.31	98.41	4.16	2.88	96.92
Total	4.11	9.58	91.77	6.27	5.58	95.20	6.99	6.38	95.70	7.49	5.80	94.84

	1999			2000			2001			2002		
	Mean[+]	St. dev[+]	% Positive[+]	Mean[+]	St. dev[+]	% Positive[+]	Mean[+]	St. dev[+]	% Positive[+]	Mean[+]	St. dev[+]	% Positive[+]
Commercial banks	3.78	18.28	89.17	5.49	11.66	86.92	6.49	9.31	90.65	5.59	12.54	86.11
Cooperative banks	8.88	5.05	97.35	6.74	5.25	94.97	6.47	5.13	95.14	5.84	6.87	94.86
Savings banks	4.74	5.77	95.45	4.35	10.10	95.45	5.01	9.36	93.94	6.92	11.95	96.97
Total	7.41	7.77	95.51	6.28	6.91	93.51	6.34	6.30	94.18	5.89	8.40	93.37

(Continued)

Table 6.4   (Continued)

Panel (E) Return on Assets	1995			1996			1997			1998		
	Mean[+]	St. dev[+]	% Positive[+]	Mean[+]	St. dev[+]	% Positive[+]	Mean[+]	St. dev[+]	% Positive[+]	Mean[+]	St. dev[+]	% Positive[+]
Commercial banks	0.24	0.68	83.75	0.30	0.71	89.16	0.51	1.95	89.01	0.46	1.99	84.55
Cooperative banks	0.96	0.88	97.75	1.12	0.81	98.40	1.22	0.75	98.65	1.20	0.71	98.28
Savings banks	0.21	0.54	93.55	0.32	0.58	96.83	0.41	0.22	98.41	0.40	0.26	96.92
Total	0.51	0.72	91.77	0.68	0.73	95.20	0.83	1.00	95.70	0.91	0.95	94.84

	1999			2000			2001			2002		
	Mean[+]	St. dev[+]	% Positive[+]	Mean[+]	St. dev[+]	% Positive[+]	Mean[+]	St. dev[+]	% Positive[+]	Mean[+]	St. dev[+]	% Positive[+]
Commercial banks	0.58	1.54	89.17	0.49	1.65	86.92	0.50	1.80	90.65	0.53	2.79	86.11
Cooperative banks	1.14	0.68	97.35	0.87	0.78	94.97	0.87	0.63	95.14	0.73	1.05	94.86
Savings banks	0.48	0.31	95.45	0.48	0.56	95.45	0.52	0.50	93.94	0.61	0.82	96.97
Total	0.96	0.81	95.51	0.76	0.92	93.51	0.77	0.84	94.18	0.68	1.36	93.37

* [+] Values in millions of Euro and in percentage, respectively.

banks in 1996) to 27% (Italian commercial banks in 2001). On average (from all the 20,942 bank cost X-efficiency estimates obtained from running 80 annual cross-sectional domestic frontiers), the mean cost X-efficiency level over the period 1995–2002 is 78.1%, and the mean level of dispersion of average efficiency scores is 17.8%.

As for the four banking systems analysed, French banks show the greatest opportunities for improving X-efficiency, with a mean X-inefficiency of 27.6% and a dispersion of average efficiency of 11.4%. Italian and French banks exhibit similar mean levels (79.3% and 78.6%, respectively), but German banks exhibit a lower range of dispersion of average cost efficiency scores. Over the period analysed, annual mean X-efficiency follows a similar trend since, for both countries, mean annual X-efficiency increased between 1995 and 1998, decreased between 1998 and 2001 and sharply increased in 2002.

As for the different bank specializations, commercial banks display a lower mean level of cost X-efficiency (75.0%) than savings and cooperative banks (77.7% and 79.4%, respectively) over the period 1995–2002. Higher mean levels of cost X-efficiency for cooperative and savings banks than those for commercial banks are found to be almost constant in every year analysed except 1995 and 2001.

As for the banking systems analysed, cooperative banks show higher mean levels of cost X-efficiency than savings banks and, especially, than commercial banks in Italy and Germany in almost every year over the period analysed. German commercial banks exhibit a mean X-efficiency similar to the other two bank categories. In France, all categories of bank display similar cost X-efficiency levels over time. When our findings are compared across countries, all French banks show the greatest mean cost X-inefficiency on average over the period 1995–2002, while Italian cooperative banks and German savings banks achieved the highest mean cost X-efficiency in their ownership category.

Table 6.5 reports descriptive statistics of the cost X-efficiency measures derived from DEA. The average cost X-inefficiency over the eight years analysed is 25.0%, which seems to be generated in almost equal proportions by allocative and technical inefficiency (12.6% and 13.5% respectively), while scale inefficiency displays a lesser significance (5.8%). The three countries analysed display similar mean levels of cost X-efficiency. Italian banks show a mean cost X-efficiency level of 58.2%, which is due to a mean technical inefficiency of 25.0%, to an allocative inefficiency of 14.5% and to a scale inefficiency of 8.6%. In Germany, the average cost efficiency over the eight years analysed is 55.3%, which seems to be generated mainly by allocative inefficiency (38.6%),

Table 6.5   SFA cost X-efficiency mean levels in European banking, 1995–2002*.

		France		Germany		Italy	
		Mean (%)	St. dev (%)	Mean (%)	St. dev (%)	Mean (%)	St. dev (%)
1995	Commercial banks	72.03	13.67	77.94	6.70	83.47	13.36
	Cooperative banks	70.17	10.25	78.18	8.88	79.62	14.67
	Savings banks	76.36	8.52	78.00	10.38	76.78	14.46
	Total	71.83	12.21	78.08	9.29	79.95	14.20
1996	Commercial banks	68.66	13.92	83.53	4.89	79.46	18.39
	Cooperative banks	66.63	8.39	84.44	4.86	83.56	14.60
	Savings ban ks	70.92	6.30	83.82	4.20	81.80	13.10
	Total	68.25	11.72	84.11	4.60	81.79	15.44
1997	Commercial banks	69.55	15.62	81.41	14.22	84.26	12.95
	Cooperative banks	68.02	9.18	84.27	4.69	86.46	7.91
	Savings banks	73.66	6.78	84.04	4.51	79.73	10.52
	Total	69.41	12.91	83.91	5.53	84.28	10.02
1998	Commercial banks	87.31	9.25	78.02	16.97	74.59	21.02
	Cooperative banks	85.93	7.71	82.44	6.25	81.13	13.45
	Savings banks	87.15	7.95	82.17	6.19	76.68	11.66
	Total	86.88	8.68	81.93	7.23	78.87	15.03

1999	Commercial banks	73.67	15.45	82.09	16.82	69.09	23.85
	Cooperative banks	73.99	9.77	81.88	5.89	81.96	12.98
	Savings banks	70.95	8.83	81.05	5.36	78.02	11.38
	Total	73.56	13.14	81.63	6.60	78.89	15.01
2000	Commercial banks	67.61	14.58	74.42	17.07	65.86	25.50
	Cooperative banks	66.92	8.50	80.31	6.11	82.45	11.72
	Savings banks	66.66	6.08	80.38	6.03	79.36	14.13
	Total	67.31	11.95	79.81	7.06	78.99	14.58
2001	Commercial banks	70.67	12.22	66.31	22.75	64.03	26.68
	Cooperative banks	72.27	6.82	74.19	10.14	80.85	13.08
	Savings banks	70.76	6.80	61.07	8.49	74.77	17.91
	Total	71.19	10.02	69.80	10.72	77.20	16.02
2002	Commercial banks	70.65	13.64	66.50	20.16	81.68	6.70
	Cooperative banks	70.29	7.35	75.14	8.66	78.96	7.01
	Savings banks	69.68	7.67	74.24	8.60	74.30	6.86
	Total	70.46	11.24	74.17	9.60	79.06	6.93
Mean 1995–02	Commercial banks	72.58	13.51	75.59	15.67	74.30	18.87
	Cooperative banks	71.90	8.43	79.47	7.15	81.33	11.40
	Savings banks	73.21	7.36	77.92	6.70	77.64	12.45
	Total	72.42	11.44	78.61	7.76	79.27	13.21

* Efficiency estimates for commercial banks are obtained by estimating an efficient frontier in a sample comprizing only this category of bank, while efficiency estimates for savings and cooperative banks are obtained by estimating a common frontier using a sample comprizing both savings and cooperative banks.

while technical and scale inefficiency are 8.0% and 1.8% respectively. It is worthwhile noting that mean levels of efficiency in Germany are strongly influenced by cooperative banks, which are numerically dominant in Germany. French banks display a mean level of cost X-efficiency of 55.1%, which is a result of mean allocative inefficiency of 28.3%, technical inefficiency of 19.1% and scale inefficiency of 6.0%.

When banks' specializations are considered, commercial banks seem to be substantially less efficient (for all cost-efficiency components, that is, technical, allocative, and scale efficiency) than cooperative and savings banks in France and Italy over all eight years considered.[31] In detail, French and Italian commercial banks achieved a mean cost efficiency level between 1995 and 2002 of 48.4% and 49.9%, respectively, while cooperative and savings banks achieved substantially higher levels of cost efficiency over the same period. Although Italian and French banking systems presents similar results, there are different reasons for the superiority of cooperative and savings banks. In France, commercial banks are found to be less technical-, allocative- and scale-efficient than cooperative and savings banks. In contrast, Italian commercial banks seems to suffer lower mean cost efficiency levels, due to high levels of allocative inefficiency (in some years, above 40%), than do cooperative and savings banks, while commercial banks usually exhibit higher mean levels of technical efficiency. Italian commercial banks also show substantial opportunities for cost efficiency gains by reducing scale inefficiency (around 9% between 1995 and 2002). In Germany, commercial banks exhibit a higher cost efficiency than savings and, especially, cooperative banks over the period 1995–2002 (namely, 69.5% versus 64% and 47.4%, respectively). On average, German commercial banks seems to be slightly less technical- and scale-efficient than the other two categories of banks, but display substantially more allocative efficiency. As a possible explanation of the greater cost inefficiency of German cooperative banks, we may note that the number of cooperative banks in Germany is at least four times the number of commercial banks. Since DEA compares all banks in the sample, as the sample size increases the probability of finding more efficient banks increases and, consequently, the average distance of inefficient banks increases, too.

It is worth noting that mean level cost inefficiency estimates (obtained by running both SFA and DEA models) express the mean distance of all inefficient banks from the efficient frontier; these are estimated with a cross-section sample and, as such, change every year. As such, all mean cost efficiency levels reported in Tables 6.5 and 6.6 display the average distance from different efficient frontiers rather than a common frontier, and consequently these results should not been interpreted as

Table 6.6 DEA cost efficiency mean levels in European banking, 1995–2002[35].

Panel (A)France*		Technical efficiency		Allocative efficiency		Scale efficiency		Overall cost efficiency	
		Mean (%)	St. dev (%)	Mean (%)	St. dev (%)	Mean (%)	St. dev (%)	Mean (%)	St. dev (%)
1995	Commercial banks	80.84	14.46	72.48	22.89	91.30	4.85	55.26	27.48
	Cooperative banks	83.39	15.36	82.79	12.98	97.84	4.83	67.83	18.27
	Savings banks	87.92	6.00	79.30	7.31	99.00	2.90	68.87	6.64
	Total	82.14	14.05	76.02	18.77	93.81	4.69	60.00	23.15
1996	Commercial banks	80.93	16.67	65.96	25.69	93.11	4.21	48.88	27.95
	Cooperative banks	84.38	15.33	84.80	12.40	97.22	5.92	70.08	19.04
	Savings banks	89.35	5.69	81.09	7.04	98.95	3.45	71.60	7.20
	Total	82.57	15.48	72.65	20.39	94.75	4.66	56.83	23.80
1997	Commercial banks	82.02	16.44	65.23	21.37	93.23	5.07	49.42	28.78
	Cooperative banks	84.96	16.01	82.93	12.78	97.00	6.78	68.76	19.08
	Savings banks	90.45	5.62	80.54	7.59	99.11	3.37	72.14	8.00
	Total	83.56	15.46	71.70	17.73	94.81	5.45	56.96	24.26
1998	Commercial banks	78.47	16.47	68.47	21.83	94.32	3.28	51.14	31.63
	Cooperative banks	84.58	16.72	83.32	12.59	96.90	7.58	68.88	19.86
	Savings banks	91.02	5.75	79.18	6.02	99.06	3.45	71.43	7.65
	Total	81.22	15.73	73.65	17.92	95.44	4.56	57.89	26.35

(Continued)

Table 6.6   (Continued)

Panel (A) France*		Technical efficiency		Allocative efficiency		Scale efficiency		Overall cost efficiency	
		Mean (%)	St. dev (%)	Mean (%)	St. dev (%)	Mean (%)	St. dev (%)	Mean (%)	St. dev (%)
1999	Commercial banks	78.71	14.97	66.05	21.94	94.01	2.48	46.22	28.77
	Cooperative banks	86.75	14.56	81.40	13.09	97.65	6.65	69.46	18.45
	Savings banks	91.10	6.73	79.02	7.83	98.90	4.41	71.09	8.43
	Total	82.02	14.24	71.58	18.26	95.45	3.86	54.98	24.20
2000	Commercial banks	77.96	15.62	60.60	22.05	95.50	1.24	45.69	29.37
	Cooperative banks	82.73	24.44	78.18	15.44	95.64	11.54	63.33	24.58
	Savings banks	89.92	22.32	84.43	11.60	95.77	11.17	73.83	22.29
	Total	80.35	18.77	67.75	19.24	95.56	5.09	53.21	27.37
2001	Commercial banks	77.01	15.91	69.92	18.58	91.10	4.33	50.77	22.03
	Cooperative banks	82.57	19.52	74.42	16.49	95.86	11.04	59.45	20.71
	Savings banks	89.32	9.16	72.39	10.19	98.39	6.25	63.32	9.63
	Total	79.70	16.46	71.49	17.26	93.14	6.52	54.43	20.62
2002	Commercial banks	70.85	25.60	68.64	19.50	85.45	8.16	41.59	22.67
	Cooperative banks	84.48	17.36	72.29	16.86	96.40	10.01	59.32	20.41
	Savings banks	90.39	9.59	70.20	9.86	98.36	6.55	62.64	12.51
	Total	76.49	21.85	69.86	17.94	89.76	8.59	48.59	21.19
Mean 1995–2002	Commercial banks	78.14	17.14	67.10	21.60	92.19	4.21	48.41	27.20
	Cooperative banks	84.21	17.56	79.64	14.23	96.75	8.25	65.54	20.15
	Savings banks	89.96	9.23	78.01	8.61	98.37	5.42	69.12	10.65
	Total	80.87	16.65	71.68	18.39	94.03	5.51	55.12	23.81

Panel (B) Germany*		Technical efficiency		Allocative efficiency		Scale efficiency		Overall cost efficiency	
		Mean (%)	St. dev (%)	Mean (%)	St. dev (%)	Mean (%)	St. dev (%)	Mean (%)	St. dev (%)
1995	Commercial banks	86.99	14.80	86.26	21.24	95.00	13.87	71.47	23.22
	Cooperative banks	93.38	5.87	56.08	20.14	99.44	1.51	51.82	18.44
	Savings banks	94.60	4.48	53.97	26.81	99.53	0.78	50.85	25.54
	Total	93.14	6.34	58.73	23.02	98.96	2.65	53.71	21.92
1996	Commercial banks	85.73	16.11	88.61	18.78	96.26	12.61	73.19	22.29
	Cooperative banks	95.44	5.84	33.18	31.07	98.41	2.61	31.16	29.55
	Savings banks	94.30	4.77	62.69	25.40	99.44	0.83	59.01	24.67
	Total	93.90	6.59	50.78	27.50	98.56	3.06	46.60	26.85
1997	Commercial banks	87.03	16.42	87.42	19.01	95.64	13.06	73.77	22.39
	Cooperative banks	92.84	6.34	50.86	35.15	99.37	1.52	46.70	32.64
	Savings banks	93.90	4.86	73.27	21.87	99.43	0.76	68.51	21.20
	Total	92.57	6.93	62.99	28.58	98.97	2.54	57.55	27.39
1998	Commercial banks	87.84	15.83	86.91	17.93	92.52	14.17	71.10	22.08
	Cooperative banks	92.91	6.51	54.04	34.19	99.42	1.51	49.69	31.77
	Savings banks	93.38	5.09	74.23	19.11	98.94	1.40	68.61	18.39
	Total	92.52	7.05	64.55	27.25	98.50	2.86	58.51	26.13
1999	Commercial banks	84.91	17.50	88.50	18.75	92.57	2.69	70.21	20.47
	Cooperative banks	89.64	7.87	51.34	35.83	97.91	3.58	45.25	32.34
	Savings banks	99.13	2.75	75.98	19.02	97.11	2.67	73.23	18.77
	Total	92.12	7.27	62.93	28.78	97.11	3.20	56.62	26.85

(Continued)

Table 6.6   (Continued)

Panel (B)Germany*		Technical efficiency		Allocative efficiency		Scale efficiency		Overall cost efficiency	
		Mean (%)	St. dev (%)	Mean (%)	St. dev (%)	Mean (%)	St. dev (%)	Mean (%)	St. dev (%)
2000	Commercial banks	84.16	17.46	89.91	14.79	91.26	3.39	69.32	18.92
	Cooperative banks	89.34	7.76	44.16	34.96	97.68	2.71	38.38	30.48
	Savings banks	95.04	4.24	50.93	39.53	99.04	1.25	47.94	37.24
	Total	90.50	7.70	50.81	34.27	97.43	2.35	44.35	31.31
2001	Commercial banks	82.67	18.80	82.03	24.17	94.15	13.54	64.94	26.94
	Cooperative banks	93.03	6.90	58.98	31.90	99.30	1.62	54.40	29.85
	Savings banks	94.48	4.55	79.21	17.29	99.17	1.07	74.26	16.90
	Total	92.43	7.39	66.79	27.11	98.77	2.61	60.91	25.99
2002	Commercial banks	78.64	21.64	86.13	20.40	93.17	12.57	64.63	26.36
	Cooperative banks	91.76	7.90	61.28	25.53	99.22	1.65	55.52	23.60
	Savings banks	91.41	7.46	80.54	15.37	96.77	2.86	71.40	15.66
	Total	90.40	9.11	68.95	22.25	97.96	3.04	60.75	21.69
Mean 1995–2002	Commercial banks	84.49	17.53	86.91	19.38	93.68	10.52	69.51	22.90
	Cooperative banks	92.00	7.07	52.27	31.48	98.81	2.11	47.42	28.87
	Savings banks	94.53	4.78	69.18	22.97	98.65	1.48	64.51	22.22
	Total	92.03	7.42	61.36	27.46	98.22	2.79	55.25	26.10

Panel (C) Italy		Technical efficiency		Allocative efficiency		Scale efficiency		Overall cost efficiency	
		Mean (%)	St. dev (%)	Mean (%)	St. dev (%)	Mean (%)	St. dev (%)	Mean (%)	St. dev (%)
1995	Commercial banks	90.54	11.08	58.85	20.65	94.63	7.50	50.20	18.70
	Cooperative banks	81.75	11.08	95.84	3.74	95.87	5.59	74.86	9.88
	Savings banks	86.83	10.63	97.48	3.04	95.14	5.06	80.29	9.35
	Total	86.16	10.96	83.52	9.39	95.24	6.10	67.82	12.78
1996	Commercial banks	69.22	25.44	74.15	13.87	91.59	10.15	47.91	23.39
	Cooperative banks	83.79	10.87	94.82	4.14	97.27	3.92	77.11	9.83
	Savings banks	89.49	9.03	96.23	3.89	95.09	4.47	81.71	8.25
	Total	80.46	15.14	88.47	7.23	94.89	6.07	68.77	13.84
1997	Commercial banks	88.93	12.09	59.72	23.02	95.34	6.53	50.50	20.55
	Cooperative banks	82.51	10.93	94.71	4.12	97.59	3.92	76.21	10.83
	Savings banks	88.31	9.30	96.16	4.26	94.26	4.89	79.84	8.37
	Total	85.75	10.93	84.35	9.92	96.17	4.93	69.16	13.26
1998	Commercial banks	79.63	17.78	56.11	18.81	89.79	11.23	40.10	18.52
	Cooperative banks	79.33	10.78	92.78	5.38	95.66	4.43	70.27	10.19
	Savings banks	86.96	9.28	95.33	4.28	89.33	4.89	73.90	8.27
	Total	80.52	12.25	84.30	8.46	93.32	6.14	63.52	11.92
1999	Commercial banks	79.22	16.65	70.13	12.90	92.19	10.78	51.37	17.48
	Cooperative banks	77.18	10.79	92.73	5.37	95.66	5.01	68.35	10.40
	Savings banks	85.41	10.61	94.56	4.74	86.61	4.67	69.83	9.50
	Total	78.52	11.96	88.34	6.83	93.93	6.14	65.06	11.74

(Continued)

Table 6.6   (Continued)

Panel (C) Italy		Technical efficiency		Allocative efficiency		Scale efficiency		Overall cost efficiency	
		Mean (%)	St. dev (%)	Mean (%)	St. dev (%)	Mean (%)	St. dev (%)	Mean (%)	St. dev (%)
2000	Commercial banks	81.67	15.82	73.79	14.13	88.56	13.36	52.98	16.78
	Cooperative banks	69.35	12.41	87.61	8.84	90.54	7.16	54.39	9.45
	Savings banks	84.16	9.80	90.17	6.70	80.47	5.35	60.94	8.82
	Total	73.14	12.80	85.24	9.63	89.17	8.16	54.77	10.77
2001	Commercial banks	81.77	16.98	69.03	11.42	88.72	14.57	49.87	17.23
	Cooperative banks	63.26	13.00	85.72	9.34	89.54	8.71	47.96	9.79
	Savings banks	80.80	12.38	89.46	8.25	78.85	8.60	56.83	11.22
	Total	68.29	13.68	82.98	9.62	88.41	9.78	49.13	11.29
2002	Commercial banks	83.39	16.49	72.39	13.75	89.41	14.35	53.55	16.49
	Cooperative banks	62.48	13.06	90.49	7.58	89.99	9.23	50.14	9.38
	Savings banks	78.53	12.59	86.36	6.91	76.92	8.88	52.34	12.78
	Total	67.96	13.69	86.61	8.71	88.71	10.19	50.99	11.06
Mean 1995–2002	Commercial banks	81.75	16.56	67.49	15.51	90.87	11.59	49.85	18.28
	Cooperative banks	70.69	12.05	90.16	7.13	92.42	6.92	58.91	9.84
	Savings banks	84.99	10.47	93.13	5.30	86.91	5.88	69.20	9.60
	Total	75.04	12.85	85.48	8.76	91.35	7.83	58.24	11.69

* The mean level of efficiency reported here is disaggregated according to bank specialization. Efficiency estimates for commercial banks are obtained by estimating an efficient frontier in a sample comprizing only this category of bank, while efficiency estimates for savings and cooperative banks are obtained by estimating a common frontier using a sample comprizing both savings and cooperative banks.

clear evidence of a productivity improvement in a country; for example, a decrease in the average distance of inefficient banks from the frontier (as in France from 1998 to 1999) may be also due to worsening management practices in the current period of these banks that were best practice in the previous period (i.e. a negative shift of the efficient frontier) rather than to an efficiency improvement. In other words, the lower mean cost X-efficiency levels found over the period 1995–2002 express a greater average distance from the French cross-sectional efficient frontiers than the average distance of Italian and German banks from their cross-section efficient frontiers. However, this does not imply that bank productivity in France is lower than in Germany, Italy and United Kingdom since cost X-efficiency does not enable us to analyse comparatively the domestic efficient frontiers. Later , we estimate productivity change using the Malmquist Total Factor Productivity (TFP) index,[32] a measure that enables us to distinguish between an efficient frontier shift (i.e. technical change) and the variation of the distance of inefficient banks from the frontier (efficiency change).

Our results appear to be consistent with previous studies. Berger and Humphrey (1997) summarized more than 120 studies in banking and found an average efficiency of 79% (84% for parametric studies and 72%[33] for non-parametric studies). Our mean efficiency estimates appear slightly lower than Berger and Humphrey's (1997) mean levels.[34] Our overall (for all four countries analysed) mean level of X-cost efficiency estimated with SFA between 1995 and 2002 is 78.1%. Consistently with Berger and Humphrey (1997), our efficiency levels estimated with DEA are lower than those estimated with SFA: mean technical efficiency levels range from 75.0% (Italy) to 92.0% (Germany), mean allocative efficiency levels range from 61.36% (Germany) to 87.44% (UK), mean scale efficiency levels range from 91.35% to 98.2%, and mean overall efficiency levels range from 55.1% (France) to 75.0% (UK).

In addition, Berger and Humphrey (1997) defined a sort of confidence interval formed by the mean plus and minus one standard deviation (between 66% and 92%) that captured 82% of the observations summarized in their study. In our findings, all our domestic and annual mean levels estimated with SFA are within the Berger and Humphrey (1997) interval. Next, we identify our own domestic confidence interval by adding ± one standard deviation to each country mean value over the period 1995–2002. As such, we define a specific confidence interval for each country (France, Germany and Italy) and for each kind of efficiency estimate (cost X-efficiency, technical efficiency, allocative efficiency, scale efficiency and overall efficiency). We find that 90% of mean levels estimated with SFA and 86.5% of mean levels estimated with DEA are captured in their respective confidence intervals.

Among more recent studies dealing with the banking systems analysed in this book, we note that Resti (1997) and Casu and Girardone (2004) focus on Italy, Dietsch and Lozano-Vives (2000) analyse French banks, Altunbas et al. (2000) focus on the German banking, while Carbo et al. (2000) analyse savings banks in several European countries, Altunbas et al. (2001) assess cost efficiency for a large sample of European banks, and Beccalli et al. (2006) assess the efficiency of a sample of European listed banks.

Regarding France, we estimated over the period 1995–2002 a mean cost X-inefficiency of 27.6%, technical inefficiency of 19.1%, allocative inefficiency of 28.3%, scale inefficiency of 6.0% and overall inefficiency of 44.9%. Our findings seem consistent with previous studies. In estimating a French domestic frontier, Dietsch and Lozano-Vives (2000) found that the mean level of cost X-inefficiency of commercial banks between 1988–92 is 22.5%. Altunbas et al. (2001) estimate that French commercial banks reduced their cost X-inefficiency between 1989 and 1997 from 28.8% to 24.4%. Focusing on listed banks, Beccalli et al. (2006) found mean technical inefficiency levels (using DEA) in 1999 and 2000 to be 29.4% and 28.0%, respectively, and mean cost X-inefficiency (using SFA) in 1999 and 2000 to be 14.9% and 17.3%, respectively. Focusing on savings banks between 1989 and 1996, Carbo et al. (2000) estimated a mean scale inefficiency of 12.1% and a mean cost X-inefficiency of 23.1%. Our findings on French savings banks slightly differ from these results: we estimate smaller scale inefficiency (1.6%) and larger cost X-inefficiency (26.8%).

In Germany, we estimated over the period 1995–2002 a mean X-inefficiency of 21.4%, technical inefficiency of 8.0%, allocative inefficiency of 28.6%, scale inefficiency of 1.8% and overall inefficiency of 44.7%. Altunbas et al. (2000), using SFA and DFA, found a mean cost X-efficiency level of 83.8% between 1989 and 1996 and found that public and mutual banks have a slight cost advantage in terms of the lower cost of funds. Altunbas and Chakravarty (2001) estimate that German commercial banks reduced their mean X-inefficiency between 1989 and 1997 from 21.8% to 13.5%. Beccalli et al. (2006) found that the mean technical inefficiency levels (using DEA) of German listed banks in 1999 and 2000 was 6.7% and 13.8%, respectively, and mean cost X-inefficiency (using SFA) in 1999 and 2000 was 14.3% and 18.1%, respectively. Focusing on savings banks between 1989 and 1996, Carbo et al. (2000) estimated a mean scale inefficiency of 7.4% and a mean cost X-inefficiency of 21.3%. Our findings on Italian savings banks are similar to these results, and although we estimate substantially smaller scale inefficiency of 1.4%, our cost X-inefficiency results of 22.0% are broadly similar.

In Italy, over the period 1995–2002 banks measured X-inefficiency stood at 20.7%, technical inefficiency at 25.0%, allocative inefficiency at 15.5%, scale inefficiency at 8.7% and overall inefficiency at 41.8%. Resti (1997) estimated using SFA that mean levels of productive efficiency of Italian banks between 1988 and 1992 were around 69.5% (ranging from 69.4% to 69.8%) and mean levels of technical efficiency of 74.0% (ranging from 73.4% to 75.7%). Altunbas and Chakravarty (2001) estimate that Italian commercial banks improved their cost X-inefficiency between 1989 and 1997, reducing their mean inefficiency from 21.7% to 12.6%. Beccalli et al. (2006) found that the mean technical inefficiency levels (using DEA) of Italian listed banks in 1999 and 2000 was 20.0% and 23.8%, respectively, and mean cost X-inefficiency (using SFA) in 1999 and 2000 was 9.8% and 11.5%, respectively. Focusing on savings banks between 1989 and 1996, Carbo et al. (2000) estimated a mean scale inefficiency of 12.1% and a mean cost X-inefficiency of 22.5%. Our findings on Italian savings banks are similar to these results: we estimate smaller scale inefficiency of 13.1% and cost X-inefficiency of 22.4%.

In conclusion, it is worthwhile noting that although it is not possible to directly compare our findings with previous studies (since these studies assess different time periods, use different definitions of bank inputs and outputs, select different samples and use partly differing investigation techniques), our findings are broadly similar to those found in previous empirical studies.

6.4 Conclusions

This chapter has analysed the shareholder value created by cooperative banks and their cost-efficiency levels using a large sample of cooperative banks in France, Germany, Italy and United Kingdom over the period 1995–2002.

Regarding profitability, French banks appear to generate substantially superior mean profits to those in Italy and Germany. The analysis of profitability ratios reveals that French cooperative banks are, on average, more able to remunerate equity capital with profits, while cooperative and commercial banks have similar ROA mean levels between 1995 and 2002. In terms of shareholder value created, we found that mean levels of EVA_{bkg} are usually negative in every year and for all bank categories, with only a few exceptions (e.g. commercial banks in 2001 and 2002). French banks are found to have substantially destroyed value for their shareholders in 1995, 1996 and 1998, while generating value in 1997 and annually from 1999 until 2002. We found substantial differences between commercial, cooperative and savings banks. In Italy, banks appear to generate substantially lower mean profits than in France. Italian banks registered constantly positive ROE and ROA over the period 1995–2002 that are, surprisingly higher than those of French banks. All banks in Italy achieved positive mean values, and cooperative and savings banks are, on average, more profitable than commercial banks. In terms of shareholder value created, mean levels of EVA_{bkg} are usually negative in every year and for all bank categories (with a few exceptions). We found substantial differences between commercial, cooperative and savings banks. Italian savings banks registered a lower mean ratio between EVA_{bkg} and capital invested than commercial and cooperative banks from 1995 to 1999 and a higher mean ratio from 2000 to 2002. Italian cooperative banks are usually found to have destroyed value, except in 1999 and 2000. Commercial banks seem to have destroyed value between 1995 and 1998, and since then have created value for their shareholders. German banks generate lower profits and shareholder value than those in the other two countries. The analysis of profitability ratios (both ROE and ROA) enables us to note that German cooperative and savings banks are on average more profitable than commercial banks and that these banks achieve positive profits also in 2001 and 2002. In addition, the percentage of banks with positive net income is constantly and substantially higher for cooperative and savings banks than for commercial banks. The lower profitability of German banks seems to be also confirmed in terms of shareholder value created. Mean levels of EVA_{bkg} are usually negative in every year and for all bank categories (with a few exceptions).

Regarding efficiency, French banks show the greatest opportunities for improving X-efficiency with a mean X-inefficiency of 27.6% and a dispersion of average efficiency of 11.4%. Italian and French banks exhibit similar mean levels (79.3% and 78.6%, respectively), but German banks exhibit a lower range of dispersion of average cost efficiency scores. Over the period analysed, annual mean X-efficiency follows a similar trend since, for both countries, mean annual X-efficiency increased between 1995 and 1998, decreased between 1998 and 2001 and sharply increased in 2002.

As for the different bank specializations, commercial banks display a lower mean level of cost X-efficiency (75.0%) than savings and cooperative banks (77.7% and 79.4%, respectively) over the period 1995–2002. The higher mean levels of cost X-efficiency of cooperative and savings banks over commercial banks are found to be almost constant in every year analysed, except 1995 and 2001.

Cooperative banks show higher mean levels of cost X-efficiency than savings banks and, especially, than commercial banks in Italy and Germany in almost every year over the period analysed. German commercial banks exhibit a mean X-efficiency similar to the other two bank categories. In France, all categories of bank display similar cost X-efficiency levels over time. Comparing our findings across countries reveals that all French banks show the greatest mean cost X-inefficiency on average over the period 1995–2002, while Italian cooperative banks and German savings banks achieved the highest mean cost X-efficiency in their ownership category.

In conclusion, while it is not possible to directly compare our findings with previous studies (since these studies assess different time periods, use different definitions of bank inputs and outputs, select different samples and use partly differing investigation techniques), our findings are broadly similar to those found in Berger and Humphrey (1997) and, generally, with the empirical literature.

Notes

University of Rome III, Dipartimento di Scienze Aziendali ed Economico-Giuridiche, Via Silvio d'Amico 77, 00145 Rome, Italy.

1. Studies dealing with bank efficiency focus on methodological issues (e.g. Berger, 1993; Altunbas and Chakravarty, 2001) compare estimates from different methodologies (e.g. Berger and Mester, 1997; Bauer et al., 1997), estimate efficiency focusing on countries or financial sectors poorly analysed by previous studies (e.g. Sathye, 2001; Green and Segal, 2004; Fiordelisi and Molyneux, 2004; Beccalli, 2004), and assess the source of inefficiency and the role of environmental factors (e.g. Dietsch and Lozano-Vives, 2000; Berger and De Young, 2001; Chaffai et al., 2001; Carbo and Humphrey, 2004).

2. Studies analysing shareholder value usually focus on developing and comparing new performance measures (e.g. O'Hanlon and Peasnell, 1998; Garvey and Milbourn, 2000; Fernández, 2002), assess the value relevance of different company accounting variables (e.g. Barth Beaver and Landsman, 2001; Holthausen and Watts, 2001), model the link between market value and accounting values (e.g. Ohlson, 1995; Felthman and Ohlson, 1995; Morel, 1999; Dechow et al., 1999; Lo and Lys, 2000; Ahmed et al., 2000; Liu and Ohlson, 2000; Biddle et al., 2001; Ota, 2002).

3. See Hamilton (1777) and Marshall (1890).

4. See Bacidore et al. (1997) and Rajan (2000).

5. Stern Stewart publishes annually a performance report for the 1,000 largest companies (see Stewart, 1991). In this paper, these capitalized expenses are amortized every year (i.e. from 1995 to 1999) using a proxy defined by dividing the overall amount of R&D expenses over the period 1995–99 for five years.

6. Since the limited data availability does not allow us to evaluate the present value of expected lease commitments over time, the present value of expected future lease commitments capitalized in every year between 1995 and 1999 is assumed to be equal to the overall amount of operating leases expenses over the period 1995–99. The amount amortized every year (i.e. from 1995 to 1999) is bring near the overall amount of R&D expenses over the period 1995–99 for five years.
7. These adjustments were originally suggested by Uyemura et al. (1996).
8. Otherwise, it would be necessary to distinguish between borrowed funds assigned to finance banking operations and those representing a productive input.
9. This point is also supported by Uyemura et al. (1996, p. 102) and Di Antonio (2002, p. 103).
10. Sironi (1999, p. 6).
11. See, for example, Damodaran (1999).
12. Fama and French (2002) propose a different model using dividend and earnings growth rates to measure the expected rate of capital gain and to estimate the equity risk premium: this model was labelled 'earning growth model'.
13. Regarding the US risk premium, the estimation provided by Damodaran (2008) has been adopted: 6.10%.
14. Since one would expect the country equity risk premium to be larger than the country default risk spread, the country equity spread is obtained by adjusting the country bond spreads as follows:
Country Equity Risk Premium = Country Bond Spread $\times\ \sigma_{equity}/\sigma_{bond}$
Where: (1) the volatility of the equity market (σ_{equity}) has been estimated focusing on *CAC 40, DAX 30, MIBTEL storico, FTSE 100*; (2) the volatility of the bond market (σ_{bond}) has been estimated focusing on the French-, Italian-, German-, British- J. P. MORGAN Government Bond return indices.
15. Namely, the French-, Italian-, German-, British- J. P. MORGAN Government Bond return indices.
16. Namely, CAC 40 for France, DAX 30 for Germany, MIBTEL storico for Italy and FTSE100 for UK.
17. Namely: Beta = Regression Beta (0.67) + 1.00 (0.33).
18. We use unconsolidated balance-sheet information.
19. The use of translog has been chosen for two reasons: first, Altunbas and Chakravraty (2001) identified some problems associated with using the Fourier functional form, especially when dealing with heterogeneous data sets. Second, Berger and Mester (1997) observe that the translog functional form and Fourier-flexible form are substantially equivalent from an economic viewpoint, and rank individual bank efficiency in almost the same order.
20. For further details, see Ali and Seiford (1993).
21. Such as, for example, the two-stages DEA suggested in Ali and Seiford (1993).
22. Although the steps 1 and 2 are carried out in the standard two-stage method (proposed by Ali and Seiford, 1993), the projected points obtained in this second step are not used in the method. The second step aims simply to identify the '"Koopmans" efficient set' and to 'have slack set'.
23. Potential slacks exist in that input when the contraction is achieved.
24. For a proof of the Units Invariance Theorem, see Cooper et al. (2000).
25. It is also possible to consider revenue maximization and allocative inefficiency in output mix selection in a similar manner. For further details, see Lovell (1993, p. 33).

26. For the DEA model used to measure allocative efficiency, see Cooper et al. (2000).
27. This selection of inputs and outputs follows the studies by Sathye (2001) and Dietsch and Lozano (2000); Aly et al. (1990) and Hancock (1986), wherein the author develops a methodology based on user costs to determine the outputs and inputs of a banking firm.
28. We use unconsolidated balance-sheet information.
29. In Italy and France the number of savings banks is quite small. In order to have enough degrees of freedom in estimating the SFA models, we prefer pooling savings banks and cooperative banks in a unique sample and estimating a common frontier for the two categories of bank.
30. For both DEA and SFA, we estimate an annual cross-section efficient frontier for eight years (1995–2002), for two bank categories (first, commercial banks and, second cooperative and saving banks) and for three countries (France, Italy and Germany).
31. It is worth bearing in mind that mean cost efficiency measures express the mean distance of inefficient banks from an efficient frontier, that is, estimated with a cross-sectional sample, and, as such, it changes every year. All comparison among mean efficiency levels obtained in different countries or by different kind of bank, for example, focuses on the mean distance of inefficient banks from their own efficient frontier. As such, the expression 'more/less cost efficient' means that the mean distance of inefficient banks from their own efficient frontier is smaller/larger than the mean distance of inefficient banks of another category/country. Lower/higher mean cost efficiency does not amount to evidence of lower/higher Total Factor Productivity.
32. See Malmquist (1953).
33. This mean value is mostly accounted for by technical efficiency levels.
34. It is worth noting that most of the studies summarized by Berger and Humphrey (1997) focus on the US banking system and on different time periods, and use different bank input and output definitions than those used in our analysis.
35. Technical efficiency is estimated by assuming Variable Return of Scale, Allocative Efficiency is estimated by assuming Variable Return of Scale, cost efficiency is obtained by multiplying technical efficiency, allocative efficiency and scale efficiency estimates obtained on the assumption of Variable Return of Scale (i.e. equivalent to estimate cost efficiency under constant return of scale). The total scores are calculated by taking all commercial, cooperative and saving banks into account.

References

Ahmed A. S., Morton R. M. and Schaefer T. F. (2000), Accounting conservatism and the valuation of accounting numbers: Evidence on the Felthman–Ohlson (1996) model, *Journal of Accounting, Auditing and Finance*, 15, 3, 271–92.

Ali A. I. and Seiford L. M. (1993), The mathematical programming approach to efficiency analysis, in Fried et al., pp.120–59.

Altunbas Y. and Chakravarty S. (2001), Frontier cost functions and bank efficiency, *Economic letters*, 72, 233–40.

Altunbas Y., Evans L. and Molyneux P. (2000), Bank ownership and efficiency, *Journal of Money, Credit and Banking*, 33, 926–54.

Altunbas Y., Gardener E. P. M., Molyneux P. and Moore B. (2001), Efficiency in European banking, *European Economic Review*, 45, 10, 1931–55.

Bacidore J. M., Boquist J. A., Milbourn T. T. and Thakor A. V. (1997), The search for the best financial performance measure, *Financial Analysts Journal*, May/June, 11–20.

Banker R. D, Charnes A. and Cooper W. W. (1984), Some models for estimating technical and scale inefficiencies in Data Envelopment Analysis, *Management Science*, 30, 1078–92.

Barth, M. E., Beaver W. H. and Landsman W. R. (2001), The relevance of the value relevance literature for financial accounting standard setting: another view. *Journal of Accounting and Economics*, 31, 77–104.

Battese G. E. and Coelli T. J. (1992), Frontier production functions, technical efficiency and panel data: With application to paddy farmers in India, *Journal of Productivity Analysis*, 3, 153–69.

Battese G. E. and Coelli T. J. (1995), A model for technical inefficiency effects in a stochastic frontier production function for panel data, *Empirical Economics*, 20, 325–32.

Bauer P. W., Berger A. N., Ferrier G. D. and Humphrey D. B. (1997), Consistency conditions for regulatory analysis of financial institutions: A comparison of frontier efficiency methods, *The Federal Reserve Board, Finance and Economics Discussion Series*, no. 1997–50.

Beccalli E., (2004), Cross-country comparisons of efficiency: Evidence from the UK and Italian investment firms, *Journal of Banking and Finance*, 28, 1363–83.

Beccalli E. Casu B. and Girardone C. (2006), Efficiency and stock performance in European banking, *Journal of Business Finance and Accounting*, 33, 218–35.

Berger A. N. (1993), Distribution-free estimates of efficiency in the US banking system and tests of the standard distributional assumptions, *Journal of Productivity Analysis*, 4, 261–83.

Berger A. N. and De Young R. (2001), The effect of geographic expansion on bank efficiency, *Journal of Financial Service Research*, 19, 2/3, 163–84.

Berger A. N. and Humphrey D. B. (1992), Measurement and efficiency issues in commercial banking, in Zvi Griliches, Output Measurement in the service Sectors, *The University of Chicago Press*, Chapter 7, p. 245–79.

Berger A. N. and Humphrey D. B. (1997), Efficiency of financial institution: International survey and direction for future research, FRB Finance and Economics Discussion Paper, no.11.

Berger A. N. and Mester L. J (1997), Inside the black box: What explains differences in the efficiency of financial institutions, *Journal of Banking and Finance*, 21, 7, 895–947.

Biddle G. C., Chen P. and Zhang G. (2001), When capital follows profitability: Non linear residual income dynamics, *Review of Accounting Studies*, 6, 229–65.

Carbo S., Gardener E. P. M. and Williams J. (2000), Efficiency and technical change in Europe's savings banks industry, *Revue de la Banque*, 6, 381–94

Carbo S. and Humphrey D. B. (2004), Opening the black box: Finding the source of cost inefficiency, Paper presented at the annual conference of the European Association of University Teachers in Banking and Finance, Krakow University, September.

Casu B. and Girardone C. (2004), Financial conglomerates: Strategic drive and impact on bank efficiency and productivity, *Applied Financial Economics*, 14, 10, 687–96.

Chaffai M. E., Dietsch M. and Lozano-Vivas A. (2001), Technological and environmental differences in the European banking industries, *Journal of Financial Services Research*, 19, 147–62.

Charnes A., Cooper W. W. and Rhodes E. (1978), Measuring for efficiency of decision making units, *European Journal of Operational Research*, 2, 429–44.

Coelli T. (1998), A multi-stage methodology for the solution of oriented DEA models, CEPA Working Paper, no. 1

Cooper W. W., Seiford L. M. and Tone K. (2000), *Data Envelopment Analysis*, Kluwer Academic Publisher, Boston U.S.

Damodaran A. (1999), Estimating risk free rates, Leonard N. Stern School of Business, The Department of Finance, Working Paper Series, no. 19 (FIN-99-021).

Damodaran A. (2005), *Applied Corporate Finance: A User's Manual, John Wiley & Sons, inc, New York*, Second edition, forthcoming in 2005 (available at: http://pages.stern.nyu.edu/~adamodar/)

Damodaran A. (2008), *Equity Risk Premiums (ERP): Determinants, Estimation and Implications*, available at http://pages.stern.nyu.edu/~adamodar/

Dechow P. M., Hutton A. P. and Sloan R. G. (1999), An empirical assessment of the residual income valuation model, *Journal of Accounting and Economics*, 26, 1–34.

Di Antonio M. (2002), Creazione di valore e controllo strategico nella banca, *Bancaria Editrice*, Rome.

Dietsch M. and Lozano-Vives A. (2000), How the environment determines banking efficiency: A comparison between French and Spanish industries, *Journal of Banking and Finance*, 24, 985–1004.

Eisenbeis R. A., Ferrier G. D. and Kwan S. H. (1999), 'The informativeness of stochastic frontier and programming frontier efficiency scores: Cost efficiency and other measures of bank holding company performance', Federal Reserve Bank of Atlanta, Working Paper, 99–23.

Fama E. F. and French R. K. (2002), The equity premium, Journal of Finance, 57, 637–59.

Farrell M. J. (1957), The measurement of productive efficiency, *Journal of Royal Statistical Society*, Series A, CXX, Part 3, 253–90.

Felthman G. and Ohlson J. A., (1995), Valuation and clean surplus accounting for operating and financial activities, *Contemporary Accounting Research*, 11, 689–731.

Fernández P. (2002), A definition of shareholder value creation, University of Navarra, IESE, Research Paper no. 448.

Fiordelisi F. and Molyneux P. (2004), 'Efficiency in the factoring industry', *Applied Economics*, vol. 36, pp. 947–59.

Fiordelisi F. and Molyneux P. (2006), *Creating Shareholder Value in Banking*, Palgrave Macmillan, London.

Garvey G. T. and Milbourn T. T. (2000), EVA versus earnings: Does it matter which is more highly correlated with stock returns?, *Journal of Accounting Research*, 38, supplement, 209–45.

Green W. H. and Segal D. (2004), 'Profitability and efficiency in the U.S. Life Insurance Industry', *Journal of Productivity Analysis*, vol. 21, pp. 229–47.

Hamilton R. (1777), An introduction to merchandise. Containing a complete system of arithmetic. A system of algebra... in two volumes. Printed for the author, sold by Y. Cadell, London and John Balfour, Edinburgh.

Holthausen R. W. and Watts R. L. (2001), The relevance of the value-relevance literature for financial accounting standard setting, *Journal of Accounting and Economics*, 31, 3–75.

Koopmans T. C. (1951), An analysis of production as an efficient combination of activities, in Koopmans T. C., ed. *Activity Analysis Of Production And Allocation*, Cowles Commission for research in Economics, Monograph No. 13, New York.

Lim G. H. and Chu-Chun-Lin (1998), S, Efficiency and returns: an empirical study of six Singapore-listed banks. *Asia Pacific Journal of Finance*, 1, 191–207.

Liu J. and Ohlson J. A. (2000), The Feltham-Ohlson (1995) model: Empirical implications, *Journal of Accounting, Auditing and Finance*, 15, 321–31.

Lo K. and Lys T. (2000), The Ohlson model: Contribution to valuation theory, limitations, and empirical applications, *Journal of Accounting, Auditing and Finance*, 15, 3, 337–67.

Lovell C. A. K. (1993), Production frontiers and productive efficiency, in Fried H., Lovell C. A. K., Schmidt S. (eds.), *The Measurement of Productive Efficiency: Techniques and Applications*, Oxford University Press, Oxford, 3–67.

Malmquist S. (1953), Index numbers and indifference surfaces, *Trabajos de Estatica*, 4, 209–42.

Marshall A. (1890), *Principle of Economics*, The Macmillan Press Ltd, London, New York.

Morel M. (1999), Multi-lagged specification of the Ohlson model, *Journal of Accounting, Auditing and Finance*, 12, 147–61.

O'Hanlon J. F. and Peasnell K.V. (1998), Wall Street's contribution to management accounting: the Stern Stewart EVA® financial management system. *Management Accounting Research*, 9, 421–444.

Ohlson J. A. (1995), Earnings, book values, and dividends in equity valuation, *Contemporary Accounting Research*, 11, 661–87.

Ota K. (2002), A test of the Ohlson (1995) model: Empirical evidence from Japan, SSRN working papers, *International Journal of Accounting*, 37, 157–82.

Rajan M. V. (2000), Discussion of EVA versus earnings: Does it matter which is more highly correlated with stock returns? *Journal of Accounting Research*, 38, supplement, 247–54.

Resti A. (1997), Evaluating the cost efficiency of the Italian banking system: What we can be learned from the joint application of parametric and non parametric techniques, *Journal of Banking and Finance*, 21, 221–50.

Sathye M. (2001), X-efficiency in Australian banking: An empirical investigation, *Journal of Banking and Finance*, 25, 613–30.

Sironi A. (1999), Estimating banks' cost of equity capital: Evidence from an international comparison, *Quaderno Newfin*, Università Commerciale L. Bocconi, Milan.

Spong K., Sullivan R. J. and De Young R. (1995), What makes a bank efficient? A look at financial characteristics and bank management and ownership structure, *FRB of Kansas City Review*, December, 1–19.

Stewart B. G. (1991), The quest for value, *HarperBusiness*.

Uyemura D. G., Kantor G. C. and Pettit J. M., (1996), EVA for banks: Value creation, risk management and profitability measurement, *Journal of Applied Corporate Finance*, 9, 2, 94–105.

7
Rating Methodology for Cooperative Banks

C. Giannotti

7.1 Introduction

The assignment on the part of specialized agencies of ratings to the bond issues of enterprises, financial institutions, and governments assumes crucial significance from the point of view of issuers, investors and the financial system as a whole.

The bond credit rating is an expression of the bond default risk. Requested, as a rule, by the issuers themselves, it indicates their capacity to pay the contractual interest and principal on their debt obligations.

As far as banks are concerned, the rating agencies should in principle adopt methodologies of analysis that are consistent with the general characteristics of those issuers as well as flexible with respect to their distinctive features, as in the case of cooperative banks.

This chapter sets out to analyze the credit ratings published by the major agencies with reference to bond issues (section 7.2), the general methodology used in the case of banks (section 7.3), and the specific methodology used to assess cooperative banks (section 7.4).

7.2 Credit rating of bond issues

At any given moment, the creditworthiness of a bond issuer depends on a variety of factors, such as the industry risk, the dimension that shows the market diversification and power, the managerial competence, the capital structure, as well as the profitability and ability to generate cash flows.

After having assigned a credit rating to the issuer, the agencies determine the credit rating of the issue, which depends on the debt seniority and the presence of collateral (notching), if any. For instance, a very well-secured bond will be rated one notch above a rating for investment grade categories and two notches above for speculative grade categories.

The rating is inversely linked to the yield bond and, therefore, plays a fundamental role for both issuers and investors. Indeed, it contributes to determining funding costs as well as expected yields.

The rating helps to reduce the asymmetry in information on the creditworthiness of the issuer. Rather than disclosing private information, the issuer prefers to request the rating from specialized agencies that operate in the capacity of certifiers.

The three best-known agencies that assign and publish credit ratings are Fitch, Moody's Investors Service (hereinafter referred to as "Moody's"), and Standard & Poor's.[1]

A credit rating from Fitch provides an opinion on the ability of an entity to meet financial commitments. Investors use it as an indication of the likelihood of receiving their money back in accordance with the terms on which they invested.[2] Fitch's ratings cover corporate, sovereign (including supranational and sub-national), financial, bank, insurance, municipal, and other public finance entities, as well as securities or other obligations they issue.

Depending on their applications, credit ratings address benchmark measures of probability of default as well as relative expectations of loss in the event of default. For instance, issuers are typically assigned Issuer Default Ratings that are relative measures of default probability. Short-term credit ratings depend mostly on the likelihood that obligations will be met on a timely basis. Securities, are rated with the probability of default and loss in the event of default taken into consideration.

Structured finance ratings are typically assigned to each individual security or tranche in a transaction, and not to an issuer.[3]

Moody's credit ratings are opinions of the credit quality of individual obligations or of an issuer's creditworthiness (for example, long term obligation, syndicated loan, bank deposit and insurance financial strength).[4]

Moody's has two separate bond rating systems (or scales): the Moody's Global Scale and the Moody's US Municipal Scale. The former applies to ratings assigned to non-financial and financial institutions, sovereigns and sub-sovereign issuers outside the United States, and structured finance obligations. The latter encompasses ratings assigned to state and local governments, non-profit organizations, and related entities that issue debt in the U.S. tax-exempt bond market.

The Moody's Global Scale is a mapping between rating categories and relative expected loss rates across multiple horizons, comprising an assessment of the probability of default as well as expectation of loss in the event of default. The expected loss rate associated with a given rating and time horizon is the same across obligations and issuers rated on the scale.

A Standard & Poor's issue credit rating is a judgment of the creditworthiness of an obligor with respect to a specific financial obligation, a specific class of financial obligations, or a specific financial program.[5] It considers the creditworthiness of guarantors, insurers, or other forms of credit enhancement on the obligation, as well as the currency in which the obligation is denominated.

The opinion evaluates the obligor's capacity and willingness to meet its financial commitments, and may assess terms, such as collateral security and subordination, which could affect ultimate payment in the event of default. Therefore, issue ratings are an assessment of default risk, but may incorporate an assessment of relative seniority or ultimate recovery in the event of default. Junior obligations are typically rated lower than senior obligations, to reflect the lower priority in bankruptcy.

The issuer credit rating is a current opinion of the obligor's capacity and willingness to meet its financial commitments. This rating does not apply to any specific financial obligation. It does not take into account the nature and provisions of the obligation, its standing in bankruptcy or liquidation, statutory preferences, or the legality and enforceability of the obligation. It does not consider the creditworthiness of the guarantors nor other forms of credit enhancement on the obligation.

7.3   Bank rating methodology

In case of banks, the credit rating seems relevant for at least two reasons.[6] It affects the cost of liabilities and the amount of marketable debt, owing to the indirect relations that exist between rating and bond yield, with evident effects on the competitiveness of financial intermediaries. Furthermore, the rating contributes to measuring the credit risk of bank assets and, therefore, to determining the capital requirements related to unexpected losses, according to the principles of the New Basel Capital Accord (Basel 2).[7]

In principle, the bank assessment should be undertaken by the rating agencies in keeping with a methodology that is likely to detect the peculiar features of those financial institutions, while enhancing the specific peculiarities that may exist among banks or among countries.

The issue ratings quality in the case of banks and the ability of the specialized agencies to detect all the available information are debated in the international literature.[8]

The major rating agencies quite often assign different ratings to bank bond issues (split rating) and the differences from other issues by other firms with similar features are more marked. The probability of disagreement between bond raters increases as the risk profile and maturity (being risk equal) increase, while it decreases with the size of the issue, given that issuers of smaller sizes are more opaque.[9]

The split rating may be explained by a greater opacity of banks vis-à-vis other types of firms that, according to financial intermediation theories, is unavoidable, being linked to the business characteristics. Only insurance companies would seem to attract more raters' disagreement than banks.[10]

In fact, in dealings with banks, the uncertainty originates in the characteristics of their assets, which consists for the most part of credits and trading assets. The depositors delegate the bank to monitor over time the creditworthiness of the firms, households, and institutions to whom they indirectly lend their financial resources,[11] but lending to opaque borrowers may give rise to opaque banks. Trading assets are not necessarily opaque and illiquid like loans. Nonetheless, trading positions may change rapidly and the relative risks may be hardly monitored from outside the bank. While real estate assets could favor an alignment of the raters' opinions, in the case of banks they are definitely residual compared with financial assets.

This is compounded by the high level of leverage and, therefore, financial risk that typically characterizes the capital structure of banks. Once debt has been sold, the shareholders of leveraged firms are inclined to take more risk than creditors expected when they bought the debt (risk shifting).[12]

The characteristics of the business, activities and liabilities of the banks, and the opacity of these financial intermediaries warrant, inter alia, supervision from the supervisory authorities. On this subject, it seems worthwhile stressing the increased market discipline favored by Basel 2 that is likely to force banks to operate more transparently (market discipline).

The following paragraphs outline the methodology adopted by Fitch to analyze banks in general.[13] Fitch assigns to banks four different types of rating:[14] support, individual, short-term, and long-term ratings.

7.3.1 Support ratings

Support ratings are the product of Fitch's assessment of the ability and propensity of a potential provider (either a sovereign state or an institutional owner) to support a bank should the bank experience financial difficulties.[15] Its ability is determined by the potential supporter's own long-term rating. Its propensity is assessed by Fitch based on a few specific variables (Table 7.1).

The support has to be provided on a timely basis and will be sufficiently sustained so that the bank being supported is able to continue meeting its financial commitments until the crisis is over.

Therefore, support ratings do not assess the bank's credit quality. These represent the long-term ratings floor (Table 7.2).

Table 7.1   Determinants of the propensity to support banks

Type of potential support	Categories of criteria
Sovereign unitary or federal state support	• state guarantees and commitments • relationship with the state • importance of the bank to the state
Institutional owner or owners	• guarantees and commitments • percentage control • nature of the owner • importance of the bank to the owning institution

Source: Processed by the author from Fitch (2004a).

Table 7.2   Support ratings

Rating	Definition
1	A bank for which there is an extremely high probability of external support. The minimum long-term rating floor is "A–."
2	A bank for which there is a high probability of external support. The minimum long-term rating floor is "BBB–."
3	A bank for which there is moderate probability of external support. The minimum long-term rating floor is "BB–."
4	A bank for which there is limited probability of external support. The minimum long-term rating floor is "B."
5	A bank for which external support, although possible, cannot be relied upon. It indicates a long-term rating floor no higher than "B–" and in many cases no floor at all.

Source: Processed by the author from Fitch (2003a).

Table 7.3 Individual ratings

Rating	Definition
A	A very strong bank.
B	A strong bank.
C	An adequate bank.
D	A bank which has a weakness of internal and/or external origin.
E	A bank with serious problems, which either requires or is likely to require external support.

Source: Processed by the author from Fitch (2003a).

In emerging markets, the propensity and ability of potential supporters are subject to many more debilitating extraneous influences than in developed countries. Therefore, the support ratings are more volatile.

7.3.2   Individual ratings

Individual ratings determine the likelihood that a bank would fail and, therefore, require support to prevent it from defaulting. These ratings are internationally comparable (Table 7.3).

With reference to the current situation and, in particular, future developments, the analysis takes into consideration a number of factors, such as profitability, balance sheet integrity and capitalization, franchise, management, operating environment, consistency, size in terms of equity capital, and diversification in terms of activities and/or geographical sector.

For rating assessing purposes, the agencies resort to a comparison between the bank and a peer group, at both a domestic and an international level. The analysis calculates different ratios that, although shared usually by all the analyzes, take into account different national banking practices and differing reporting standards and conventions.

7.3.3   Short-term and long-term credit ratings

Short-term and long-term issuer ratings assigned to banks assess their general creditworthiness on a senior basis. They are driven by their support and individual ratings. Support ratings are directly related to long-term debt ratings, as they represent the long-term rating floor; depending on the level of a bank's support rating, its long-term credit rating cannot fall below a specific floor. Otherwise, a good individual rating may raise the long-term rating above its support rating floor.

Ratings assigned to specific issues made by a bank depend on the relative preferential position of the bondholder and the terms, conditions, and covenants attaching to that security. International short-term and long-term ratings may be assigned to both foreign-currency and local-currency debt issues.

National ratings are generally assigned to banks in emerging markets, where such ratings are demanded.

Fitch proposes also to show in what direction long-term ratings may move over a one- to two-year period. Therefore, the agency assigns outlooks to these ratings: "Positive", "Stable", "Negative", or, occasionally, "Evolving."

All ratings except for support ratings may be placed on Rating Watch, meaning that there is a reasonable probability of a rating change in a relatively short period, and the likely direction of such change ("Positive", "Negative", or "Evolving").

7.4   Cooperative banks rating methodology

7.4.1   The need to rate cooperative banks fairly

As far as the analysis of financial ratios for individual rating purposes is concerned, cooperative banks have historically benefited from a series of positive factors that, in recent years, have partly weakened:[16]

- relatively high margins that originated in the low costs of funding and in loans to private individuals and small businesses.

  Over the years, with a view to countering growing competitive pressure, cooperative banks have adopted important strategies aiming at their rationalization, integration, and centralization, as well as the search for new distribution channels, new market outlets, and new funding opportunities (bond market).
- a relatively low risk profile due for the most part to the main strong point of this category of banks, that is to say, their proximity to their substantial retail client base.

  This has nonetheless resulted in a high degree of vulnerability in the event of economic downturns, as happened for instance in Finland in the early 1990s owing to the economic recession, and in France owing to the crisis in the real estate sector and in the domestic fishing industry.

- strong capitalization, ensured, as a rule, by the lack of constraints on the distribution of dividends to their shareholders. Insofar as ownership structure is concerned, as everyone knows, the "one-member-one-vote" rule applies.

A recent study analyzes a few current strong and weak points of cooperative banks in order to evaluate their role in financial stability.[17]

Cooperative banks seem to be more stable than commercial banks. The reason for this lies in the lower volatility of yields rather than in the level of capitalization and profitability, which, on average, is lower than in commercial banks. In fact, the objective of cooperative banks is to maximize their members' consumer surplus, delivering financial services at below-market prices to their clients. As a result, the yield level is low on average, although the consumer surplus may be considered the front line of defense of cooperative banks during hard times as it succeeds in abating the negative effects on performance. Confirming that the low yield level does not result from economic inefficiency, the level of the cost-to-income ratio is in line with that of commercial banks.

Cooperative banks seem to increase the stability of the financial system. Their presence weakens poorly performing commercial banks, forcing them to move their business activity from the retail market to corporate and investment banking, whose revenues are nonetheless more variable.

It is quite a time since operators and the literature alike have stressed the need for a specific methodology of analysis to rate cooperative banks that might be consistent with the nature and characteristics of these financial intermediaries.

The fairness of the rating process affects not only the competitiveness of cooperative banks in financial markets, but also their members through rates on their credit and, therefore, the benefits owed to them.[18]

According to a few studies, rating agencies – unlike investors – have not consistently expressed a fair rating.[19] In particular, the assets risk level and the default risk of bonds issued seem to be lower in cooperative banks than in stock banks. In any event, these differences were not always considered by the specialized agencies in their ratings, while they have usually been incorporated in the expected bond yields required by the market. In fact, investors requested a spread on average on cooperative banks that was significantly smaller than that required on average from stock banks, sometimes even ignoring the assigned rating. The insolvency risk premium is lower.

A few studies have tried to highlight the major determinants of the rating of cooperative banks, assessing the significance of the characteristic features of this type of financial intermediary in comparison with commercial banks.[20] The results show that cooperative bond ratings appear to be affected to a greater extent by asset quality and size. On the other hand, commercial banks' bond ratings are more sensitive to debt level and the issuer's capacity to cover its interest payments. It would seem that the factors determining rating are not the same, owing to the specific characteristics of cooperative banks (for instance, their cohesion and internal support).

7.4.2   Methodology of analysis

The methodology of analysis adopted by the rating agencies has undergone considerable development in recent years in order to take account of the distinctive features of cooperative banks.

The rating assigned to cooperative banks (as well as to other financial institutions) depends on the evaluation of a range of variables, such as ownership and the likelihood of external support should it ever be needed, the quality and the strategy of management, asset quality, liquidity and funding, profitability, and capitalization.

For instance, with reference to the external supports present in Italy, the ratings take also into consideration the potential external support from the bank's adherence to the depositors' guarantee fund ("Fondo di Garanzia dei Depositanti del Credito Cooperativo") specific to Italian cooperative banks.[21] Besides, the fund has the option of stepping in to help the associated banks to overcome temporary difficulties.

In general, Fitch assigns ratings exclusively to legal entities. In any event, in the presence of a group of banks that take advantage of a mutual support system, the rating agency determines a set of ratings for the group itself, even though the latter is not legally a single entity. Although lacking a standard group structure, many banking groups now publish consolidated accounts, and the analysis of groups is based on this financial information. Audited consolidated accounts are a prerequisite for the rating of any group.

In principle, the methodology of analysis may be applied to both cooperative banks and savings banks, even though in the latter case few European banks have given rise to a mutual support mechanism.[22]

Table 7.4   Ratings assigned in the presence of a formal support mechanism

	Support	**Individual**	**Short-term**	**IDR**
Group	Assigned	Assigned	Assigned	Assigned
Central body	Group rating	None	Group rating	Group rating
Individual banks	None	None	Group rating (blanket)	Group rating (blanket)

Therefore, within the context of the cooperative banking movements in Europe, a fundamental element is represented by the mutual support system (risk sharing), which varies to a considerable extent from one country to another and from one group to another (Table 7.4). The rating agencies attach fundamental importance to the analysis and evaluation of the characteristics of this support.[23]

The formal cross-guarantee mechanism is the strongest form of mutual support; it means that, in the event of liquidity or solvency problems, any bank sharing in the mechanism can rely on timely support from within the group. If this is not sufficient, then the group looks to the sovereign state for support. In Western Europe, such support mechanisms have proved completely effective. There are a variety of legally binding mechanisms in Europe, such as in the Netherlands (Rabobank Group), in Finland (Okogroup), and the five French cooperative groups.[24]

These supports must not be mistaken with the liquidity funds present within a few banking groups, to which member banks may be required to contribute amounts often determined by their central bodies. Mutual support mechanisms are legally binding and explicit in what they seek to remedy, namely, liquidity or solvency problems of the banks. Liquidity funds, in contrast, and supposed to deal with the banks' short-term liquidity problems but, as a rule, they are insufficient to resolve serious liquidity or insolvency crises afflicting the entire group. While formal cross-guarantee mechanisms are a decisive factor influencing the debt rating assigned to member banks, liquidity funds are usually taken into account within the context of the evaluation of the group's liquidity level.

The methodology of analysis adopted by Fitch needs to be analyzed, first when formal support mechanisms among cooperative banks of a group are present and, second, when they are absent.[25]

7.4.2.1   Groups with a formal cross-guarantee mechanism

When a group has a formal cross-guarantee mechanism, Fitch assigns a full set of ratings to it: individual, support, short-term and Issuer Default Rating (IDR).

The short-term ratings and IDRs applied to the group will be automatically assigned to all the entities sharing the support mechanism, since the consolidated equity of an entire group is available to protect the creditors of every member subject to the guarantee. The short-term ratings and IDRs are, as for any financial institution, driven by either support ratings or individual ratings.

The support rating of the group takes into account the relevance of the group within the domestic and the international financial system ("too big to fail"). This contributes to determining the propensity of the government to support the group.

With a view to assigning an individual rating to the group, Fitch analyzes the group's audited consolidated financial statements, evaluating the trend of the traditional ratios used to analyze banks. In general, the determination of an individual rating for the group is favored by the presence of a group risk management system, which ensures a fair degree of harmonization.

Fitch assigns ratings also to the group's central body, itself a legal entity sharing in the cross-guarantee mechanism. Given the likelihood that any outside support provided to the group will be channeled through the central body responsible for the liquidity and solvency of the group's members, the support rating of the central body will be the same as that assigned to the group. In accordance with the same logic, that entity will receive the same short-term rating and IDR as those assigned to the group.

As a rule, Fitch does not assign individual ratings to central bodies, since they rarely carry out the activities typical of commercial banks, given the role they play within the group. The central body has the responsibility for determining group strategies, defining and monitoring risk management policies, and issuing debt on behalf of the group. Otherwise, an individual rating, which may differ from the group rating, is also assigned to the central body.

There is no specific need to assign ratings to individual local banks belonging to a group, given that issues on the capital market are usually made by the central body. Therefore, it is understandable that the blanket short-term ratings and IDRs being determined are identical to those of the group.

No individual ratings are assigned to members, owing to issues of integration and the lack of autonomy of these small banks. In many cases, these banks may be unable to undertake certain functions independently (for example, treasury management and credit assessment). Their equity does not solely belong to them, as it can be used at any time to support other members.

Support ratings are not assigned to individual banks, since it is quite hard to evaluate the size and role of members within the domestic economy case-by-case. Furthermore, the potential sources of support may be, forthcoming from the state, the group's central body, or other member banks.

Finally, the rating agency analyzes any subsidiaries within a group that is excluded from the support mechanism. In this event, the evaluation is made on a case-by-case basis and, as a rule, all the anticipated ratings are assigned. Even an individual rating may be determined, provided that the independence and autonomy needed for the evaluation are not completely absent. The support rating, the short-term rating and the IDR being assigned may be the same as that of the group or different, depending on the level of integration, the relevance of the bank being analyzed, and the evaluation of all the forms of support present within the group.

7.4.2.2   *Groups without a formal cross-guarantee mechanism*

The procedure for rating groups that have no formal support mechanism appears more complex and requires evaluations to be carried out on a case-by-case basis.

In the past, the want of an automatic support mechanism caused Fitch to assign ratings merely to individual banks. The support rating, the short-term rating and the IDR of the individual entities were generally assigned taking into consideration also the group's overall creditworthiness. The financial condition and the importance of the sector within the banking system make it possible to identify the potentially available support level.

In any event, with reference to groups with no formal support mechanism, a full set of ratings may be assigned to the group, provided that a number of conditions are met:

- published, audited consolidated financial accounts;
- common strategy and joint marketing activities;
- uniform risk management system;
- strong mutual support mechanism, providing for support for any bank that may run into financial difficulties; and
- attitude and treatment of such groups by the local banking regulator.

The first such case was S-Verbund H-T in Germany, in October 2004. A year later, a full set of group ratings was assigned to the member banks of the support mechanism of Germany's cooperative sector (Genossenscaftlicher FinanzVerbund).[26]

A mutual support mechanism may consist of liquid funds, provided directly by the individual banks or deposited in a central fund set up for that purpose. The presence of a central authority, to be promptly informed in the event of potential problems at an early stage, is required in order to ensure timely support.

Special attention must be devoted to the presence of support mechanisms, if any, from outside the group. In fact, in the event of financial difficulties, a bank could have recourse to potential outside support should internal support prove insufficient.

If the banking groups comply with the aforementioned criteria to a more limited extent, Fitch may publish a short-term or IDR rating "floor," representing a minimum level that may be exceeded by those banks having a sounder risk profile. In any event, the possibility of exceeding the floor ratings diminishes in the presence of a stronger mutual support mechanism. In fact, in that event the banks that are in better condition need to support the weaker ones, presenting a contingent liability that must be considered in the respective individual ratings.

7.5 Conclusions

The long-term credit ratings of an issuer measure its probability of default (Issuer Default Rating). In the case of issues or securities, long-term credit ratings may be higher or lower to reflect relative differences in recovery expectations.

In recent years, the rating agencies have largely modified their processes to rating cooperative banks with a view to adjusting the analysis to that type of bond issuer, which is unquestionably characterized by features that are distinct from those of commercial banks.

In the presence of formal support mechanisms within the group, the agencies assign a complete set of ratings to the entire group, which may be considered a single entity in terms of creditworthiness even though it is not so from a strictly formal point of view. Support ratings are directly related to long-term debt ratings, since they amount to their long-term debt rating floor.

Therefore, the assessment of the credit risk of cooperative banks is affected to a considerable extent by the presence and effectiveness of legally binding support mechanisms. Each initiative that promotes support among group banks improves the issuers' risk profile, with clear advantages in respect of the issue costs and the competitiveness of cooperative banks.

On this subject, one should stress the significance of the project to set up an institutional guarantee fund among Italian cooperative banks (so called "Fondo di Garanzia Istituzionale del Credito Cooperativo") that has been instituted in July 2008.[27] The fund will consist of voluntary contributions by the banks and will aim to reduce illiquidity and insolvency risks of cooperative banks and agricultural banks. The Italian fund would allow banks to obtain a system rating from specialized agencies, promoting the funding of financial resources on the international markets at lower cost, as well as the granting of loans on favorable economic terms to clients. Such a guarantee mechanism would make possible a rating floor for all the member banks. Furthermore, the fund would allow reducing the level of capital requirements that banks face in relation to credit risk, according to Basel 2, for the inner exposure to the network, so freeing up financial resources.

Appendix: The credit ratings of the main international rating agencies

7.1   Fitch's credit ratings[28]

7.1.1   International credit ratings

International credit ratings assess the capacity to meet foreign currency or local currency commitments. The rating scale applies to foreign currency and local currency ratings; both ratings are internationally comparable assessments.

Short-term and long-term Issuer Default Ratings (IDRs) may be assigned to entities in certain sectors (corporate, financial institution and sovereign entities). These are drawn from the international long-term and short-term ratings scales.

The short-term IDR takes into consideration the liquidity profile of the entity and relates to its ongoing capacity to meet financial obligations in a timely manner within a relatively short time horizon (less than 13 months, except for public finance where short-term ratings may be assigned up to a three-year horizon, in line with industry standards).

The long-term IDR is related to issuers and counterparties, reflecting their ability to meet all of their most senior financial obligations on a timely basis over the term of the obligation. The long-term IDR, there-fore, is effectively a benchmark likelihood of default rating.

Securities may be rated higher than, lower than, or the same as the long-term IDR to reflect expectations of the security's relative recovery prospects, as well as differences in ability and willingness to pay.

Credit ratings express risk in relative rank order, which is to say they are ordinal measures of credit risk and are not predictive of a specific frequency of default or loss. Entities or issues with the same rating are of similar but not necessarily identical quality, given that the ratings are relative measures of risk and that the rating classes may fail to reflect minor differences in the risk level (Tables 7.5 and 7.6).

Fitch adds the "+" or "–" sign to a generic rating to denote relative status within major rating categories. Such suffixes are not added to the "AAA" long-term rating category or to categories below "CCC", or to ratings other than "F1" short-term rating category.

Table 7.5   International long-term credit ratings

Rating	Definition
AAA	Highest credit quality with the lowest expectation of credit risk.
AA	Very high credit quality with very low credit risk.
A	High credit quality with low credit risk.
BBB	Good credit quality with low credit risk.
BB	Speculative with possibility of credit risk developing.
B	Highly speculative: • significant credit risk with a limited margin of safety (for issuers and performing obligations); • distressed or defaulted obligations with potential for extremely high recoveries (for individual obligations).
CCC	Default a real possibility (for issuers and performing obligations). Distressed or defaulted obligations with potential for average to superior levels of recovery (for individual obligations).
CC	Default of some kind probable (for issuers and performing obligations). Distressed or defaulted obligations with average or below-average levels of recovery (for individual obligations).
C	Default imminent (for issuers and performing obligations). Distressed or defaulted obligations with potential for below-average to poor recoveries (for individual obligations).
RD	The entity has failed to make due payments (within the applicable grace period) on some but not all material financial obligations.
D	The entity has defaulted on all of its financial obligations.

Source: www.fitchratings.com.

Table 7.6   International short-term credit ratings

Rating	Definition
F1	Highest credit quality.
F2	Good credit quality.
F3	Fair credit quality.
B	Speculative.
C	High default risk.
D	The entity has defaulted on all of its financial obligations.

Source: www.fitchratings.com.

Table 7.7   National long-term credit ratings

Rating	Definition
AAA	Highest rating assigned in its national rating scale for the country.
AA	Very strong credit risk.
A	Strong credit risk.
BBB	Adequate credit risk.
BB	Fairly weak credit risk.
B	Significantly weak credit risk .
CCC, CC, C	Extremely weak credit risk .
DDD, DD, D	Entities or financial commitments that are currently in default.
E	Adequate information unavailable to meet the obligations of the rating.

Source: www.fitchratings.com.

The recovery analysis plays a relevant role all along the rating scale. It becomes more critical at lower rating levels (the likelihood of default is often quite high and differences in recoveries have a more meaningful impact on loss expectations), where Fitch often publishes recovery ratings that are complementary to credit ratings.

7.1.2   National credit ratings

National long-term ratings are an assessment of credit quality relative to the rating of the "best" credit risk in a country that will normally be assigned to all financial commitments issued or guaranteed by the sovereign state. National short-term credit ratings indicate the strongest capacity for timely payment of financial commitments relative to other issuers or issues in the same country. Therefore, national ratings in one country are not comparable with those assigned in another country, nor are they comparable to international rating scales (Tables 7.7 and 7.8).

Table 7.8   National short-term credit ratings

Rating	Definition
F1	Strongest capacity.
F2	Satisfactory capacity.
F3	Adequate capacity.
B	Uncertain capacity.
C	Highly uncertain capacity.
D	Actual or imminent payment default.

Source: www.fitchratings.com.

Table 7.9 Long-term corporate obligation ratings

Rating	Definition
Aaa	Highest quality with minimal credit risk.
Aa	High quality with very low credit risk.
A	Upper-medium grade with low credit risk.
Baa	Medium grade with moderate credit risk.
Ba	Speculative elements with substantial credit risk.
B	Speculative and high credit risk.
Caa	Poor standing and very high credit risk.
Ca	Highly speculative and likely in default.
C	Typically in default.

Source: Moody's (2007).

7.2   Moody's credit ratings[29]

Long-term obligation ratings are judgments of the relative credit risk of fixed-income obligations with an original maturity of one year or more, addressing the possibility that a financial obligation will not be honored as promised. Such ratings reflect both the likelihood of default and any financial loss suffered in the event of default (Table 7.9).

The modifiers "1", "2", and "3" may be appended to each generic rating classification from "Aa" through "Caa." These modifiers indicate that the obligation ranks in the higher end of its rating category ("1"), or a mid-range ranking ("2"), or a ranking in the lower end of that rating category ("3").

Short-term ratings are judgments of the ability of issuers to honor short-term financial obligations that have an original maturity generally not exceeding 13 months, unless explicitly noted. Ratings may be assigned to issuers, short-term programs, or individual short-term debt instruments (Table 7.10).

Table 7.10 Short-term ratings

Rating	Definition
P-1	Issuers (or supporting institutions) with a superior ability to repay short-term obligations.
P-2	Issuers (or supporting institutions) with a strong ability to repay short-term obligations.
P-3	Issuers (or supporting institutions) with an acceptable ability to repay short-term obligations.
NP[30]	Issuers (or supporting institutions) do not fall within any of the prime rating categories.

Source: Moody's (2007).

Issuer ratings are judgments of the ability of entities to honor senior unsecured financial obligations. These ratings are expressed on general long-term and short-term scales.

In certain local jurisdictions, the agency assigns national scale ratings, which are judgments of the relative creditworthiness of issuers and issues within a particular country and are not suitable for global comparison.[31]

7.3 Standard & Poor's credit ratings[32]

Issue credit ratings can be either long-term or short-term. Short-term ratings are generally assigned to those obligations considered short-term in the relevant market (for example, in U.S. obligations with an original maturity of no more than 365 days).

There are two forms of issuer credit ratings: counterparty credit ratings and sovereign credit ratings. Issuer credit ratings can be either long-term or short-term; short-term issuer credit ratings reflect the obligor's creditworthiness over a short-term time horizon.

The issue or issuer ratings from "AA" to "CCC" may be modified by the addition of a "+" or "−" to show relative standing within the major rating categories. The Tables from 7.11 to 7.16 provide the ratings and definitions used by Standard & Poor's.

7.4 The classification of obligations

The rating assigned by the rating agencies allows for classifying the obligations into two categories (Table 7.17):

- investment grade, which indicates relatively low to moderate credit risk;
- speculative grade (or "non-investment grade", or "junk bonds") signals either a higher level of credit risk or a default that has already occurred.

Table 7.11   Long-term issue or issuer credit ratings[33]

Rating	Definition
AAA	The obligation (or obligor) has the highest rating. The obligor's capacity is extremely strong.
AA	The obligation (or obligor) differs from the highest-rated obligation (or obligor) only to a small degree. The obligor's capacity is very strong.
A	The obligation (or obligor) is somewhat more susceptible to the adverse effects of changes in circumstances and economic conditions than obligations (or obligors) in higher-rated categories. The obligor's capacity is still strong.
BBB	The obligation exhibits adequate protection parameters. The obligor has adequate capacity to honor commitments. However, adverse economic conditions or changing circumstances are more likely to lead to a weakened capacity on the part of the obligor.
BB	The obligation (or the obligor) is less vulnerable to nonpayment than other lower-rated issues (or obligors). However, the obligor faces major ongoing uncertainties or exposure to adverse business, financial, or economic conditions that could lead to the obligor's capacity being inadequate.
B	The obligation (or obligor) is more vulnerable to nonpayment than obligations (or obligors) rated "BB", but the obligor currently has the capacity to honor commitments. Adverse business, financial, or economic conditions will likely impair the obligor's capacity or willingness to meet its financial commitments on the obligation.
CCC	The obligation (or obligor) is currently vulnerable to nonpayment. In the event of adverse business, financial, or economic conditions, the obligor is not likely to have the capacity to meet its financial commitment on the obligation.
CC	The obligation (or obligor) is currently highly vulnerable to nonpayment.

Source: www.standardandpoors.com.

Table 7.12   Long-term issue lowest ratings

Rating	Definition
C	The obligation is currently highly vulnerable to nonpayment. This rating may be used to cover a situation where a bankruptcy petition has been filed or similar action taken, but payments on this obligation are being continued.
D	The obligation is in payment default.
NR	No rating has been requested.

Source: www.standardandpoors.com.

Table 7.13   Long-term issuer lowest ratings

Rating	Definition
R	The obligor is under regulatory supervision owing to its financial condition.
SD and D[34]	The obligor has failed to pay one or more of its financial obligations (rated or unrated).
NR	The issuer is not rated.

Source: www.standardandpoors.com.

Table 7.14   Short-term issue or issuer credit ratings[35]

Rating	Definition
A-1	The obligation (or obligor) is rated in the highest category. The obligor's capacity to meet its financial commitments is strong.[36]
A-2	The obligation (or obligor) is somewhat more susceptible to the adverse effects of changes in circumstances and economic conditions than obligations (or obligors) in higher rating categories. However, the obligor's capacity is satisfactory.
A-3	The obligation exhibits adequate protection parameters. The obligor has adequate capacity to honor commitments. However, adverse economic conditions or changing circumstances are more likely to lead to a weakened capacity on the part of the obligor to meet its financial commitment.
B-1	The obligation is regarded as having significant speculative characteristics. The obligor has a relatively stronger capacity to meet its financial commitments over the short term than other speculative-grade obligors.
B-2	The obligation is regarded as having significant speculative characteristics. The obligor has an average speculative-grade capacity to meet its financial commitments over the short term compared with other speculative-grade obligors.
B-3	The obligation is regarded as having significant speculative characteristics. The obligor has a relatively weaker capacity to meet its financial commitments over the short term than other speculative-grade obligors.
C	The obligation is currently vulnerable to nonpayment and is dependent upon favorable business, financial, and economic conditions for the obligor to meet its financial commitments.

Source: www.standardandpoors.com.

Table 7.15   Long-term issue lowest rating

Rating	Definition
D	The obligation is in payment default.

Source: www.standardandpoors.com.

Table 7.16   Long-term issuer lowest ratings

Rating	Definition
R	The obligor is under regulatory supervision owing to its financial condition.
SD and D[37]	The obligor has failed to pay one or more of its financial obligations (rated or unrated).
NR	The issuer is not rated.

Source: www.standardandpoors.com.

Table 7.17   Rating-based classification of bonds

		Long term		Short term	
Investment grade	Fitch	"AAA" to "BBB–"	Fitch	"F1" to "F3"
	Moody's	"Aaa" to "Baa3"	Moody's	"P-1" to "P-3"
	Standard & Poor's	"AAA" to "BBB–"	Standard & Poor's	"A1" to "A3"
Speculative grade	Fitch	"BB+" to "D"	Fitch	"B" to "D"
	Moody's	"Ba1" to "C"	Moody's	"NP"
	Standard & Poor's	"BB+" to "D"	Standard & Poor's	"B1" to "D"

Notes

1. See Appendix.
2. See www.fitchratings.com
3. Each tranche is rated on the basis of stress scenarios in combination with its relative seniority, prioritization of cash flows, and other structural mechanisms.
4. See www.moodys.com and Moody's (2007).
5. See www.standardandpoors.com
6. See Fischer and Mahfoundhi (2002).
7. See Basel Committee on Banking Supervision (2004).
8. See, *inter alia*, Fischer and Mahfoundhi (2002), Galil (2003), and Gropp and Richards (2001).
9. See Morgan (2002).
10. See Morgan (2002).
11. See Diamond (1984).
12. See Jensen and Meckling (1976).
13. For a more detailed analysis, refer to the rating methodology of the leading agencies, e.g. Moody's (1999).
14. See Fitch (2004a).
15. See Fitch (2006a).
16. See Dalmaz and De Toytot (2002); Fitch (2001; 2003b); Flageole and Roy (2005); Moody's (2003).

17. See Hesse and Čihák (2007).
18. See Fisher (2002).
19. See Fischer and Mahfoundhi (2002); Fisher (2002).
20. See Flageole and Roy (2005).
21. See Standard & Poor's (2007).
22. See Fitch (2006b).
23. See Moody's (2000; 2003).
24. See Fitch (2001; 2003b; 2004b; 2006b).
25. See Fitch (2004b; 2006b).
26. See Fitch (2006c).
27. See www.creditocooperativo.it
28. See www.fitchratings.com
29. See www.moodys.com and Moody's (2007).
30. Not prime.
31. On Moody's national scale ratings, see Moody's (2007).
32. See www.standardandpoors.com
33. For the sake of expository convenience, ratings below "CC" are analyzed in two other tables differentiating issue ratings (Table 7.12) from issuer ratings (Table 7.13).
34. SD = selective default; D = default.
35. For the sake of expository convenience, ratings below "C" are analyzed in two other tables differentiating issue ratings (Table 7.15) from issuer ratings (Table 7.16).
36. Within this category, certain obligations (or obligors) are designated with a plus sign (+); this indicates that the obligor's capacity to meet its financial commitment is extremely strong.
37. SD = selective default; D = default.

References

Basel Committee on Banking Supervision (2004), *International Convergence of Capital Measurement and Capital Standards*, A Revised Framework, June, Bank for International Settlements, www.bib.org

Dalmaz S. and De Toytot A. (2002), Le banche cooperative europee continuano ad evolversi, *Cooperazione di Credito*, no. 176/7.

Diamond D. W. (1984), Financial Intermediation and Delegated Monitoring, *The Review of Economic Studies*, vol. 51, no. 3, pp. 393–414.

Fischer K. P. and Mahfoundhi R. M. (2002), Corporate Governance and Rating: Do Agencies Rate Mutual Bank Bonds Fairly?, CREFA Working Paper No. 01–12.

Fisher K. P. (2002), Le agenzie attribuiscono un rating equo alle obbligazioni emesse dalle banche cooperative?, *Cooperazione di Credito*, no. 176/7.

Fitch (2001), *The European Co-operative Banking Sector*, Financial Institutions Special Report, www.fitchratings.com

Fitch (2003a), *Launch of Fitch's Bank Support Rating Methodology*, Criteria Report, 22 July, www.fitchratings.com

Fitch (2003b), *Update on European Co-operative Banking*, Special Report, 6 October, www.fitchratings.com

Fitch (2004a), *Bank Rating Methodology*, Criteria Report, 25 May, www.fitchratings.com

Fitch (2004b), *Methodology for Assigning Ratings to European Banking Structures Backed by Mutual Support Mechanism*, Criteria Report, 21 October, www.fitchratings.com

Fitch (2006a), *The Role of Support and Joint Probability Analysis in Bank Ratings*, Special Report, 25 July, www.fitchratings.com

Fitch (2006b), *Updated Methodology for Assigning Ratings to European Banking Structures Backed by Mutual Support Mechanism*, Criteria Report, 11 August, www.fitchratings.com

Fitch (2006c), *Verbundratings. Rating of German Banking Group Backed by Mutual Support*, Special Report, 10 August, www.fitchratings.com

Flageole M. A. and Roy J. (2005), Rating Cooperative and Commercial Bank Bonds: A Comparative Approach, *Annals of Public and Cooperative Economics*, vol. 76, no. 3, pp. 407–35.

Galil K. (2003), The Quality of Corporate Credit Rating: An Empirical Investigation, Center for Financial Studies, Goethe University of Frankfurt, Working Paper, www.ssrn.com

Gropp R. and Richards A. J. (2001), Rating Agency Actions and the Pricing of Debt and Equity of European Banks: What Can We Infer About Private Sector Monitoring of Bank Soundness?, *Economic Notes*, Monte dei Paschi di Siena, vol. 30, no. 3, pp. 373–98.

Hesse H. and Čihák M. (2007), Cooperative Banks and Financial Stability, IMF Working Paper, January, www.imf.org

Jensen M. C. and Meckling W. (1976), Theory of the Firm: Managerial Behavior, Agency Costs and Ownership Structure, *Journal of Financial Economics*, vol. 3, no. 4.

Moody's (1999), *Rating Methodology. Bank Credit Risk*, Rating Methodology, April, www.moodys.com

Moody's (2000), *French Mutual Banking Groups*, Rating Methodology, August, www.moodys.com

Moody's (2003), *European Co-operative Banks: Moving beyond Issues of Cost and Efficiency*, Special Comment, October, www.moodys.com

Moody's (2007), *Moody's Rating Symbols & Definitions*, March, www.moodys.com

Morgan D. P. (2002), Rating Banks: Risk and Uncertainty in an Opaque Industry, *The American Economic Review*, vol. 92, no. 4, pp. 874–88.

Standard & Poor's (2007), Banca di Credito Cooperativo San Marzano di San Giuseppe Rated "BBB-/A-3"; Outlook Stable, Research Update, 31 May, www.bccsanmarzano.it

Part Two Specific Features and Innovations in Cooperative Banking

8
The Impact of Basel 2 on Cooperative Banking

S. Cosma

8.1 Introduction

Among the new challenges facing cooperative banking, a central role is played by the regulations governing capital adequacy.

Besides having to calculate their economic capital on the basis of commonly used risk assessment models, banks are bound to calculate and keep the 'regulatory capital' (capital for supervisory purposes). Under equal risk conditions, they generally end up with more regulatory capital than economic capital (Gumerlock, 1993; Arak, 1992; Heldring, 1995). The minimum capital requirements imposed by supervisory authorities represent exogenous ties exerting a significant impact on the management of a bank and, above all, on the configuration of systems designed to measure and contain the absorption of capital connected with risk assumption, capitalization level, capital composition, and the process of capital allocation to the various business units.

The capital ratio instrument, dealt with in the Accord drafted by the Basel Committee on Banking Supervision in July 1988, was recognized by the supervisory authorities of more than 150 developed countries, and applied to banks of all sizes and complexity levels. The instrument is once again a subject of great interest as a consequence of the capital adequacy scheme reform process that was initiated by the Basel Committee in 1999 and concluded in 2004 with the final version of the New Capital Accord (BCBS, 2004). The Accord was updated in November 2005 to embody a revised version of the 1996 amendment concerning market risks as well as the contents of paper *The Application of Basel II to Trading Activities and the Treatment of Double Default Effects* (BCBS, 2005b) relating to the conservative treatment of certain exposures connected with trading activities, the counterparty credit risk, and the *double default* effects (the risk that both obligor and guarantor may default in relation to the same debt). On 4 July 2006 the Committee issued a comprehensive version of the Basel II Framework. This document is a combination of the June 2004 Basel II Framework, the 1996 Amendment to the Capital Accord to incorporate market risk, the 2005 paper on the application of Basel II to trading activities and the treatment of double default effects, and the elements of the 1988 Accord that were not revised during the Basel II process. No new elements have been introduced in this comprehensive version.

The New Accord was scheduled to become effective in late 2006. The New Accord came into force in EU countries following its ratification by the EU Council and to the issue of new instructions for supervision at a national level. The New Accord application perimeter remains, as per Basel 1, that of banks and banking groups (i.e. of groups mainly involved in banking) operating at an international level.

Although this application perimeter may seem to exclude cooperative banking systems operating at a national or regional level, such systems are instead included in the EU application perimeter directive published in June 2006 incorporating capital adequacy international rules. The EU directive matches the structure and instruments provided in the international Accord; any differences are intended only to take into account certain specific features of the Continental context, for example, the role of small and medium-sized enterprises (SMEs) in the economy of the EU.

8.2   Structure of the New Basel Accord

In addition to the traditional objectives of the regulations, that is, the overall stability obtainable through guaranteed banking system solvency and the development of uniform competitive conditions for international banks in all countries, the New Accord aims to provide a capital adequacy system that better meets the risk profile of individual institutions, as well as at securing a growing responsibilization of financial intermediaries. The pursuit of these new objectives rests on the adoption of a more meritocratic approach, under which the banks' levels of operational freedom are linked to the quality of the risk management process and to the presence of effective control systems.

The New Accord seems to overcome the limitations of the preceding regulation, which promoted the stability of financial institutions solely through the fixing of solvency coefficients. The capital adequacy framework proposed by the Basel Committee rests on three pillars: first, on banks' obligation to allocate a specific portion of their capital to the risk (credit, market, and operational) connected with the banks' activity (First Pillar); second, on the need for banks to submit their risk assessment and control system as well as their capital adequacy assessment system to further review by the supervisory authorities (Second Pillar); and third, on the disclosure of information about capital needs and about the methodologies followed for assessing those needs (Third Pillar).

Despite some grey areas and unresolved problems, the reform should lessen the 'regulatory arbitrage' problems favoured by financial innovations (securitization, credit derivatives, and so on) and reduce regulatory costs, thus persuading financial intermediaries to adopt cooperative and collaborative behaviours by virtue of the convergence between management and supervision logics.

In the First Pillar, the New Basel Accord revises significantly the methodologies for the assessment of minimum capital requirements for credit risk, introduces a new specific capital requirement for operational risk, and partially modifies the discipline of capital requirements for market risk contained in the Amendment of January 1996.

The logics underlying the new discipline regarding capital requirements for credit and operational risks are the same as those underlying the 1996 Amendment as far as market risk discipline is concerned:

- an assessment methodology range characterized by a growing refinement and improved compliance with internal risk management systems;
- an expected capital requirement inversely proportional to the refinement level of the approach used; and
- the provision of adequacy criteria – of an organizational and operational nature – on the observance of which depends the adoption of more complex methodologies.

As far as credit risk is concerned, two approaches are proposed by the Committee:

- *A standardized approach*. This method follows the assessment logics provided by Basel 1 when envisaging a subdivision of assets into obligor/exposure categories and the application of standard risk weights to those assets. At the same time, the standardized method differs from the previous Accord as it provides for a more complex range of obligors/exposures, acknowledges risk-mitigation techniques such as financial collaterals, physical collaterals, or credit derivatives, and it replaces the weights defined in the previous regulations by obligor category with risk weights depending on external rating classes produced by agencies such as Standard & Poor's, Moody's, and FitchlBCA, by export credit agencies, and by other institutions qualified in complying with precise requirements.

- *The internal rating based (IRB) method.* The IRB method recognizes the banks' capacity to make autonomous assessments of relevant parameters for the determination of risk weights (resulting from a continuous function defined by the Committee for the various portfolio types) to be applied to five exposure categories into which assets will be subdivided: corporate, retail, banks, sovereign, and equity. The parameters are constituted by the probability of default (PD), the loss given default (LGD), the exposure at default (EAD), and the residual life (maturity, M) of the operation. The IRB method can be implemented in two versions: a simpler one (foundation IRB, FIRB) that limits the banks' autonomy to the sole assessment of PD, and a more complex version (advanced IRB, AIRB) that allows banks to perform an internal assessment of all the indicated parameters but, at the same time, demands compliance with more stringent minimum qualitative requirements.

As far as operational risk is concerned, the Committee has proposed two macro-categories of approaches to the calculation of the relevant capital adequacy: quantitative *top-down* standardized methodologies based on balance sheet indicators (basic indicator approach and standardized approach), on the one hand, and qualitative and quantitative methodologies (advanced measurement approach), on the other.

The first approach category (standardized approach) is based on the use of exposure indicators (gross income) and of risk weights established at a system level. The decision-making autonomy granted to intermediaries is confined to two activities: the process of allocation of the activities performed to the eight business units indicated by the Basel Committee, preparatory to the application of the standardized method, and compliance with the qualitative requirements imposed by the use of the standardized method. Conversely, the second approach category (approach) allows banks to choose among the numerous operational risk measurement methodologies available to the banking system, while requesting banks to provide exposure and loss data. Regarding the operational freedom granted to banks that opt for models, the regulation provides for the observance of precise qualitative and quantitative requirements. The greater complexity and higher implementation costs involved in the   methodologies when compared with standardized methodologies are balanced by specific recognitions capable of reducing the expected capital requirements.

As far as market risk is concerned, the Basel Committee proposes two methodologies for the calculation of capital requirements:

- A standardized approach that, through simplified schemes and risk weights established at a system level, allows a separate calculation of requirements regarding positions in debt securities, equities, foreign exchange, and commodities. In particular, as far as debt securities and equities in the trading book are concerned, the calculation is based on the building block methodology that yields distinct capital charges for specific risk and for general market risk, respectively.
- An approach based on internal models that, subject to compliance with given conditions, makes it possible to determine minimum capital requirements using internal data and the models adopted for management purposes. The minimum capital requirements are at least three times the risk value assessed by the banks for a ten-day time horizon.

The updating of the 1996 Amendment consists in practice of a revision of the trading portfolio definition, the introduction of ratings for the assessment of the specific risk (in the previous version the specific risk would be assessed according to a table that associated a risk weight with the security issuer typology and to the security residual life), and the introduction of two sections spelling out further criteria to be followed for the use of VAR-type (value at risk) internal models.

The Accord's Second Pillar lays stress on the importance of bank organization and management in the assessment of the bank's degree of exposure to risk, in the determination of capital adequacy to face risks, and in the provision of an effective risk-management and control system. Moreover, it is up to supervisory authorities to evaluate banks' capital adequacy vis-à-vis specific risk profiles, and also to take immediate action in case of need, even by way of requesting additional capital, mainly for risks either not falling within the scope of the First Pillar (interest rate risk in the banking book, sectorial, strategic, and reputational risks) or tied to external factors (economic cycle effects).

The Third Pillar requires banks to disclose information of a qualitative and quantitative nature (targets and risk management policies, approaches used to measure exposure to various types of risk, description of internal models, capital requirements, regulatory capital structure, accounting), allowing the market to assess, price, and control the relevant degree of risk, so as to start an effective market discipline process.

8.3   The expected effects of Basel 2 on cooperative banking

The Basel Committee's proposals contained in the Accord are such that they can be applied by banks differing in legal status, institutional model, size, and degree of operational sophistication, but all of them have a common feature: internationalization.

Neither legal category nor organizational model is expressly referred to in the Accord. Hence, neither of them plays any discriminating role in relation to specific provisions.

It can, however, be considered that the specificity of the organizational models adopted in cooperative banking, particularly the decentralized network model widespread in a number of countries (let us mention, in particular, cooperative credit banks in Italy, rural banks in Spain, Raiffeisen banks in Germany and Austria, and *Volksbanken* – people's banks – in Germany), may imply competitive advantages or disadvantages in relation to the following:

- Within the scope of the IRB method, the risk weight of equities, whether listed or not, turns out to be far higher than in the case of other counterparty credit risks. The EU cooperative banking systems featuring a decentralized labour-sharing network structure own a great number of equities in the service undertakings of their own network, such as data processing centres and central banks (EACB, 2003). Owing to the treatment envisaged for such equities that are not speculative and are meant to be held for a long time in the banking book (not in the trading book), decentralized banking groups are at a disadvantage in comparison with those featuring more centralized operational models.
- A bank that decides to adopt the IRB system for a portion of its portfolio is bound to extend the application of that system to the whole banking group, although through a gradual implementation planned formally in a binding and realistic way. The construction of a history of data such as to comply with the requirements set out by the IRB approach may turn out to be very difficult in the case of subsidiaries or branch offices of cooperative groups operating on a decentralized basis. Apart from the size of the institution, it may be difficult to collect data for the calculation of PD and LGD for some classes of exposure (such

as those with sovereigns) because default cases are insufficient (EACB, 2003). Moreover, cooperative banks often have significant credits with a reduced number of sovereigns and banks. Such a circumstance makes PD calculation more complicated. But the Accord does not provide for the possibility of a permanent partial implementation of the IRB approach whereby the standardized method would be applied to certain subsidiaries or branch offices of the banking group, unless in the case of irrelevant operating units or of class of assets that are insignificant in terms of magnitude and expected risk.

- In the case of decentralized network structures, small- and medium-sized cooperative banks – even if they use rating systems and scoring techniques provided by the central institutions of the groups – do not have the potential to meet all the organizational requirements set out for the adoption of the IRB approach (number of units or controls by independent units) because in most cases the number of people on the payroll is below 50 (EACB, 2003). These requirements, therefore, impair the competitiveness of the mentioned institutions to the advantage of banks that feature centralized institutional models and encourage restructuring through mergers or takeovers.

- A bank that opts for methodologies of operational risk calculation can avail itself, for risk mitigation, of insurance coverage meeting stringent regulatory requirements. In cooperative banking systems, however, the concentration of competence in their central institutions, and the cross-guarantee systems (such as the Rabobank system in the Netherlands, the Raiffeisen banks in Austria, and the Okobank group in Finland), improve the operational risk profile. This leads us to believe that regulations should treat such factors as risk mitigation techniques, so as not to penalize the cooperative banks in terms of minimum capital requirements.

- In the case of network structure banks, the measurement of operational risks with methodologies turns out to be complicated by recourse to the outsourcing of a large share of production processes. This circumstance makes it difficult to identify either the process whereby the prejudicial event that generates the economic loss takes place or the risk factor, a true obstacle to the construction of a data model meeting regulatory requirements. Furthermore, network structure banks find it more difficult than centralized structure banks to perform an adequate monitoring of outsourcers. In consideration of the retail side of cooperative banks, their measurement of operational risks with the standardized approach should, when compared with banks characterized by an otherwise unbalance portfolio (corporate finance, negotiation and sale, and so on), involve a saving in terms of minimum capital requirements. In fact, the beta factor for retail banking is the lowest among those envisaged by the Basel Accord, that is, 12 per cent.

Unlike in the case of the institutional or organizational model, the size of the banks and the groups for which the Accord is meant is expressly considered to be a regulatory discriminatory factor in relation to the following prescriptions, which can, therefore, be held to be of a special interest to minor cooperative banks and groups:

- The choice between the simplified method and the internal rating method for the calculation of the risk weight in the case of capital instrument exposures not included in the trading book – subject to the use of the market-based method being allowed by national supervisory authorities (the calculation can also be made according to the PD/LGD method) – must be guided by principles securing consistency with the institution's overall size and the degree of sophistication. Smaller banks should, therefore, opt for the simplified method, and apply a 300 per cent risk weight to equity holdings that are publicly traded and a 400 per cent risk weight to all other equity holdings.
- Relevant information (Third Pillar) should be disclosed as soon as it is available. However, in the case of small-sized banks characterized by steady risk profiles, information disclosure can be made yearly subject to explanations being provided about the adequacy of this kind of frequency.

Size plays a major role also with respect to the methodological approach that banks choose for credit risks. Although the size of EU cooperative banks and groups may broadly vary, most institutions – even those belonging to groups operating at an international level – are small or medium-sized (EACB, 2003; 2005c). The construction of an internal rating system capable of meeting the regulatory validation requirements seems to be problematic for small-sized cooperative banks because of the costs, the characteristics of information about customers (generally not structured and not organized as historical data), the reduced dimensions of the organization structure, and the difficulty in estimating the PD for every single debtor owing to the limited number of customers. The cost of learning and implementing the IRB method are fixed, which is likely to accelerate the process of consolidation between minor banks (Resti, 2004).

Apart from factors complicating the implementation of an internal rating system, there is cause to wonder whether it is truly advantageous to introduce a new analytical method in the more risk-sensitive credit process. From an economic viewpoint, the incentives deriving from the capital requirements under the IRB approach turn out to be mitigated by cooperative banks capitalization mechanism. This mechanism, based on reserve accumulation and on the very rare, almost non-existent, distribution of dividends, has provided EU cooperative banks with capital ratios significantly higher than those of other bank categories (EACB, 2004a). From a strategic viewpoint, the fear is that the IRB approach may weaken the lending relationship model underlying cooperative banking, while failing properly to enhance the basic elements of the relevant competitive advantage (Stein, 2002; Berger and Udell, 2002). The elements referred to are represented by 'soft' information connected with the bank's being deeply rooted in the territory, with long-term relations with customers (Boot, 2000), with the direct and personal knowledge of entrepreneurs and of the underlying socio-economic texture, and with the wealth of 'distinctive' competence linked to a consolidated 'informal' credit analysis experience.

If, in consideration of the reasons set forth above, many banks in the cooperative system (mainly small) tend to adopt the standardized approach, the Basel 2 impact might manifest itself mainly in relative terms, that is, in coexistence with the other banks, thus generating various effects, as frequently emphasized in the literature (Sironi and Zazzara, 2002; Comana, 2003; Carosio, 2003; Di Salvo, 2002; Sironi, 2005; De Laurentis and Caselli, 2005; Antonicelli et al., 2005; Resti, 2004; Berger, 2006, namely:

- Minimum capital requirements are differentiated from those of larger banks under equal approach conditions (standardized).

  The standardized approach should spur credit to higher-rating enterprises, for the purpose of reducing regulatory costs. Most of the customers of the cooperative banking system, however, fall within the category of small, unrated enterprises, for which the risk weight is 100 per cent. The result, in terms of capital requirements, would involve no saving in respect of the current weighting system and would penalize smaller banks vis-à-vis larger ones. The latter, in fact, are traditionally characterized by customer enterprises either having, or capable of asking for, an external rating.

- Retail customers could be lost in relation to larger banks, under equal approach conditions (standardized).

Under the standardized credit risk assessment approach, retail exposures may be risk-weighted at 75 per cent. If a bank intends to include a claim in the regulatory retail portfolio via the treatment reserved to retail exposures within the frame of the standardized approach, one of the criteria to be met is the granularity criterion (no aggregate exposure to any one counterparty can exceed 0.2 per cent of the overall regulatory portfolio). Meeting this criterion depends, therefore, on the size of the retail portfolio. Banks having retail portfolios of different size could be compelled to weight the same exposure in different ways, hence to price the same credit in different ways. This would lead the retail debtor to quit the smaller bank with a reduced capital in favour of other banks.

- *Adverse selection.*In the presence of banks opting for the IRB approach (which larger banks are likely to do), lower-quality enterprises would find it advantageous to migrate to banks using the standardized method so as to avoid higher debt costs or credit rationing. This behaviour on the part of 'bad' enterprises will involve an evident downgrading of the loan portfolio of 'standard' banks if these do not have proper competence and instruments to make a risk-weighted credit selection and resist the temptation of growing indiscriminately by replacing the credits that have migrated to banks using the IRB approach with the credits of the "bad" enterprises. The loan portfolios of said banks would also be downgraded by the fact that unrated high-grade enterprises that do not meet the requirements for entering the retail portfolios of banks using the standardized approach would find it advantageous to migrate towards IRB banks offering better conditions, thanks to a lower capital absorption being involved. The target of limiting the impact of adverse selection will lead smaller banks to develop rating systems; since such rating systems are probably not sufficiently sophisticated to obtain the Basel Committee's validation, they represent a further indirect cost of Basel 2.

- *New opportunities in respect of SMEs.* The possible adoption by larger banks of rating systems strongly oriented to quantitative analysis and of loan selection policies mainly based on automatic mechanisms could penalize, in terms of credit, SMEs featuring weak economic or financial indices. This would create new opportunities for SMEs to apply to smaller banks, which would clearly entail the risk of a downgraded loan portfolio if smaller banks were not in a position to assess and carefully select the new prospective customers. From another viewpoint, the more favourable treatment envisaged for SMEs under AIRB (as opposed to standardized) approaches has prompted fears that large banks may attack the market segments traditionally controlled by smaller banks, with a modification of the lending model (transactional versus relationship). Such fears are mitigated by empirical research (Hannan, 1991; Berger and Udell, 1996; Carter et al., 2004; Berger et al., 2004; 2005; Berger, 2006; Cole et al., 2004; Keeton, 1995; Strahan and Weston, 1996; 1998; Peek and Rosengren, 1998; Avery and Samolyk, 2004), which finds that large international banks likely to opt for the AIRB approach will tend to grant loans to SMEs in technical forms and with targets that are different from those of small banks because of different comparative advantages. At the same time, Berger (2006) and Altman and Sabato (2005) confirm a reduction, albeit modest, in the competitive advantages of small banks in the SME sector, based on privileged 'relationship lending' vis-à-vis well-diversified large banks that will first adopt the AIRB approaches.

- *Greater differentiation of the retail portfolio management modalities than for banks using the IRB approach.* When compared with the current regulations, the new rules governing the determination of the capital required to cover credit risks make possible capital savings in the case of retail portfolio credits; they favour, in particular, cooperative banking traditionally featuring portfolios oriented towards such a component. In this case, too, however, the dual character of the new rules is may have a different impact on banks, depending of the approach adopted, both in terms of capital requirements and in terms of credit management modalities. Variations in capital requirements in the presence of retail portfolios can hardly be foreseen as they depend on the method used and, in addition, on the technical form and specific characteristics of the credits. The second effect – that concerning the retail credit management modalities – is connected with the criteria required to include claims in the retail portfolio. Under the standardized approach, for the purpose of being included in the regulatory retail portfolio claims must meet the orientation criterion, the product typology criterion, the granularity criterion, and the maximum aggregated exposure criterion. Under the IRB approach, in addition to the role of size, technical form, and the orientation criterion, a major role is also played by the management modalities (credits cannot be managed on an individual basis, but as a portion of a portfolio segment with similar risk features for the purpose of risk assessment and quantification). Thus, banks using the IRB approach are likely to enhance the development of retail portfolio management modalities based on quantitative methodologies or segmentation statistics (Altman and Sabato, 2005, in this sense too), while banks using the standardized approach are likely to consolidate management modalities based on direct knowledge and personal relationships.

To conclude, the Basel 2 Accord seems to penalize groups featuring a decentralized network structure relative to more centralized systems, mainly through the following: treatment reserved to equity exposure, ban on a permanent partial implementation of the IRB approach, stringent organizational requirements for the adoption of the IRB model, failure to consider cross-guarantee systems (typical of cooperative banking) for the purpose of mitigating operational risks, and criteria for the construction of a data model necessary for the adoption of methodologies in connection with operational risks.

The medium-to-small size of cooperative banks – also belonging to groups operating at an international level – in particular, of decentralized local banks, makes it possible to extend to cooperative banking the considerations made in the literature about the consequences of regulatory reform for the traditional equilibrium between larger and smaller banks, given that smaller banks will likely adopt the standardized approach to credit risks. The effects expected for smaller banks are likely to consist in higher minimum capital requirements than those applying to larger banks, under equal (standardized) approach conditions, in a possible loss of retail customers in favour of larger banks, still under equal (standardized) approach conditions, in adverse selection, in new opportunities in respect of SMEs, and in a greater differentiation of retail portfolio management modalities than in the case of banks adopting the IRB approach.

8.4. The impact of Basel 2 on capital requirements: some empirical evidence

With a view to ascertaining the consequences of the rules proposed for the calculation of banks' minimum capital requirements, the Basel Committee undertook quantitative impact studies that involved a wide range of banks of different countries. The impact of the new rules was not analysed as a function of the institutional or legal category of those to whom the rules were addressed, but as a function of the size and of the portfolio owned.

The latest study whose results are known (Quantitative Impact Study – QIS 5), published in 2006 (BCBS, 2006a) involves a sample of

357 banks, of which 202 belong to G10 countries and 155 to other countries, and refers to the impact of the rules proposed in the final version of the Basel Accord (BCBS, 2005c). Banks are subdivided into two groups: group 1, formed by large banks operating at an international level, with a Tier 1 more than 3 billion euros, and group 2, formed by smaller banks mainly operating in a single country or in specific business sectors, with a Tier 1 less than 3 billion euros. Each group of banks is subdivided into three subgroups:

- G10, formed by banks belonging to the 13 member states of the Basel Committee;
- CEBS (Committee of European Banking Supervisors), formed by banks belonging to member countries of the EU or to EU candidate countries, or to member countries of the European Economic Area (EEA); and
- non-G10, formed by banks belonging neither to the G10 nor to the CEBS group.

The results concerning group 2, which is more relevant to the European cooperative banking systems on account of their size (Tier 1 of European cooperative banks is far below the 3 billion euro upper limit of group 2), show the following:

- Apart from the selected credit risk measurement approach, group 2 banks (belonging to subgroups G10 and CEBS) attain an overall mean reduction in minimum capital requirements in respect of the current Accord. This reduction is of little significance if the standardized approach is selected (a few percentage points), significant if FIRB approaches are selected (12 to 16 percentage points), and considerable in cases of the adoption of AIRB approaches (around 26 percentage points). In relative terms, smaller banks (group 2) will benefit from significantly higher capital savings than large banks belonging to group 1.
- In the case of the group 2 banks belonging to subgroup CEBS, the overall mean reduction in minimum capital requirements is higher, on average, than in the case of the banks belonging to subgroup G10.
- The increase in the overall minimum capital requirements for group 2 banks belonging to subgroups G10 and CEBS that adopt the standardized approach is due to the effect of the minimum capital requirements vis-à-vis operational risks, in both cases capable of balancing the negative variation of the capital requirements of credit

risks. Anyway, minimum capital requirements vis-à-vis operational risks are significantly lower in the case of banks performing traditional banking activity and using the alternative standardized approach instead of the basic indicator approach.

- Minimum capital requirements broadly vary from one bank to another, such variability being ascribable to the quality of exposures (reflected in PD in the case of the FIRB approach) and also to the retail activity weight.

- The reduction in minimum capital requirements vis-à-vis credit risks attained by banks through the standardized approach and, to a larger extent, through the IRB approach, is largely due to capital saving connected with retail exposures, in particular residential mortgage loans. The capital saving connected with such exposures is greater with smaller banks (group 2) than with larger banks (group 1). The latter banks, in fact, are characterized by a small portion of capital used in this portfolio clusters.

- Corporate portfolio and the portfolio of those SMEs treated as corporate generate a reduction in minimum capital requirements that becomes significant for banks adopting the IRB approach. A slight increase in minimum capital requirements connected with the portfolios of SMEs treated as corporate occurs solely with group 2 banks belonging to the CEBS subgroup that opt for the standardized approach. This phenomenon can be interpreted as a result of the absence of an external rating for most smaller banks' corporate counterparties as well as of the treatment envisaged for past due loans, weighted on the basis of the difference between allowances and the loan amount.

- Sovereign exposures and, to a decidedly larger extent, equity exposures are responsible for an increase in the minimum capital requirements of the banks that adopt the IRB approach.

- The reduction in the minimum capital requirements for retail exposures generated by the use of the standardized approach is considerably smaller than that brought about by the use of the IRB approach, mainly in the case of group 2 banks belonging to subgroups G10 and CEBS. Likewise, the reduction in minimum capital requirements generated by the residential mortgage portfolio is by far greater for banks (groups 1 and 2, subgroups G10 and CEBS) using the IRB than for those using the standardized approach.

To conclude, the impact of the new regulations on cooperative banking seems to be positive. Banks should, in fact, record more limited minimum capital requirements for operational risks than other institutions, as they operate chiefly in the traditional banking sector. Moreover, when referred to the current risk weighting system, and irrespective of the approach selected, banks should benefit from a significant reduction in minimum capital requirements for credit risks on account of the high incidence of retail exposures and residential mortgage portfolio. Conversely, the situation of the portfolio of SMEs treated as corporate raises some concern. Larger banks that will probably adopt the IRB approach will benefit from considerably improved minimum capital requirements for SMEs, and thus jeopardize the competitiveness, in that sector, of smaller banks that are likely to use the standardized or FIRB approach. A further competitive disadvantage for smaller banks would stem from the fact that the treatment envisaged both for retail exposures and for the residential mortgage portfolio reduces the minimum capital requirements of banks using the IRB approach by more than two and a half times the reduction generated to banks using the standardized approach. Although retail is the main component of the portfolio of small financial institutions that are likely to opt for the standardized approach, the quantitative impact study demonstrates that it is just this kind of portfolio that is most affected by regulatory discrimination between different approaches.

8.5. The EU capital adequacy rules: the relevant aspects for cooperative banking

At the same time as the Basel Committee was drafting the New Capital Accord, the EU Commission was preparing a capital requirements directive for banks and investment enterprises. The EU Council and Parliament formally adopted the directive on 14 June 2006. The capital requirements directive (CRD), including both directive 2006/48/EC and directive 2006/49/EC, was published in the EU Official Journal of 30 June 2006.

The EC directive faithfully follows the structure and proposals of the Basel Committee; there are significant deviations in connection with the following:

- Scope of application, extended to all banks and investment enterprises, on a consolidated and individual basis.
- Grant of power to the authority responsible for consolidated supervision (generally corresponding to the national supervisory authorities of the member state where a parent undertaking with undertakings operating in other member states is based) to establish the approval

of recourse to more sophisticated methods of calculation of capital requirements by a European group, should the various supervisory authorities concerned fail to reach a unanimous resolution.

- Greater information transparency, from a supervision viewpoint; actually, supervisory authorities are bound to make publicly available information concerning the enforcement of the regulations as well as the methodologies used in assessing the soundness of the institutions supervised.
- The amount of data to be disseminated by banks in compliance with the Third Pillar.

The elements that differentiate the EC directive from the international Accord in connection with First Pillar discipline, and that are significant for the cooperative banking system in consideration of certain specific features of the sector – such as prevailing customer target (dealers, craftsmen, professionals, farmers), the privileged relationship between local banks and SMEs, and the organizational structure adopted (decentralized, capillary territorial networks in the areas of operation, recourse to outsourcing for back-office functions and for the production of given services and products) – are listed below:

(1) *The retail exposure identification criteria.* In compliance with the international Accord, the EC directive identifies – under the standardized approach – four criteria for including credits in the regulatory retail portfolio, namely, the orientation criterion, the product criterion, the granularity criterion, and criterion of the low value of individual exposures. When setting out the granularity criterion, however, the EC directive requires solely a proper portfolio diversification, without fixing a quantitative limit to the ratio between aggregate exposure to one counterparty and the overall regulatory portfolio (equal to 0.2 per cent in the Basel Accord).

(2) *The recognition of collateral instruments in the form of mutual funds, a broadened range of guarantors and counter-guarantors.* For credit risk mitigation, Basel Accord 2 recognizes physical and financial collaterals characterized by special features that limit the role of mutual fund collaterals, while hindering small enterprises' access to credit. The admitted physical collaterals, in fact, are those given by certain categories of providers: sovereigns, certain central banks, other international organizations such as the BIS and the IMF, multilateral development banks, public sector entities, brokerage firms and banks, and other entities with ratings equal to or more than A–. In any case,

the guarantor's risk weight must be lower than the counterparty's. In the case of IRB approaches, the perimeter of accepted guarantors extends to firms that have received an internal rating representing a PD equivalent to that of category A–. Moreover, the admitted physical collaterals must also meet operational requirements (the collateral must involve a direct obligation of the guarantor's; it must be expressly referred to a specific exposure or to a pool of exposures; it must be clearly defined as to the amount; it must be irrevocable; it must be unconditional and enforceable in a timely manner). In Italy, for instance, the *confidi* (joint-surety associations on bank loans) system, formed by SMEs with public and private funds, eases the access of associated firms to loans. Non-compliance with subjective requirements (very few consortiums have an international rating and, in any case, far from A–) and with objective requirements (the guarantee given is not direct, irrevocable, unconditional, and enforceable in a timely manner) by such associations prevents banks from benefiting from a reduction in the minimum capital requirements vis-à-vis collaterals. Even when the collateral given by *confidi* is of the financial type, it is not admissible for the purpose of a reduction in minimum capital requirements because it has the nature of an irregular pledge. A financial collateral wins recognition if there is legal certainty, that is, a financial collateral must be supported by suitable documentation and be enforceable in a legal environment; also, it must be able to require an execution of it and, in order to gain lawful possession of it, the bank must comply with all requirements of law; it must be in cash and readily receivable; finally it must not have a significant correlation with the guaranteed debt. Unlike Basel 2, the EC directive expressly recognizes as eligible for banks' credit risk mitigation mutual fund collateral schemes and collateral schemes that do not become available on non-payment, but provide for the possibility of provisional payments being made by the guarantor (advances). It also broadens the perimeter of guarantors to include financial intermediaries other than banks and investment firms on condition that they are subject to prudential supervision equivalent to that of banks and investment firms (in Italy, for instance, such intermediaries are the financial firms registered in the special list under art. 107 TUB (Testo Unico Bancario – Banking Consolidation), as factoring, leasing, consumer credit firms, and so on). A further possibility of reducing the minimum capital requirements for banks operating, in particular, with small enterprises, whose access to credit is favoured by forms of mutual fund collaterals, is connected with the extension of the range of counter-guarantors so as to include local entities and multilateral development banks (Basel 2 limits the perimeter of counter-guarantors to sovereigns). For example, in Italy the collaterals secured by *confidi* and counter-guaranteed by public entities of either a state or a local nature will be able to benefit from the latter's better risk weighting.

(3) *Partial implementation (i.e. limited to a portion of the portfolio) of the most sophisticated methods on a permanent basis.* Recognition of the difficulties that would be faced by small credit institutions in developing a rating system for given counterparties has led to the proposal, for this class of exposures, for the partial permanent use of the standardized approach in the case of insignificant exposures. Such exposures are listed in article 89 of directive 2006/48/EC.

(4) *The possibility of using aggregate data to estimate the internal rating system parameters, subject to compliance with certain conditions set forth in Annex VII, part 4.* Credit risk assessment can be made at the system level rather than by individual banks, or under 'mixed' systems at the cooperative network integration level. The directive affords advantages, also in terms of economies of scale, to cooperative banks by making it possible to outsource the following:

○ production of information relevant to testing and monitoring credit grades;
○ production of summary reports from the credit institution's rating system;
○ production of information relevant for reviewing whether the rating criteria remain predictive of risk;
○ documentation of changes in rating processes, evaluation criteria, or individual rating parameters; and
○ production of information relevant to ongoing regulatory review.

(5) *The principle of proportionality, on the basis of which regulations take into account the specific situations of risk of small banks and of cooperative systems with regard to the application of the IRB methodologies and compliance with the qualitative requirements of the standardized approach to operational risks.*

In the EC directive the principle of proportionality plays a major role as far as the provisions regarding the Second Pillar are concerned. It is reiterated and emphasized in the document wherein CEBS set out the guidelines for the application of the Second Pillar in June 2005 (CEBS, 2005). The Committee was established for the implementation of more detailed technical measures (second-level legislation), for the purpose of providing the EU Commission with consultancy about EU legislation in the banking sector, of contributing to the sound and coherent implementation of the EU legislation in the various countries, and of promoting convergence in regulatory practice as well as the cooperation of supervisory authorities.

Supervisory authorities will consider the size and complexity of intermediaries when determining the depth, frequency, and intensity of the review and evaluation of the procedures adopted by banks both to comply with regulations and to measure their own exposure to risk. In particular, proportionality concerns the Internal Capital Adequacy Assessment Process (ICAAP) and the prudential Supervisory Review and Evaluation Process (SREP) by the supervisory authorities.

Regardless of the approach adopted under the First Pillar, banks are called on to make organizational efforts to meet the regulatory framework, by complying with the internal governance model and ICAAP requirements.

As far as internal governance is concerned, CEBS's guidelines (CEBS, 2006a) consider corporate structure and organization, body management, internal control, public disclosure, and transparency. More precisely, intermediaries are called on to provide themselves with transparent organization structures, enabling them to conduct sound and prudential management, as well as with clear and well-defined reporting lines and a responsibility allocation system, and with a risk management function capable of supervising and facilitating both the implementation of risk policies and the risk management process. The guidelines request a clear documentation of the responsibilities of the management body in charge of establishing business objectives, along with the institution's strategies and risk profile, of adopting the ensuing policies, and of developing a sound internal control system. It is the management's duty to establish the maintenance of internal capital and regulatory capital suitable for the actual risk profile, to monitor and evaluate periodically the effectiveness of the internal governance structure, and to spread an internal control culture. Strengthened internal control system-oriented requests are particularly interesting for cooperative credit banks because of the limited size of the existing organization structures. Such requests envisage the establishment of three precise functions – risk control function, compliance function, and internal audit function – all of them independent, from operational and organizational viewpoints, of the controlled units. The first function must secure conformity with risk policies; the second must report any breaches of law, regulations, codes, and regulatory criteria, and also assist the management in promoting compliance; the third must detect failures, if any, in control systems, suggest possible improvements, and evaluate the conformity of the activity with the established policies and procedures. Eventually, banks are invited to disclose information regarding the organization, the present and expected future situation, financial and operating results, potential risk factors, and governance structures and policies.

As far as ICAAP is concerned, CEBS's guidelines require a well-defined and well-documented internal capital adequacy evaluation process, subject to periodic review both by top management and by independent auditors. This process must take into account all the risks actually incurred by the business (credit and operational risks underestimated by simplified methods of minimum capital requirements calculation, residual risks issuing from credit risk mitigation techniques and securitizations, settlement risks, strategic and reputation risks, and banking book interest risks), exogenous risk factors, and all factors that, based on the institution's strategic plans, may entail future greater capital absorption. The internal capital adequacy definition must be connected not only with the application of quantitative methodologies, but also with qualitative evaluations and subjective judgments.

The features that are of specific interest for small banks can be found in the provisions relating to banks that are organized on simpler lines. They concern the following:

- *ICAAP integration level in management processes.* Less sophisticated banks are exempted from integrating ICAAP into daily management processes (capital allocation to business units, resolutions concerning credit and business in general, budgets). ICAAP must allow the management body continuously to assess the key risks proper to the activity performed, so as to contain them (consolidation of assets, use of mitigation instruments) and either bring them back within the set limits or align them to the expected variations of the capital for supervisory purposes.
- *ICAAP design modalities.* Less sophisticated banks can calculate internal capital by adding the results of very simple internal models for the assessment of the risks not covered by the First Pillar and expressly referred to in the Second Pillar to the capital requirements resulting from the application of First Pillar methodologies. The stress test

procedures, too, or the scenario analyses adopted can display a low sophistication level.

8.6 Expected effects of the EC directive on cooperative banking

A critical analysis of the new EC directive concerning capital requirements shows that, despite efforts aimed at avoiding competitive distortions, in some cases the legal or institutional structure of cooperative credit banks represents a source of competitive advantages and disadvantages.

A possible disadvantage for cooperative groups might ensue from the provisions relating to the consolidated supervision of groups. The supervisory authorities of the various member states can decide whether to ask for compliance with capital requirements exclusively on a consolidated basis, thus exempting credit institutions from compliance on an individual basis. The conditions that institutions must meet to benefit from this opportunity seem to advantage listed companies and parent undertakings or subsidiaries based on capital holdings, the specificity of cooperative networks failing to be considered. Such networks are characterized by cross-liability systems, according to which banks are jointly and severally liable for the obligations undertaken by other system members, in case these obligations fail to be fulfilled (articles 68–9 of directive 2006/48/EC).

As already noted in connection with the Basel Accord, a further competitive disadvantage for banks belonging to decentralized-structure cooperative systems is represented by the equity exposure risk weight under the IRB approach. Equities in service undertakings, investment firms, and central banks constitute the largest portion of investments in equities made by banks belonging to cooperative networks, but, owing to their amount, they do not fall within the consolidation procedure (EACB, 2005c). A reduction in the risk weight for such exposures would be desirable.

Under the standardized approach, the rules governing the determination of intra-group exposure risk weights seem to afford a competitive advantage to cooperative banks (and savings banks) over other bank categories (Rym, 2005). The competent authorities, in fact, can allow the application of a risk weight equal to 0 per cent, in lieu of 20 per cent, to the exposures of a credit institution to a counterparty that is a parent undertaking, or its subsidiary, or a subsidiary of its parent undertaking, provided that particularly stringent conditions are met (art. 80,

2006/48/EC). The same possibility is granted to the competent authorities for intra-group exposures when both the institution that claims a credit and the counterparty meet only a portion of the relevant requirements and adopt the same institutional guarantee scheme (typical of cooperative systems). Such a scheme must comply with precise requirements (capacity to secure the liquidity and solvency of adhering banks, timely intervention, a full view of the risk profile of adhering banks, information to adhering banks about risk monitoring, and reports about the accounting and risk situation). The requirements on both the institution claiming the credit and the counterparty are as follows:

(a) The counterparty must be an institution or a financial holding company, a financial institution, an asset management company, or an ancillary services undertaking subject to appropriate prudential requirements.
(b) The counterparty must be established in the same member state as the credit institution.
(c) There must be no current or foreseen material, practical, or legal impediment to the prompt transfer of own funds or repayment of liabilities by counterparty to creditor.

The reduced number of requirements (a, b, c) to be met by counterparties in the last case, when compared with those to be met by institutions not adhering to guarantee schemes, creates a true competitive advantage for cooperative banks. In order to allow institutions that do not adhere to guarantee schemes to benefit from the treatment for intra-group exposures, the counterparty must be fully included in the same consolidation as the credit institution and be subject to the same risk evaluation, measurement and control procedures as the credit institution.

As for the supervisory review process (Second Pillar), the decentralized network model of cooperative credit banks, on the basis of which certain central institutions construct and provide risk management and mitigation systems meant for a number of network banks, leads us to believe that review of such banks by the competent authorities will focus exclusively on the adequacy of the implementation modalities.

Apart from the institutional or organizational model, the adoption of models of internal governance, risk management, and ICAAP complying with CEBS's guidelines imply new organizational requirements, namely:

- greater formalization: risk management policies and strategies, objectives in terms of risk and business, management's liabilities and

working procedures, risk management system, and capital policy must be suitably supported by documents;
- increased review: risk management strategies and policies, internal governance model, and capital policy must be periodically reviewed by top management. ICAAP is subject to independent internal review;
- enhanced reporting system: the risks inherent in the activities, the outcome of the activity of control functions, as well as capital planning and management policies must be the subject of an internal communication;
- creation or development of the planning and management control function for the purpose of strengthening strategic activities (growth and development plans, income prospects, definition of propensity to risk, and so forth); and
- enhanced information system for the sharing, analysis, and filing of major risk measurement data.

In the case of small banks, compliance with regulations is hindered by organizational encumbrances due to the limited number of people on the payroll, as well as to insufficient formalization of risk management processes and insufficient professional skill adequacy.

With regard to the internal governance model, the first encumbrance, that is, the limited number of people on the payroll, hinders the creation of a 'second level' control function (for risk management control) and of a compliance function, both independent, from an organizational and operational viewpoint, of the controlled units.

The second encumbrance, that is, insufficient formalization of risk management processes, hinders the precise definition of the contents of the risk control function that would require a pre-definition of the policies and objectives in terms of risk, of management strategies, and of a coherent limit system (Antonicelli et al., 2005). An outsourcing of this function, on the other hand, appears to be inappropriate owing to the close interconnection between risk management controls and the bank's major decision-making processes.

The third encumbrance, that is, insufficient professional skill adequacy, hinders the creation of a compliance function capable of filling its multiple tasks (BCBS, 2005a), of a protective nature (pre-emptive identification of risks of non-conformity that might occur in connection with changes in regulations, consultancy and assistance in respect of regulations), of an inspective nature (detection of breaches), and of a reporting nature (reporting of major breaches to control functions). Even in the case of outsourcing of the compliance activity to associative structures, rather frequent for cooperative banks, the responsibility for internal control system rests with the management; this means that the bank is compelled to own adequate internal competent skills coordinating or monitoring compliance activity.

With regard to ICAAP, small cooperative credit banks' compliance with regulatory requirements is a problem because of the investments required and the present level of development of risk management methodologies and instruments, mainly of a traditional type. Indeed, in view of the complexity and extent of regulatory requirements for individual cooperative banks, there will be an ever-more qualified and complex offer of services by the top levels of the associative structure of the cooperative credit system.

The proportionality criterion, furthermore, seems to be disregarded, to the detriment of small banks, in the framework of the supervisory review process, when the supervisory authorities' review and evaluation of banks' compliance with the directive are requested to be updated once a year at least. While such frequency is suitable for large banks, where supervision is performed at a consolidated level, in small banks it would increase bureaucracy in an unjustified manner and jeopardize bank efficiency (EACB, 2005c).

In brief, the EC directive concerning capital requirements seems to lessen the impact of Basel 2 on the cooperative banking system if certain specific features of the sector are duly taken into account.

The mitigation of the effects of Basel 2 on cooperative banks derives from the flexibility granted for the purpose of credit inclusion in the retail portfolio (with reference to the granularity criterion); from the recognition of mutual fund collaterals and from the expanded range of guarantors and counter-guarantors; from the possibility of permanent partial implementation (i.e. limited to a portion of the portfolio) of more sophisticated methods (IRB and advanced measurement approaches, AMA); from the possibility of using aggregate data for an evaluation of internal rating system parameters and of having recourse to outsourcing for the production of information relevant to supervisory activity under the IRB approach; and from the recognition of the proportionality criterion, particularly significant in respect of the Second Pillar.

The EC directive, however, does not solve all the problems connected with fair conditions of competition between institutions characterized by different legal or institutional structures.

Cooperative banking draws competitive advantages from the recognition of the specificity of network-structured cooperative banks, which, although decentralized, at the same time have solidarity mechanisms of their own, capable of making them more credible, stable and efficient than other institutions in relation to the weight to be applied to intra-group exposures under the credit risk standardized approach.

Conversely, cooperative banking suffer from competitive disadvantages that flow from the fact that the prospects concerning the consolidated supervision of groups seem to advantage listed companies and parent undertakings or subsidiaries based on capital holdings. Further disadvantages derive from the provisions regarding the weight of equity exposure under the IRB approach as they penalize decentralized cooperative credit banks owing to the amount of equities owned in services undertakings, investment firms, central banks, and so forth.

The medium-to-small size of most of cooperative credit banks – as far as this involves a limited number of people on the payroll, insufficient formalization of risk management processes, and inadequate professional skills – becomes an encumbrance in respect of the adoption of models of internal governance, risk management, and ICAAP meeting the CEBS guidelines.

8.7   The impact of EU regulations governing capital requirements: empirical evidence

With a view to evaluating the effects of the Capital Requirements Directive on the minimum capital requirements of EU banks, the EU Commission conducted a quantitative impact analysis on the banks in 18 EU member states as well as on banks of Bulgaria and Norway (CEBS, 2006b). Banks were subdivided into two groups according to the same criterion as used in the Basel Committee's QIS 5: 49 banks belong to group 1 and 262 to group 2. The results relating to the banks of group 2, which are closer in terms of size to EU cooperative banks, are perfectly aligned with those of QIS 5. Indeed, the study reveals the following:

- Almost half the banks of group 2 will adopt the standardized approach to credit risk measurement, and most of them will adopt the basic indicator approach to operational risk.
- Minimum capital requirements will decrease, on average, regardless of the approach used.
- There are strong incentives to move from the standardized approach to FIRB in the case of credit risks, and from the basic indicator approach to the standardized approach in the case of operational risks.
- The main item responsible for a reduction in capital requirements under the standardized approach and, to a greater extent, under

the IRB approach remains the retail portfolio and, in particular, the mortgage portfolio. However, since residential mortgage loans are long-term, the bank is exposed to interest rate risk. The advantage obtainable in consideration of the First Pillar prospects risks being nullified by the Second Pillar prospects in connection with interest rate risk.

- The corporate portfolio and the portfolio of SMEs treated as corporate involve a decrease in minimum capital requirements that turns out to be significant in the case of the adoption of IRB approaches. Exposures to SMEs treated as corporate generate a slight increase in minimum capital requirements solely in banks of group 2 that opt for the standardized approach.
- Sovereign exposures expand capital requirements, justified by the expected 0 per cent weight in the Accord in force. The same effect is produced by the equity portfolio.
- Obviously, the operational risk remains a driver of the increase in regulatory capital.

Results concerning the consequences of the proposal for new capital requirements contained in the Basel Consultative Paper of April 2003 (CP3) and in the Madrid Compromise of October 2003 (CAD 3) on EU credit institutions are expressed in a study carried out by PricewaterhouseCoopers on behalf of the EU Commission (PricewaterhouseCoopers, 2004). The main source of data for this study is Quantitative Impact Study 3 (QIS 3) conducted, at a national level, by 12 of the 15 EU member states in 2003 (Italy, Ireland, and Luxembourg did not participate).

Put very briefly, the study shows that:

- The capital requirements of EU credit institutions should be reduced by 5 per cent, small credit institutions will not be penalized, and most EU member states will not be subject to the effects feared for SMEs in terms of financing availability and cost.
- Consistently with the results of QIS 3 conducted by the Basel Committee, the banks that operate chiefly with SMEs or with retail customers should record significant reduction of the capital requirements vis-à-vis credit risk, partially balanced by higher requirements due to operational risk. Otherwise, banks operating mainly with sovereigns, large enterprises, or in the investment banking sector will record minimal or even no capital saving at all.

Eventually, the proposal impact is analysed by type of institution (commercial, retail bank or building society, and specialist institution):

- In terms of capital requirements, the consequences for commercial banks are extremely variable as a function of the composition of the bank portfolio. For instance, large German banks (group 1) have an extremely reduced retail portfolio when compared with British or Spanish banks; thus, they benefit less from a smaller capital absorption connected with that portfolio. Large Dutch banks have significant exposures to banks, sovereigns, and large non-domestic enterprises that offset the capital saving connected with their significant domestic retail activity.
- Retail banks and building societies are the institutions that will benefit most from the capital saving connected with residential mortgage loans and, more generally, with retail activity, even if – as in the case of commercial banks – the effects vary according to geographic area. Germany, Denmark, and Austria will obtain the most benefits as their geographic areas are characterized by low losses on residential mortgage loans – unlike Italy, for instance.
- In terms of capital requirements, specialist institutions will experience extremely differentiated effects as a function of the composition of their portfolio and of the approach selected. Investment banks and those specialist institutions that are subject to low credit and market risks vis-à-vis their business activity will be penalized by the operational risk capital requirement introduced by the new regulation.

In line with the outcome of the quantitative impact study made by the Basel Committee, the new regulations should bring about positive effects for cooperative banking in terms of minimum capital requirements, in consideration both of the fact that such system mainly operates in the traditional banking sector and of the high incidence of retail exposures and residential mortgage loans. These results are confirmed by a study of a wide range of Italian cooperative credit banks (190) conducted by a working group constituted by Federasse (Lopez, 2003). The study, however, reveals that an improvement in terms of capital requirements vis-à-vis credit risk might be eroded by the introduction of a 150 per cent risk weight on loans that are overdue for more than 90 days. Moreover, the retail portfolio granularity criterion equal to 0.2 per cent (as provided by the Basel Committee) would penalize small banks that, owing to the limited amount of retail portfolio owned, would not be in a position to benefit from the treatment reserved to the specific sector for many exposures, with immediate consequences in terms of higher capital requirements.

8.8   Conclusions

This chapter provides an analysis of the possible effects of the implementation of the New Capital Accord on cooperative banking. The capital adequacy reform carried out by the Basel Committee has a number of implications.

For the analysis of the expected impact, the institutional or organizational model was considered first, then due consideration was given to the size characteristics of the EU cooperative banking systems.

The analysis developed from the first survey perspective rests on the examination of the position papers produced by various EU associations (EACB, 2001, 2004a, 2004b, 2005a, 2005b; World Council of credit unions, Inc 2003, ESBG, 2003a; World Savings Banks Institute and The European Savings Banks, 2003) about the most recent provisional version of the New Accord, as well as on the check that the viewpoints contained in these papers have been accepted in the final version. The New Accord provisions were examined on the basis of indications given by the various associations as to the possibility that these provisions may result in a competitive disadvantage for banks organized on the lines of different legal or organizational models. This makes it possible to infer the possible effects on cooperative banking, in terms of competitive disadvantages and advantages following the implementation of the New Accord.

The analysis developed from the second survey perspective rests on the theoretical and empirical contributions found in the literature, as well as on the results of the Basel Committee's latest quantitative impact study.

Since the survey is limited to EU cooperative systems, it was deemed advisable to check the presence of alignments and misalignments of the effects of the New Accord with those brought about by the issue of directives 2006/48/EC and 2006/49/EC on cooperative banking.

First, stress was laid on the elements differentiating the EC directive from the international Accord, as they play a major role in cooperative banking on account of certain specific features of the sector.

Second, efforts were made to understand whether, also within the framework of the EC directive, the legal or organizational structure and the medium-to-small size of the banks of the cooperative credit system may constitute sources of competitive advantages or disadvantages.

The method used in conducting the analysis was the same as used previously. A comparison between viewpoints about the directive expressed by bank associations (EAPB, 2002, 2003, 2004, 2006; ESBG, 2003b, 2005a, 2005b) organized according to different models, on the one hand, and the evidence given in certain theoretical and empirical contributions as well as in the quantitative impact studies made on behalf of EU authorities, on the other, made it possible to infer the expected effects of the EC directive on cooperative banking in relation to the legal or institutional structure and the typical size of the sector.

In practice, after an examination of the new regulations, theoretical contributions, and empirical evidence, three questions remain unanswered:

- If regulatory instruments are aimed at securing competitive parity, and hence a regulatory cost proportional to risk, is it correct – when establishing the capital coefficient calculation rules – not to consider the better quality of the composition of the cooperative credit banks' capital, which in the European context has historically been little characterized by junior debt and hybrid financial instruments?
- Apart from the cooperative credit banks' usefulness in improving method of analysis of the credit process for the purpose of avoiding problems of adverse selection and competitive disparity in relation to more sophisticated banks, does not the adoption of IRB methods complying with the First Pillar risk to weaken the business model underlying the competitive advantage of cooperative banking?
- What is the business dimension justifying the information and organizational effort connected with the adoption of an IRB system? Is it possible to charge these costs to common structures?

In considering the foregoing questions, one feels the need for further theoretical in-depth studies and for more empirical evidence.

Bibliography

Altman E. I. and Sabato G., 2005, 'Effect of the New Basel Capital Accord on Bank Capital Requirements for SMEs', *Journal Of Financial Services Research*, no. 28.

Antonicelli M. A., Bernasconi F. and Di Salvo R., 2005, 'La conformità a Basilea 2 nelle piccole banche. Il caso delle banche di credito cooperativo', *Cooperazione di credito*, January–March.

Arak M., 1992, 'The Effect of the New Risk-based Capital Requirements on the Market for Swaps', *Journal of Financial Services Research*, vol. 6, no. 1, May.

Avery R. B. and Samolyk K. A., 2004, 'Bank Consolidation and the Provision of Banking Services: Small Commercial Loans', *Journal of Financial Services Research*, no. 25, April.

BCBS, 2004, *International Convergence of Capital Measurement and Capital Standards*, June, 26.

BCBS, 2005a, Compliance and Compliance Function in Banks, April.

BCBS, 2005b, *The Application of Basel II to Trading Activities and the Treatment of Double Default Effects*, July.

BCBS, 2005c, *International Convergence of Capital Measurement and Capital Standards – A Revised Framework*, November.

BCBS, 2006a, *Results of the Fifth Quantitative Impact Study (QIS 5)*, June.

BCBS, 2006b, *International Convergence of Capital Measurement and Capital Standards. A Revised Framework Comprehensive Version*, July.

Berger A. N., 2006, 'Potential Competitive Effects of Basel II on Banks in SME Credit Market in The United States', *Journal of Financial Services Research*, no. 29.

Berger A. N. and Udell G. F., 1996, 'Universal Banking and the Future of Small Business Lending', in: Saunders A. and Walter I., eds, *Financial System Design: The Case for Universal Banking*, Burr Ridge, IL: Irwin Publishing.

Berger A. N. and Udell G. F., 2002, 'Small Business Credit Availability and Relationship Lending: The Importance of Bank Organizational Structure', *Economic Journal*, vol. 112, no. 477, February.

Berger A. N., Bonime S. D., Goldberg, L. G. and White, L. J., 2004, 'The Dynamics of Market Entry: The Effects of Mergers and Acquisitions on Entry in the Banking Industry', *Journal of Business*, no. 77, October.

Berger A. N., Miller N. H. and Petersen M. A., Rajan R. G. and Stein J. C., 2005, 'Does Function Follow Organizational Form? Evidence from the Lending Practices of Large and Small Banks', *Journal of Financial Economics*, no. 76, May.

Boot A. A. W., 2000, 'Relationship Banking: What Do We Know?', *Journal of Financial Intermediation*, vol. 9, no. 1.

Carosio G., 2003, 'Basilea 2, piccole banche e piccole imprese', *Cooperazione di credito*, no. 182, October–December.

Carter D. A., McNulty J. E. and Verbrugge J. A., 2004, 'Do Small Banks have an Advantage in Lending? An Examination of Risk-adjusted Yields on Business Loans at Large and Small Banks', *Journal of Financial Services Research*, no. 25, April.

CEBS (Committee of European Banking Supervisors) 2005, *Consultation Paper Application of the Supervisory Review Process under Pillar 2* (CP03 Revised), June.

CEBS, 2006a, *Guidelines on the Implementation, Validation and Assessment of Measurement (AMA) and Internal Ratings Based (IRB) Approaches*, 20 January.

CEBS, 2006b, *Quantitative Impact Study. Overview on the Results of the EU Countries*, 16 June.

Cole R. A., Goldberg L. G. and White L. J., 2004, 'Cookie-cutter Versus Character: The Micro Structure of Small Business Lending by Large and Small Banks', *Journal of Financial and Quantitative Analysis*, no. 39, June.

Comana M., 2003, 'Basilea 2: le BCC di fronte alla riforma della vigilanza', *Cooperazione di credito*, no. 181, July/September.

De Laurentis G and Caselli S., 2005, *Miti e verità di Basilea 2*, EGEA, Milano.

Di Salvo R, 2002, 'Il rischio di credito, Basilea 2 e piccole banche: quale sviluppo per i controlli prudenziali', *Cooperazione di credito*, no. 176/177, April September.

EACB (European Association of Co-operative Banks), 2001, 'Position Paper on the 2nd Consultative Document of the Basel Committee on Banking Supervision on the New Basel Capital Accord', http://www.eurocoopbanks.coop/

EACB, 2003, 'Comments on the Third Consultative Document: The New Basel Capital Accord', Brussels, July, http://www.bis.org

EACB, 2004a, 'EACB Study on Co-operative Banks in Europe: Values and Practices to Promote Development', http://www.eurocoopbanks.coop/, December.

EACB, 2004b, Annual Report, http://www.eurocoopbanks.coop/

EACB, 2005a, 'Application of the Supervisory Review Process under Pillar 2 (CP 03 rev)', Position Paper, Brussels, 21 October, http://www.eurocoopbanks.coop/

EACB, 2005b, 'Consultation Paper 10: Guidelines on the Implementation, Validation and Assessment of Measurement (AMA) and Internal Ratings Based (IRB) Approaches', Position Paper, Brussels, October 28, http://www.eurocoopbanks.coop/

EACB, 2005c, Comments on the Proposal for New Capital Requirements Regime for Credit Institutions and Investment Firms, Brussels, March, http://www.eurocoopbanks.coop/

EAPB (European Association of Public Banks), 2002: Capital Requirements for Credit Institutions and Investment Firms', Brussels, www.eapb.be, 31 January.

EAPB, 2003, 'Position of the EAPB on the EU Commission Working Document of 18 November.

EAPB, 2004, 'EAPB Position on the European Commission Proposal for the Amendment of the Consolidated Banking Directive (2000/12/EC) and the Capital Adequacy Directive (93/6/EEC): Capital Adequacy Rules for Credit Institutions and Investment Firms Brussels', www.eapb.be, 8 November.

EAPB, 2006, 'EAPB Position Paper on the 2nd Draft of CEBS: Guidelines on the Implementation, Validation and Assessment of Measurement (AMA) and Internal Ratings Based (IRB) Approaches', www.eapb.be, Brussels, 14 February.

ESBG (European Savings Banks Group), 2003a, 'Statements on Third Consultation Paper of the Basel Committee on the Revision of the Basel Accord', 25 July, Brussels.

ESBG, 2003b, 'Position Paper on the European Commission Third Consultation Working Document on Capital Requirements for Credit Institutions and Investment Firms' Brussels, 22 December.

ESBG, 2005a, '"Response to CEBS" Consultation on the Application of the Supervisory Review Process under Pillar 2 (CP 03 revised)', Brussels, 21 October.

ESBG, 2005b, '"Response to CEBS" Guidelines on the Implementation, Validation and Assessment of Measurement (AMA) and Internal Ratings Based (IRB) Approaches', Brussels, 8 November.

Gumerlock R., 1993, 'Double Trouble', *Risk*, vol. 6, no.9, September.

Hannan T. H., 1991, 'Bank Commercial Loan Markets and the Role of Market Structure: Evidence from Surveys of Commercial Lending', *Journal of Banking and Finance*, no. 15, February.

Heldring O., 1995, 'Alpha Plus', *Risk*, vol. 8, no. 1.

Keeton W. R., 1995, 'Multi-Office Bank Lending to Small Businesses: Some New Evidence', *Federal Reserve Bank of Kansas City Economic Review*, 80, no. 2.

Lopez J., 2003, 'Il nuovo accordo di Basilea: una simulazione dell'impatto del calcolo del coefficiente di capitale sulle banche di credito cooperativo', *Cooperazione di credito*, no. 181, July–September.

Peek J. and Rosengren E. S., 1998, 'Bank Consolidation and Small Business Lending: It's Not Just Bank Size That Matters', *Journal of Banking and Finance*, vol. 22, no. 6, August.

PricewaterhouseCoopers, 2004, 'Study on the Financial and Macroeconomic Consequences of the Draft Proposed New Capital Requirements for Banks and Investment Firms in the EU', Final Report, 8 April.

Resti A., 2004, 'Impact of Basel 2 on Small and Medium Sized Credit Institutions', in The New Basel Capital Accord and the Future of the European Financial System, Report of a CEPS Task Force, no. 51, April.

Rym A., 2005, 'The New Capital Requirement Directive: What Pieces Are Still Missing from the Puzzle?', http://www.ceps.be, September.

Sironi A., 2005, *Rischio e valore nelle banche*, EGEA, Milano.

Sironi A. and Zazzara C., 2002, 'Il processo di riforma dello schema di adeguatezza patrimoniale: le implicazioni per le banche di piccola e media dimensione', Research ASSBANK-ACRI, Newfin centre.

Standard & Poor's, 2003, 'Basel Committee on Banking Supervision: Third Consultation Paper', Standard & Poor's Response, August 22.

Stein J. C., 2002, 'Information Production and Capital Allocation: Decentralized vs. Hierarchical Firms', *Journal of Finance*, no. 57, October.

Strahan P. E. and Weston J. P., 1996, 'Small Business Lending and Bank Consolidation: Is There Cause for Concern?', *Federal Reserve Bank of New York Current Issues in Economics and Finance*, no. 2.

Strahan P. E. and Weston J. P., 1998, 'Small Business Lending and the Changing Structure of the Banking Industry', *Journal of Banking and Finance*, no. 22, August.

World Council of credit unions, Inc, 2003, 'Basel capital accord II', September, www.woccu.org

World Savings Banks Institute and The European Savings Banks, 2003, 'Group Statements On Third Consultation Paper Of The Basel Committee On The Revision Of The Basel Accord', 25 July.

9
Internal Controls and Cooperative Banks

V. Stefanelli

9.1   Internal controls in banking regulation

The increase in competition in European banking and the dangers of the erosion of market shares have pushed financial intermediaries to critically review their competitive models in the search for the correct business equilibrium required in the new market scene.

From this point of view, the variety of strategic paths recently adopted by various intermediaries can be justified: from the realization of mergers usually aimed at strengthening market power to the creation of strategic alliances, entry into new business areas, diversification and outsourcing of specific financial activities in the pursuit of economies of scale, and the use of new distributive channels for products and services increasingly 'engineered' and oriented to increasing customer satisfaction.[1]

The effects of competition are equally visible in the cooperative credit industry, which can no longer postpone rethinking traditional banking business (EACB, 2004a; Dalmaz and De Toytot, 2002). Faced with new opportunities for profit, however, it has increased its organizational complexity and widened the potential risk factors for intermediaries. For example, virtual distributive channels have been adopted which, if they failed to function, in the absence of adequate plans of disaster recovery could compromise the banks' operations in the market; the specific risks of outsourcing, if not effectively managed, could affect intermediaries' reputations; and diversification, correlated to the banking activity, could, by taking advantage of economic resources and focusing on the financial intermediation sectors, broaden intermediaries' exposure to risk.

The sustainability of change in the banking competitive models must ultimately and necessarily find a certain degree of correspondence in the introduction of adequate organizational standards and suitable control instruments to guarantee the strategic and economic consolidation of innovatory projects.

The importance of organizational arrangements and control in respect of financial intermediaries is also recognized in current prudential regulation schemes (Basel Committee on Banking Supervision, 1998). Under banking standards, financial intermediaries, even smaller ones, are called on to constantly adapt their organizational structures and control processes to the complexity of management and the degree of risk undertaken.

At the international level, the regulators also specify in the organizational (and equity) variables the instruments for safeguarding healthy and prudent management, with which all intermediaries must comply. Although they intervene in a balanced way, outlining an organic and complete picture of the principles referring to the subject of internal controls in banks, the normative order offers minimal guidelines setting out the space in which individual parties can take independent organizational initiatives.

On the other hand, the design of an 'optimal' and 'global' model of organization and control, besides not being among the tasks of the regulatory process, would have displayed only limited theoretical consistency. Various authors claim that the instrument of internal control does not and cannot have an 'atomistic' dimension, since it is not about a block of procedures that, explained by fixed principles, can be introduced sic et simpliciter into another one: this is fully a part of an enterprise and, as such, is interdependent on the organization, the quality of the human resources, and the level of technological innovation, as well as the culture of the enterprise itself (Patalano, 1995; Bernardini and Paterna, 1999, 2000; Carretta et al., 2003).

From a regulatory perspective, in fact, internal control in financial intermediaries is not viewed simply as an instrument for certifying that the activities of individual intermediaries conform to current standards but, rather, as a 'system' that is a part of the entire organizational structure of the intermediaries and assigns specific roles and responsibilities to each business organ, weaving them into an overall control structure that is organized on different levels and provided with a reliable information and communication system.

Therefore, the impact of the standards on business behaviours is decidedly broad and pervasive, in that it relates to organizational aspects, processes, procedures, decision-making mechanisms and business communication and control systems; at the same time, it is also particularly varied, given that every intermediary, in complying with the regulatory provisions, is called on to autonomously implement a control system capable of governing the complexity of its own managerial organization and the specificity of its risk exposure. In spite of the introduction of regulatory standards vis-à-vis internal controls at the end of the 1990s, the topic is still highly current, from a twofold perspective.

From a business perspective the organizational changes connected to the process of regulatory transition have driven intermediaries to undertake numerous transformations and continued adaptations within structures that require sufficiently long-term time horizons to be able to be really and fully understood at all levels of the hierarchy. The studies completed at the supervision level reveal that certain technical aspects of the internal controls of financial intermediaries still do not appear to be completely in line with the standards prescribed by the regulations.[2]

From an international perspective the topic is even more significant in the light of the recent reforms of banking legislation. In particular, reference is made here to the review of the prudential principles relating to the banks' equity adequacy (Basel 2). Parallel analysis of the provisions of Basel 2 and the regulatory standards relating to internal control systems highlights strong interdependence between the two, given that the latter seem to be necessary conditions for the former. Those banks which, having adopted a 'standard-compliant' internal control system, already possess most of the organizational requirements for the validation of internal methods for calculating the equity requirements for lending and operating risks obviously have a potential competitive advantage.[3]

The new international accounting principles also have a special focus on banks' internal controls. From the point of view of the harmonization of financial reporting, the recent European provisions require some companies to adopt more transparent, strict and suitable accounting and control systems in order to produce fair and more realistic estimates of business management, inspired by market evaluation rather than historical rationales.[4]

In the present chapter we adopt a purely business perspective and tackle the basic theme of internal controls by surveying the distinctive features of the regulatory authorities' proposed framework in order to establish the range of changes required from the supervised entities and, subsequently, the characteristics of the control model adopted by cooperative lending banks. In the final part, where possible, the problems faced by European systems in respect of the transition to the prescribed system are highlighted.

9.2   The internal control framework in banks: organizational roles, structure and levels of control

The evolution of the style of control in banking supervision has increasingly focused on the conditions under which financial intermediaries organize typical processes of production, administration and distribution in their respective business areas. The supervisory authorities have intervened by prescribing principles and rules aimed at the promotion of organization structures designed to pursue the resolved and suitable strategic goals required to face increased business risks and market selectivity.[5]

This greater interest is partially the consequence of the remarkable losses sustained by various banks. An analysis of the genesis of these losses indicates that they could probably have been avoided if effective internal control systems had been in place. Such systems would have prevented, or at least promptly highlighted, the appearance of the problems that eventually caused the losses, thus limiting the damage to the banking organizations (Basel Committee on Banking Supervision, 1998).

For those reasons, the supervisory authorities, interacting with the supervised intermediaries, encourage them to improve their organizational and internal control processes, from a certification rather than a regulatory point of view. They become almost consultants to financial institutions, contributing to the circulation of knowledge of best practices: supervision of and support for the intermediaries' management tend to become a unitary activity, sharing the goals of stability and efficiency by stimulating healthy and prudent management (Carretta et al., 2003).

The authorities' efforts obviously transpire from the European Union provisions and the banking standards issued at the end of the 1990s by the international supervisory bodies (European Monetary Institute, European Central Bank and Basel Committee on Banking Supervision).[6] More precisely, at the international level the documents produced aim to encourage individual national authorities to define, in a unitary fashion, the criteria of appraisal with respect to the adequacy of intermediaries' internal control systems, within a framework of harmonization and improvement of the systems themselves: '(...)Supervisors should require that all banks, regardless of size, have an effective system of internal controls that is consistent with nature, complexity, and risk inherent in their on-and-off-balance-sheet activities and that responds to changes in the bank's environment and conditions (Basel Committee on Banking Supervision, 1998).'

The main document on internal control, issued in 1998 by the Basel Committee on the subject of banking supervision, is entitled Framework for Internal Control Systems in Banking Organizations. It defines rules of conduct for national authorities and principles of a general nature that qualify the attributes of adequacy and functionality of the organizational and internal control systems of financial intermediaries.

In the framework drafted by the Basel Committee, and subsequently transposed into national law by individual Member States[7], the system of internal controls is defined as the set of rules, procedures and organizational structures that support the bank in the pursuit of business strategies that are in harmony with the business context and consistent with the applicable standards, in safeguarding asset values, in protecting intermediaries from losses, and in making available, at all organizational levels, reliable and timely accounting and management information. The process of internal control, which traditionally constitutes a mechanism capable of reducing the incidence of fraud and wilful and erroneous misappropriation in the current regulatory framework, has assumed a broader and 'systemic' scope, similar to a network model, where the business responsibilities of the individual bodies are interwoven with those aimed at providing protection from the various types of risk undertaken.

Such an arrangement promotes among intermediaries a progressive approach to control by processes achievable through organizational and across-the-board work methods, with respect to the structure and the various business activities, which in some cases could require the implementation of mechanisms of incentives, integration and mutual adjustment, in support of effective control actions (Schwizer, 2005; Cosma and Stefanelli, 2005).

Equally important changes necessarily focus on a process of 'internalization' of the control instruments adopted by the organizational structure, to achieve, through remarkable knowledge-broadening, learning and development efforts, a 'culture of control', considered to be the basis for the acceptance of controls by the various individuals (Carretta et al., 2003).

Aware of the complexity of the organizational functioning and controls of an enterprise, the authorities have formulated an articulated set of guiding principles capable of integrating, in a balanced way, the various organizational levers and having due regard both to the 'hard' profiles (processes, activities and operative mechanisms) and to the 'soft' profiles (business culture), with respect to the structures.

In this chapter we have decided to relate the characteristics of the internal control model outlined by the organs of instrumental supervision to the subsequent appraisal of the normative impact on the cooperative sector, referring any further investigation to the broad corpus of literature on the topic.

Under the provisions contained in international regulations, the architecture of an effective internal control system, in respect of the pursuit of the goals that have been set, must consist of five strongly interdependent elements: the supervision of management; the supervision of the business culture of control; identification and appraisal of the internal and external factors of risk; the structure of the controls; and the information, communication and monitoring systems.

The regulation assigns a prominent role to companies' administrative bodies (board of directors, top management, board of statutory auditors) and to the business functions in charge of the maintenance and the management of the control processes (board of statutory auditors, internal auditing, staff units or committees in charge of protecting specific management aspects), a characteristic which is then included in the broader debate on the organization of corporate governance under way in several European countries.[8]

The principles prescribed by the authorities in this area emphasize the need for bank organizations to provide for appropriate levels of responsibility and suitable systems of checks and balance, with the twofold aim of providing the proper incentives for managers to pursue the adopted strategic goals and of facilitating supervisory bodies' 'active' surveillance activities, encouraging the efficient allocation of resources.

In other words, the adequacy of the internal control model is based on its involvement in the various roles of business bodies, according to the rules, organizational structures and procedures (systems of corporate governance) that constitute the formal outline of internal control systems.

The model proposed by the authorities is not limited, however, to aspects of governance. It also examines the operating features of the intermediary that contribute to strengthening the adequacy of the system. The architecture of the control system first of all envisages a mapping of business processes in order to identify the implications in terms of level and type of assumed risks; and in this area it foresees the adoption of specific control instruments in respect of the business risks. In this area, the standards further increase the degree of detail and propose a to-the-point and strict organization of the instruments, broken down into three different levels, each overseeing a sector of substantial (quantifiable and non-quantifiable) risks that could negatively affect the attainment of the business goals.

Generally speaking, three levels of control by the authorities can be identified, as follows:

- Line controls (level I) are integrated into the day-to-day operations of the intermediary, and consist of the routine controls normally carried out by the same productive structures while the processes are under way, in order to ensure their proper development.
- Risk control (level II) can be achieved through specific risk-management functions which, hierarchically independent from the productive and commercial structures, oversee the business risks as part of an integrated vision, in order to identify in a clear and unambiguous manner the risk profile/business performance and adjust it to the limits assigned and connected to the business strategy.
- Internal auditing activity (level III) is carried out by an organizational function that is hierarchically independent from the operating functions, and provided with resources and operating tools that are qualitatively and quantitatively suitable for the implementation of controls that are not only of the static and 'assertive-repressive' type, that is, from assessment to penalty, but also of the dynamic and 'propositive-planned' type, that is, from assessment to organizational implementation[9].

At this last level of control, the regulatory indications bring together an elevated degree of professional qualification and a constant modernization of both knowledge and auditing techniques. From a reliable accomplishment of internal auditing activities, in fact, there can flow a useful contribution to the action of regulatory supervision, due to its ability to identify time dysfunctions or anomalies in the control system and to punctually point out specific areas of potential risk.

In confirmation of the particular emphasis placed on the role of internal auditing in internal controls, reference is made to a further document issued by the same prescribed authorities, and aimed at regulating in a more punctual manner the tasks and the responsibilities of such a supervisory body (Basel Committee on Banking Supervision, 2001a).

The document acknowledges the possibility of the intermediary outsourcing the internal audit function for reasons of cost or lack of suitable internal competence. In such cases, the risks normally associated with the loss of control over an outsourced function assumes peculiar features, because they are associated with activities that concern the very exercise of control over business management; the intermediaries must, therefore, for surveillance purposes implement all the necessary organizational, procedural and contractual measures aimed at ensuring effective monitoring and integration vis-à-vis the outsourced functions within the complex system of internal control.

Conditions of procedural control and contractual protection are imposed by the regulatory bodies also in cases of outsourcing various functions of the internal audit. More and more often the banks adopt flexible organizational conditions, outsourcing the non-core links of the value chain and specializing in a predetermined phase of the services cycle, regardless of whether this is the phase of planning, production, distribution or regulation (BCE, 2006).

In all cases, according to the supervisory authorities, the choices of outsourcing cannot be realized without regard to the responsibilities for the controls on the part of the business management level, and this appears to be consistent with the profile of the specific risk associated with similar strategies: the economic development of particular activities reduces exposure to reputational risk, but widens exposure to operating risks. In a contrary hypothesis, the choice to give in outsourcing a business activity against a certain reduction of the operational risk for the bank increases reputational risk.

After all, regardless of the nature of the strategy (in/outsourcing), the intermediary runs in a combined way all types of risk (credit risk, country and currency exchange risk, market risk, interest rate risk, liquidity risk, operating risk, legal risk, risk of reputation, strategic risk), and is called on to maintain adequate protection, including in an indirect form, of the various links in the value chain.

The attempt to harmonize different European banking approaches to risk management with business outsourcing decisions, and the need to further enhance awareness of bank management with respect to overseeing the same risks, has persuaded the international supervisory authorities to propose a protection control model for the outsourcing of business functions (Committee of European Banking Supervisors, 2006).

The currently proposed model, which is susceptible to further modification and review by the authorities, recognizes the possibility of intermediaries delegating the development of the activity of specific business functions; such delegation, however, does not exempt the intermediary from responsibility for control over the outsourced activities. Intermediaries that entrust an activity to a third party must formalize the relationship in a written contract in which the goal and the limits of the conferred delegation and the guidelines of the activity are defined; moreover, it is a task of the bank's board of directors to define the goals of the outsourcing decisions, with respect to the business strategy and the qualitative and quantitative parameters expected from the process, to identify selection criteria and appraise the outsourcer, and to plan for timely instruments and procedures (also of a contractual nature) in the event that the service supplied is inadequate.

Some postulates of the risk-control model stemming from outsourcing appear at first sight, particularly onerous, mainly for smaller banks, which are often characterized by a strategy of category outsourcing. For example, in order to avoid the possibility that the intermediary suffers high losses from dependency on the outsourcer, the model outlined by the supervisory authorities proposes that bank management decides internally the ability and competences such that the outsourced activities can be performed in an economic manner: 'The ultimate responsibility for the proper management of the risks associated with outsourcing or the outsourced activities lies with an outsourcing institution's senior management. Outsourcing institutions should be required to retain adequate core competence at a senior operational level in house to enable them to have the capability to resume direct control over an outsourced activity, in extremis' (Committee of European Banking Supervisors, 2006).

The framework of internal controls, outlined by the supervisory authorities and supplemented in the subsequent documents described above, ensures that the development of the various phases of the value chain conform to the required risk profile decided by the management, to avoid jeopardizing the balance of the business and the banking system as a whole. As described above, it provides for the distribution among the management bodies of the competences and the tools for overseeing the different risks, but it requires control actions also based on ongoing dialogue between the bodies themselves, so that they can perform their individual control responsibilities in an aware and 'informed' manner.

The last element that qualifies the articulation of the internal control framework defined by the Basel Committee is, in fact, represented by the internal information and communications system, which has not only decision-making, coordination, operation and control functions, but also 'advanced' aims of a training, motivational and also creative type, capable of triggering collaborative business behaviours and of encouraging an active dialogue between the bodies, with a view to integrating formal communication fostering the right interpretation (Cosma and Stefanelli, 2005).

After all, the internal control regulations thus articulated encourage intermediaries to develop the ability to avoid fraudulent behaviours that can compromise their own stability and that of the system, to formulate strategic choices consistent with market evolution, to constantly adapt their own production processes, and ultimately to refine the ability of corporate management bodies to consciously take on the various types of risks associated with current competitive models.

9.3   The distinctive profiles of internal controls in cooperative banks

The internal controls framework described in the previous paragraph must be 'tailored' to the dimensions and the specific features of the organization, processes and procedures of individual businesses: an excess of control vis-à-vis any risks viewed as marginal by the supervised party can uselessly add to operating costs. On the other hand, a shortage of controls on risky and strategically important activities for the same entity can compromise management balances, generating excessive future losses.

The control models implemented by individual intermediaries must, therefore, assure a high degree of consistency, over time, with the evolution of both the management and the competitive contexts. For these reasons, and in consideration of the pervasive nature of the internal controls, the transposition into law of the standards hereunder has proved particularly onerous for the banking system as a whole: in some cases it has required specific restructuring and the introduction of measures with respect to both organization (roles and responsibilities) and business processes (activities, goals, effectiveness/efficiency measures), upgrading information systems and financial reporting. In all cases it became expedient to increase the formalization of the organizational arrangements and the related regulations. Only in the case of the more virtuous businesses has the adoption of the internal control system determined an evolution in work methods and in information processing and circulation procedures, involving the creation of a 'control culture' within individual business units (Schwizer, 2005).

With specific reference to cooperative lending banks, the appraisal of the impact of the internal control standards necessarily refers to the topic of the integration of the individual associates, consortium companies and sectoral structures; in other words, it involves the organization of the entire industry.

For present purposes it is necessary, therefore, to provide a short overview of the organizational peculiarities of the European cooperative banks that have reasonably influenced, if not slowed down or weighed down, the industry-specific control model. In this area, for example, an element that has slowed down the implementation of a standard-compliant control model is its sensitivity to organizational problems which, in companies with a less complex structure, such as cooperative banks, is traditionally thought to be rather low. One of the main challenges that cooperative systems have faced (and continue to face) is, indeed, the need to recover considerable space for organizational efficiency by optimizing their group organization.

Although the cooperative lending market features the presence of individual independent companies, such as the UK building societies, the efforts put into the search for more efficient organizational combinations have led most cooperative banks to evolve national structures with a pyramid organization, that is, two or three levels of organizational decentralization (national, regional and/or local), similar to 'integrated' or simply 'network' systems.

Such an arrangement is shaped as a coordinated system of autonomies, based on multi-tiered structures with distinct but complementary functions, strengthened by shared mechanisms for strategic guideline-setting and coordination. Such a system grants a broad degree of autonomy to the lower tiers in respect of customer relations and core business transactions, while at the same time granting control and governance powers to the upper levels for rationalizing resources and developing investments. This is the case, for example, with the cooperative networks operating in the larger European countries (Germany, Italy, Spain, France and Portugal), whose structures are based on national centralization for recovering a significant amount of efficiency and economies of scale.

The allocation of similar functions to the 'higher' structures is based on the principle of 'subsidiarity', by virtue of which the upper tiers of an organization take over in the event of the limited capability of, or crisis in, a lower tier, and also on the principle of the 'serving organ', whereby the upper tiers deliver a multiplicity of services also on behalf of the lower tiers (or the local units).

In some European cooperative systems, as in the German and Spanish cases, the upper tier of the organization also exercises control over the lower tiers, carrying out, beside the two functions described above, that of 'guarantor' (outside and the inside of the system), with wide powers of control over the affiliated companies, with a view to safeguarding their liquidity and solvency, as well as their technical, administrative and financial operations.

Such a role is consistent with the integrated system rationale, according to which the individual lending cooperatives are required to adopt uniform behaviour and to pursue strategic business goals common to the group. In light of the organizational complexity of cooperative systems, a considerable effort is required to achieve the adequacy standards defined by the authorities with respect to internal control, if one considers, in conjunction with limited sensitivity to organizational themes, the various delays and weak spots of the smaller banks (reduced participation of the management level in business management, deficient formalization of roles and organizational responsibilities, lack of sophisticated risk-assessment models and consequent limited perception of the nature of the risks).

Therefore, the adoption of an adequate internal control system for regulatory purposes has undoubtedly represented, for the entire industry, an opportunity for rethinking dominant business models and for a cultural growth of the entire structure in the area of organizational development.

As regards 'network' – rather than independent – cooperatives, the adoption process of a standard-compliant system of controls has been based, for example, on the formulation of complex and challenging strategic and operational choices, whose fulfilment has often required the participation and mobilization of trade organizations and federal structures.

The consultancy offered by such organisms has always represented a certain advantage for the cooperative banks, provided that they continue to deliver to their members specific professional services that are comparable with the market's quality standards. The growing complexity of the competitive models of cooperative banks, and the need to oversee risks that were previously neglected or were of limited importance, have also forced the federal structures and trade organizations to implement a updating process, with respect to their know-how and capabilities, in order to support the development of the entire system.

A decisive professional leap has been necessary as a result of the introduction of banking regulations on internal control, because, as will be described below, the cooperative model adopted identifies the federal bodies as control institutions. The process of transition towards the regulatory provisions on internal control has required in individual cooperative systems the definition and the sharing of programmes, of various forms, of self-appraisal of systems of internal control aimed at identifying and correcting any possible misalignments regarding the standard-compliant model.

In most cases the action plans supported by the various programmes have foreseen a different operativity in the various phases. In the initial phase, coordinated by the upper-tier structures, a system-level analysis has been put in place aimed at implementing a punctual survey scheme geared to the individual elements falling within the control field, in order to identify the companies, the functions and the responsible individual organizational units and to collect all the available information on the inside of the cooperative system. In parallel to this phase, initiatives have been launched for sharing information and action plans, and for training resources in respect of risk diagnosis and control appraisal, instrumental to the development of the successive phases of the programmes.

In fact, the latter initiatives have predicted operativity at the individual member level aimed at identifying, in various business areas, the 'gross' and 'net' risk exposure profiles of the required controls (expressed in terms of procedures, processes, actions and formalized business bodies).

In this way, the programmes have allowed the highlighting of any required interventions for strengthening and adapting the system control model by improving (a) the self-diagnosis of the procedures that govern the development of the activities, (b) the formalization of the coordination and connection procedures (for example, relating to the informative-accountant system and the methodologies for measuring and managing risks) between the various nodes of the structure, (c) the preparation of mechanisms for the monitoring and periodic assessment of the internal control system, and (d) management conduct and resources dedicated to the overseeing of risks connected to the technological innovation of the processes and outsourcing policies.

The outcome is a 'system-wide' internal control model, in which the coordination of the higher tiers of the structure assures at the same time unity of control actions and a broad involvement of the lower tiers, avoiding waste and functional duplications and thus respecting the principle of subsidiarity. A further peculiarity of the system is, as mentioned above, the supervisory role allocated to the upper tiers of the organizations, which are called on to ensure the economic, equity and financial balance of the individual entities and of the system as a whole (management control), to support the individual members in the assessment of the risk profiles of the transactions (technical-operational support), and to exercise, in the majority of cases, third-tier control (internal auditing activity) over the associates and consortium members.

The particularly critical aspects that emerged during the analysis and realization of a standard-compliant internal control system, which have required from the various companies a considerable effort in terms of economic and non-economic resources, can be comprehensively identified in the qualitative adequacy of the management, in the strictness of the technical controls of the second and third tiers, and in the preparation of special controls on the risks of outsourcing.

With regard to the first tier, the recognition of a prominent role assigned under the regulations to the supervisory activities of the management level stresses management quality and requires the launching of numerous training and staff updating projects, which, by intervening in the management models, have stimulated enhanced decentralization and a broader responsibilization of the resources, supporting cultural development with respect to the theme of the managing of business risks. On the other hand, the limited size of cooperative banks, and their organizational structure characterized by strong centralization, can certainly not be considered functional to the configuration of suitable professional pathways capable of stimulating management growth.

With regard to the second tier, the need to adequately manage the variety of business risks by means of strict risk control models requires considerable financial investments by the cooperative banks to acquire, besides the calculation methodologies and instruments, the know-how necessary to assure processing platforms and suitable safe and functional hardware and software capable of satisfying the current and future management and control requirements.

As for the third tier, a first cross-industry reading of individual case studies developed in the successive parts of this volume shows how the architecture of internal controls was adopted by individual organizational systems in the higher-level companies (rather than in all lower levels), the bodies responsible for exercising internal auditing activities in respect of all the group companies. With the goal of efficiently allocating resources, the cooperative banks prove that they have seized the opportunity offered by the regulations to outsource the third tier of internal control.

The shifting of this control function towards the higher tiers in the structure of cooperative systems has appeared necessary in order to unburden the individual cost structures and to legalize, from a formal point of view, the altogether scarcely incisive role carried out by the internal audit to date, being primarily focused on individual administrative actions and not on the analysis of processes and business procedures. The focus thus placed on the internal audit function should not, however, lead us to believe that this must replace the units responsible for measuring and managing risks (as identified inside individual companies), given that in any case it is an upper-tier control.

Also with regard to the topic of outsourcing, the last noteworthy criticality in the control model implemented by cooperative banks, it should be highlighted how the decisions taken by the cooperative industry in this field are particularly recurrent and oriented to sectoral outsourcing, which is not limited to the individual internal audit function but extends to multiple activities along the value chain until it achieves a 'cosourcing' strategy.[10]

As already anticipated, the theme of internal control in bank outsourcing is currently the subject of debate at the international level. According to the trade organizations and federal structures of the cooperative lending industry, the peculiarity of the sector's outsourcing policies should persuade the regulatory authorities to provide for expedient exceptions to the general principles of internal control laid down in these situations.

From this point of view, various proposals have been advanced with the aim of rendering the control model, currently outlined by international regulation, more suitable for grasping the peculiarities of the business of the various supervised entities, in terms of equal effectiveness in the control action (EACB, 2004b; ESBG, 2004).

More precisely, with the aim of avoiding uselessly burdening corporate business systems, strict controls should be implemented by the outsourcing company, and procedural and contractual control instruments prepared, only in cases in which the outsourcer is chosen from outside the cooperative system (outsourcing to non-consolidated entities in non-consolidating groups) and not in cases of sectoral outsourcing (outsourcing to 'superior' or to subordinated entities), in which the outsourcer is already subject to the controls laid down by the cooperative system itself.

On the whole, the process of adapting cooperative banks to the regulations governing internal control has undoubtedly represented an opportunity for growth and for strengthening the cooperative business model, allowing a stronger link between the various 'meshes' of the system and achieving a more obvious unity of direction, action and control.

Moreover, this process has paved the way for seizing further opportunities of improvement and development offered by the international framework, in respect of controls, identifying itself as the lever for reducing the costs of regulation across the entire industry (Elliehausen, 1998).

Notes

1. See ECB (2004; 2005); McCauley, Ruud and Wooldridge (2002); Borio and Tsatsaronis (1999).
2. See Basel Committee for Banking Supervision (1998; 2001b); IMF (2003a; 2003b); Banque de France (2001).
3. On Basel II on cooperative banks, see the contribution of S. Cosma in this book.
4. On IAS and cooperative banks, see the contribution of M. Cotugno in this book.
5. See Basel Committee on Banking Supervision (1997); Gabbi (1998); Schwizer (2002); Gualandri (2002); Carretta et al. (2003), Carretta and Schwizer (2003).
6. We refer to the Bank Coordination Directive No. 89/646, Framework for Internal Control Systems in Banking Organizations and Operational Risk Management, Basel Committee on Banking Supervision (1998); Basel Committee on Banking Supervision (2001a); Compliance and the compliance function in banks, Basel Committee on Banking Supervision (2005).
7. See, for example, the regulation of internal controls of Italian banks by Banca d'Italia (1998 and 2002) or of Portuguese banks by Banco de Portugal, Circular No.169/B/2002.
8. On corporate governance in the banking sector, see Comitato di Basilea (1999); Basel Committee on Banking Supervision (2006); and the chapter on corporate governance in cooperative banks by P. Schwizer and V. Stefanelli in this book.
9. See Basel Committee on Banking Supervision (2002); Institute of Internal Auditors (2002).
10. See A. Carretta in this book.

References

Banca Centrale Europea (BCE) (2006) Rapporto Annuale 2005, Febbraio (Francoforte).

Banca d'Italia (1998) Sistema dei controlli interni, compiti del Collegio Sindacale, 145 Aggiornamento del 9 Ottobre 1998 alla circolare no. 4 del 29 Marzo.

Banca d'Italia (2002) Bollettino di vigilanza, Ottobre.

Banque de France (2001) Presentation du rapport du FMI sur l'évaluation du respect par la France des principes fondamentaux pour un contrôle bancaire efficace (available at http://www.banque-de-france.fr/fr/supervi/telechar/supervi_banc/principes.pdf).

Basel Committee on Banking Supervision (1998) Framework for Internal Control Systems in Banking Organisations, September (Basel).

Basel Committee on Banking Supervision (2001a) Internal Audit in Banks and the Supervisor's Relationship with Auditors, August (Basel).

Basel Committee on Banking Supervision (2001b) Working Paper on the Regulatory Treatment of Operational Risk, September (Basel).

Basel Committee on Banking Supervision (2002) Internal Audit in Banks and the Supervisor's Relationship with Auditors: A Survey, August (Basel).

Basel Committee on Banking Supervision (2005) Compliance and the compliance function in banks, April.

Basel Committee on Banking Supervision (2006) Enhancing Corporate Governance for Banking Organisations, February (Basel).

Bernardini M. and S. Paterna (1999) 'I controlli interni delle banche nella normativa di vigilanza: sicurezza versus reddito o reddito con sicurezza?', Cooperazione di Credito, no. 164/5.

Bernardini B. and S. Paterna (2000) I controlli interni delle banche nella normativa di vigilanza: sicurezza versus reddito o reddito con sicurezza?, *Rivista del Credito Cooperativo*.

Borio C. and K. Tsatsaronis (1999) Il processo di ristrutturazione nel settore bancario mondiale, Rassegna trimestrale BRI (Agosto).

Carretta A. and P. Schwizer (2003) 'Il sistema dei controlli interni delle banche e degli intermediari finanziari: un'opportunità per lo sviluppo della conoscenza negli operatori e nelle autorità di vigilanza,' 26 convegno AIDEA, Udine 14–15 Novembre.

Carretta A., P. Schwizer and V. Stefanelli (2003) Oltre la regolamentazione: il sistema dei controlli interni degli intermediari finanziari. Cultura del controllo o controllo della cultura?, Ottavo Rapporto Fondazione Rosselli Milano: Edibank).

Comitato di Basilea per la vigilanza bancaria (1999) Rafforzamento del governo societario nelle organizzazioni bancarie, Settembre (Basilea).

Committee of European Banking Supervisors (2006) Guidelines on Outsourcing, December.

Cosma S. and V. Stefanelli (2005) 'Il ruolo della comunicazione interna nella gestione del rischio operativo in banca: aspetti innovativi alla luce di Basilea 2 (con S. Cosma)', atti del Convegno AIDEA Giovani Aspetti innovativi della comunicazione d'impresa: teoria e strumenti, Lecce, 24–5 Novembre.

Dalmaz S. and De Toytot A. (2002) 'Le banche cooperative europee continuano ad evolversi', Cooperazione di credito, no. 176–77, Aprile/Settembre.

Elliehausen G. (1998) 'The Cost of Banking Regulation: A Review of Evidence', Federal Reserve Bulletin, April (available at: http://www.federalreserve.gov/Pubs/staffstudies/1990–99/ss171.pdf).

European Association of Cooperative Banks (EACB) (2004a) Annual Report, March.

EACB (2004b) Consultation Paper 02: High Level Principles on Outsourcing, July (Brussels).

European Central Bank (ECB) (2000) Mergers and Acquisitions Involving the EU Banking Industry. Facts and Implications, December.

European Central Bank (ECB) (2004) Report on EU Banking Structure, November.

ECB (2005) EU Banking Structure, October.

European Savings Banks Groups (ESBG) (2004) Response to CEBS's Consultation Paper on High Level on Principles on Outsourcing, July (Brussels).

Gabbi G. (1998) 'Obiettivi della vigilanza e regolamentazione consensuale nel mercato bancario', in A. Carretta (ed.), Banche e intermediari non bancari: concorrenza e regolamentazione (Roma: Bancaria Editrice).

Gualandri E. (2002) 'Il ruolo della Banca Centrale e degli altri organismi di controllo: amministratori del sistema e attori nel cambiamento culturale delle banche', in A, Carretta (ed.), Il governo del cambiamento culturale in banca (Milano: Bancaria Editrice).

Institute of Internal Auditors (2002) Definition of Internal Auditing.

International Monetary Found (IMF) (2003a) Country Report no. 03/46, February.

IMF (2003b) Country Report no. 03/373, November.

McCauley R., J. Ruud and P. Wooldridge (2002) Globalizzazione dell'attività bancaria internazionale, Rassegna trimestrale BRI, Marzo.

Patalano C. (1995) Modelli organizzativi e di controllo nel sistema bancario (Milano: Edibank).

Schwizer P. (2002) 'L' innovazione technologica nel rapporto fra banca e cliente: implicazioni organizzative, culturali e di controllo', in APB News, no. 1.

Schwizer P. (2005) 'Rapporti fra il collegio sindacale e la funzione di internal auditing nelle banche', in M. Baravelli and A. Viganò (eds), Il collegio sindacale nelle banche (Roma: Bancaria Editrice).

10
The Impacts of IAS–IFRS on Cooperative Banking

M. Cotugno

10.1   Introduction

The aim of Regulation (EC) no. 1606/2002 of the European Parliament on the application of international accounting standards is to harmonize the financial information presented by publicly traded companies, in order to ensure a high degree of transparency and comparability of financial statements (Commission of the European Communities, 2003).

The harmonization process leading to the introduction of these provisions has turned into a long drawn-out story. It began in 1978, with the introduction of the first Community directives on the matter,[1] and continued until a new 'accounting strategy'[2] was finally defined in 1995. The most important episode took place in 1999, when the process of accounting integration in Europe was taken over by the much broader Financial Services Action Plan (FSAP), which provides for a complete framework of 42 coordinated actions at different levels (companies, auditors, government and supervisory authorities), with a view to accelerating the convergence process (Gualandri and Grasso, 2006).[3]

Articles 4 and 5 of Regulation 1606/2002 provide for (a) a two-tiered approach by IAS–IFRS (International Accounting Standard and International Financial Reporting Standard), that is, a minimum level for companies preparing their consolidated accounts and issuing securities admitted to trading on a publicly regulated market (irrespective of whether they are shares or bonds), in accordance with Directive 93/22/EEC of the Council,[4] and (b) a second optional level whereby the individual member states may voluntarily resolve to extend the IAS–IFRS standards to other types of companies (EC Regulation No. 1606/2002).

Therefore, it is interesting to describe how the introduction of IAS–IFRS may affect financial reporting by the European cooperative banking system, currently based on the Fourth Council Directive 78/660/EEC on the annual accounts of certain types of companies, on the Seventh Council Directive 83/349/EEC on consolidated accounts, and on the Council Directive 86/635/EEC on the annual accounts and consolidated accounts of banks and other financial institutions, and, of course, on the dedicated regulations passed by member states and translating the aforementioned directives into national law.

The effects of these changes on the accounting system, in fact, do not concern the administrative sphere alone (Vezzani, 2004). The transition from a historical cost-based to a market-value accounting system requires, first and foremost, a cultural change on the part of management, because decisions taken on credit and security portfolio management may affect short-term performance, thus also clearly affecting the relevant incentivization schemes.[5] Moreover, the new accounting system also affects organizational processes because of the organizational overlapping and synergies in the implementation of IAS-compliant audits; and it affects the internal controls of banks by way of verifying the consistency of forecasts and conjectures, which, in an IAS–IFRS environment inspired by *principles*, are much more frequent than in an accounting system based on *rules*.[6]

10.2 The hierarchy of accounting standards and the changes introduced by IAS–IFRS

The accounting system applied in a country is affected by a practically unlimited number of variables. Many empirical studies have attempted to establish models based on different factors, such as cultural, sociological, and institutional variables.[7] As a general model designed to explain the underlying reasons for the different accounting systems, reference could be made to Zysman's classification of financial systems (Zysman, 1983), with the aim of showing that there a relationship exists between corporate-financing decisions, corporate governance and the accounting system in force in a given country.[8] Financial systems can be of three types: (1) *capital market-based*, in which financial resources are found on the financial markets and the relevant pricing is governed by market rules; (2) *credit-based: governmental*, in which resources are administered by the government, and their allocation and price are determined by the pursuit of specific political objectives; and (3) *credit-based: financial institutions*, in which resources are managed by banks and other financial intermediaries and prices are the result of the interaction between credit demand and credit supply.

The concepts of 'insider' and 'outsider' are well-known in financial literature: insiders are those who have access to the privileged financial information about a company, in their capacity as company directors, banks or other stakeholders in close contact with the management, with low information asymmetry; outsiders, by contrast, are those who are unable to access privileged financial information, such as, for example, minority investors and creditors who have no long-term relations with the company. We can now outline the characteristic features of a financial system and its relations with the accounting system.

Worldwide, most economies belong to either type I or type IV in terms of financing systems (Table 10.1). In particular, type I economies feature an emphasis on credit and are insider-oriented in terms of corporate governance, as exemplified by Germany and Italy, where the preferred system of financing by companies is bank credit, and equity is held mainly by insiders. In contrast, type IV economies are typical of 'Anglo-Saxon' countries – the USA, UK and Australia – where capital markets play a major role, and equity is mostly held by outsiders. Type II systems are rather uncommon (credit-based systems and outsider-oriented corporate governance), while type III economies are exemplified by the Japanese system, with an emphasis on the equity market, but a strong presence of banks in risk capital, which results in a dominant role played by insiders.

The predominant financial systems, therefore, are, (a) the Continental European, with a strong credit market and a predominance of insider ownership, and (b) the Anglo-Saxon systems, in which the equity market plays a major role and where outsider ownership prevails. The former is a strong equity-outsider system with a focus on 'accounting for outside shareholders', while the latter is a weak equity-outsider system, where the focus is on 'accounting for tax and creditors'.

The accounting system shaped by the Community directives, therefore, is creditor-oriented and sets out a hierarchy of accounting standards whose purpose is to produce economic and financial information targeting this group of users. The key principle set out in the directives is that of prudence, observance of which produces historical cost assessments. Furthermore, the systematic application of the principle of prudence

Table 10.1 Financing system

	Strong credit	**Strong equity**
Insiders dominant	I	III
Outsiders dominant	II	IV

results in the asymmetrical treatment of latent costs and revenues, fostering the creation of hidden reserves. The final information disclosed by the financial statements concerns the company's 'distributable revenue' and the assets that can be 'seized' by creditors (Figure 10.1).

The approach adopted by the International Accounting Standard Board (IASB), by contrast, is typical of countries featuring a strong equity-outsider system, in which the focus of financial reporting is the investor. This *decision-usefulness theoretical approach* requires information to be produced by the company for economic-decision makers. The financial statements may be used by a large number of stakeholders: investors, employees, financers, suppliers, customers, government, and so on; however, it is not always possible to meet the information needs of all the stakeholders simultaneously. The Board makes a specific decision, laid down in the IAS–IFRS framework: 'since investors are the suppliers of risk capital for the company, satisfying their information requirements by means of financial statements will simultaneously satisfy most of other users' interests' (IASB, 2001).

To decide that the investor is the preferential focus of financial reporting means to decide that the accrual method is the key accounting standard, and to use market values, if possible, to remove the asymmetry of treatment between latent costs and revenues in order to provide a measure of the company's actual financial performance in terms of 'produced income' and 'economic value of the company'. This approach, of course, is not devoid of defects; above all, it produces highly volatile corporate results. The information disclosed in the notes to the accounts is of crucial importance for investors because it enables them to understand the real causes of this volatility.

Although the accounting systems shaped by the Community directives are of the historical-cost accounting type, we cannot maintain

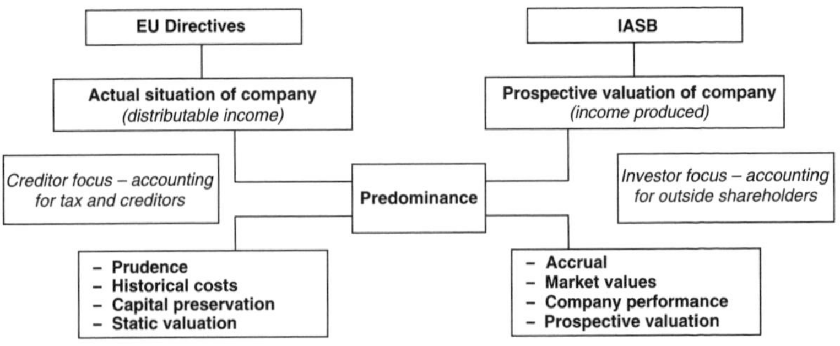

Figure 10.1   Balance sheet: The different aims.

that the IAS–IFRS standards are a full fair-value system. Such a system, in fact, requires the measurement of the fair value of all assets and liabilities, which IAS–IFRS – which can be defined as a mixed accounting system – fails to provide. The presence of market values, if available, and of fair values is in fact unquestionably is more preponderant than in the past, although the historical-cost principle still predominates in the case of capital assets, for example (International Accounting Standard 16, Property, plant and equipment), or of receivables, which are measured according to the amortized cost method.

To a greater extent, the introduction of IAS–IFRS has led to substantial changes in the accounting standards and the level of financial disclosure by European banks, based on how the Community directives have been translated into national law. As for the ten newly admitted EU member countries, the issue is entirely different, because their situations differ considerably and their distance from the IAS–IFRS standards varies accordingly.

The changes to the accounting standards affect cooperative banks more significantly than commercial banks. Financial reporting, in fact, plays a strategic role for cooperative banks, given that member-shareholders and customers coincide. The assumption whereby increased visibility on the financial markets reflects positively on a bank's core business is grounded in the academic literature. Financial intermediaries that have built a reputation for reliability, professional competence, a focus on goals and good investor relations will also receive positive feedback with respect to their characteristic business.[9] IAS–IFRS-based financial reporting, focusing on investors rather than creditors, in cooperative banking will also benefit the customer, provided that it is suitably supplemented by the disclosure of ethical and social information, which is increasingly requested by all cooperative stakeholders.

10.3   The principal effects of IAS 39 on banks

The IAS–IFRS accounting standards most strongly affecting cooperative banks are IAS 39 (International Accounting Standard 32, Financial Instruments: Disclosure and Presentation), IAS 32 (International Accounting Standard 39, Financial Instruments: Recognition and Measurement) and IFRS 7 (International Financial Reporting Standard 7, Financial Instruments: Disclosures). These three standards address 'financial instruments' in general, albeit from an entirely different perspective: IAS 32, in particular, lays down a classification of financial instruments and outlines other supplementary information, IAS 39 illustrates the valuation methods associated with each financial instrument, and IFRS 7 integrates IAS 32 with respect to the complementary information to be provided in the notes to the accounts.

Unlike the technical approach to how items in financial statements should be presented, as set out in the Seventh EEC Directive, the IAS–IFRS standards tend to focus on management decisions. Only an assessment based on the future intentions of the management give effect to the definition of a company's 'capacity to produce monetary or equivalent means'.[10]

10.3.1   Exposure and the assessment of financial assets and liabilities

The conventional division of a bank's financial assets into banking book and trading book is significantly transformed into five different types of portfolio, based on the contents of the latest version of IAS 39,[11] with obvious effects in terms of reporting and organizational complexity, risk management, and credit and security intermediation. In particular, IAS 39 provides for the portfolios as follows.

1. *Held for trading* (HFT). A financial asset is defined as being 'held for trading' when it is purchased or produced primarily with a view to generating a profit from short-term fluctuations. Assets held for trading include payables and shares, as well as receivables and payables originated by an entity with a view to making a profit from short-term price variations or a return as dealer. Derivatives are always classified as 'held for trading', unless they are used for *hedge accounting*[12] purposes. These items are always assessed at fair value, and any variations are recorded in the income statement.

2. *Financial assets designated as fair value through profit or loss* (FVTPL). From a conceptual point of view FVTPL overlaps with the HFT portfolio in that they both use the same method of measurement; the only difference is that this portfolio includes financial assets that are not ordinarily held for trading, but which the intermediary nevertheless intends to measure at fair value. This is the contested fair value option reconsidered in the current version of IAS 39. In particular, it establishes that a security that is a financial asset can be designated at fair value only in the following cases:

    (a) where the designation as FVTPL eliminates or significantly reduces a measurement or recognition inconsistency that would otherwise arise from measuring assets or liabilities; and

(b) where the asset belongs to a group of financial assets or financial liabilities, or both, that are managed, and their performance is evaluated by management, on a fair value basis in accordance with a documented risk management or investment strategy.

Therefore, the fair value option measurement is limited to a higher quality of information[13] given that two or more asset and liability items with a common management and measurement asymmetry would lead to distortions in financial statements. Consequently, it becomes impossible to designate any items at fair value, definitively abandoning the market value accounting of IAS–IFRS-based financial statements.

3. *Held-to-maturity investments* (HTM). This category is for fixed maturity financial securities with fixed or determinable payments that the company has the positive intention and ability to hold to maturity. The exceptions are loans and receivables originated by the company. The amortized cost method and impairment test is used to measure this item.

4. *Loans and receivables* (LR). Loans and receivables are financial assets originated by the company in connection with the lending of money to an entity that qualifies itself as a debtor. This category does not include any receivables originated with a view to selling them immediately or in the short term. The key defining factor here is the origin, which entails that, if the bank purchases a receivable rather than originating it directly, it must use another category. The amortized cost method and impairment test are used to measure this item.

5. *Available for sale financial assets* (AFS). These assets are the financial assets not included in any other above categories, and can thus be seen as a residual category. The valuation method used here is the fair value method, albeit in a peculiar manner: the item is recognized in financial statements at historical cost value; fair value variations are not recorded in the income statement but in a special fair value reserve among the net equity items. Only after the financial asset has been sold will it be possible to discount the reserve and record the profit or loss made in the income statement.

Financial liabilities can be classified in three portfolio categories: *held for trading* measured with the fair value method, *financial liabilities designated as fair value through profit or loss* measured according to the related fair value method, and a residual category measured with the amortized cost method (Table 10.2). Of crucial importance is compliance with certain criteria for classifying an item among the financial liabilities or the equity, as shown in § 4.

Table 10.2   The classification of financial assets and financial liabilities

Category	Type	Indicators	Valuation	Accounting treatment	Examples
	Held for trading (HFT)	Directors' resolutions, historic corporate performance, securities with secondary market	Fair value	Gains/losses in the Income Statement (I.S.) in the year they become due	Shares, bonds, Treasury bonds, units of funds, etc.
	Available for sales (AFS)	Directors' resolutions, historic corporate performance, securities with secondary market	Fair value	Gains/losses in the I.S. in the year they become due	
				Gains/losses in the Shareholders Equity (S.E.) in the year they become due and in I.S. following derecognition of the asset or impairment test	Shares, bonds, Treasury bonds, units of funds, structured products, etc.
Financial activities	Loans and receivables (LS) originated for trading purpose	Directors' resolutions, historic corporate performance, nature of transaction	Fair value	Gains/losses in the I.S. in the year they become due	Loans receivable
	Loans and receivables (LS)	Directors' resolutions, historic corporate performance, nature of transaction	Amortized cost and impairment test	Gains/losses in the I.S. in the year they become due	Loans receivable

	Held to maturity (HTM)	Directors' resolutions, historic corporate performance, securities with a less liquid secondary market, higher value if security is maintained until expiry	Amortized cost and impairment test	Gains/losses in I.S. following derecognition of the asset at impairment test or amortization	Bonds, Treasury bonds, capitalized-return insurance policies, deposits, structured products
Financial liabilities	Held for trading (HFT)	Directors' resolutions, historic corporate performance, nature of transaction	Fair value	Gains/losses in I.S. following derecognition of the asset at impairment test or amortization	Uncovered sales
	Others financial liabilites	Directors' resolutions, historic corporate performance, nature of transaction	Amortized cost and impairment test	Gains/losses in the I.S. in the year they become due	Loans payable in general
Derivatives	Held for Trading (HFT)	Directors' resolutions, historic corporate performance, hedge effectiveness test, application of hedging objectives and strategies	Fair value	Gains/losses in I.S. in they year they become due, together with the underlying asset (fair value hedge) Gains/losses in S.E. in they year they become due and in the I.S. on derecognition of the following, even in advance compared with the derivative (cash flow hedge) Gains/losses in S.E. in they year they become due and in the I.S. on derecognition of the following, even in advance compared to the derivative (net investment hedge in a foreign entity)	

Source: Author's processing based on Vitali and Vinzia (2004).

10.3.2   The Hedge accounting methodology

Another important innovation introduced by the IAS–IFRS standards concerns hedging management. In particular, as regards banking, hedge accounting generates management difficulties because it is necessary to verify punctually the actual effectiveness of the derivative, and the management of net items becomes more difficult (macro hedge methodology). In the case of cooperative banks, the method in question features a further criticality because the effectiveness of the hedge is subject – at consolidated level – to the requirement of impartiality, that is to say, the contracting parties must be unrelated and must not have an interest in each other, including a controlling interest, in order to be able to use the derivative also at the level of consolidated financial reporting. An overview of how IAS–IFRS applies to this issue follows.

Derivative instruments are valued and measured exclusively at fair value and recorded above the line in the balance sheet (IAS 39, § 69, 2004). They may be for the purpose of trading or hedging. In the latter case, in given conditions the hedge accounting rules can be applied to offset the gains or losses made by the hedged item with the gains or losses made with the hedging derivative. Therefore, the hedging takes place at the fair value of the hedged item, so that there is an offset with the fair value of the derivative.

Under IAS 39 there are two hedging possibilities:[14]

- *Fair value hedge*, that is, a hedge of exposure to changes in the fair value of fixed rate debt, as a result of changes in interest rates. The fair value variation of the derivative and of the hedged financial instrument is included directly in net profit or loss; therefore, the effectiveness of the hedging operation is immediately visible.
- *Cash flow hedge*, that is, a hedge of a forecast asset and liability acquisition, and therefore not necessarily from a financial asset or liability obviously subject to potential rate variations. To a certain extent, the accounting method is based on that used for *available for sale* assets. In particular, the fair value variations of the derivative are recognized to an equity reserve and are subsequently included in net profit or loss only after the derivative's sale; in contrast, the fair value variation of hedged cash flows is included directly in net profit and loss. Under to this method, hedging is carried out by instalments, based on hedged cash flows (Maspero, 2005).

The possibility of designating a derivative for hedging is subject to effectiveness testing. In short, the ratio between profit and loss of the hedged and hedging asset must be between 0.8 and 1.23. Outside this range the hedging is deemed to be ineffective, and therefore it is no longer possible to exercise the hedge accounting option (IAS 39, § 142, 2004).

IAS 39 enables the application of hedge accounting at consolidated level only if it is entered into with third parties, which makes the hedge accounting rules practically inapplicable to internal deals. This might represent a criticality for cooperative banks in the form of integrated networks (e.g. Rabobank, Crédit Mutuel and Crédito Agrícola Mútuo) because the derivative hedging contracts entered into by a local coop-erative bank and the central federation cannot be accepted for hedg-ing purposes at consolidated level. The result is that hedging in the individual financial statements of a single local bank is effective and produces its effects for financial reporting purposes; but it loses its effec-tiveness at consolidation, being classed as an internal deal that cannot be accepted for financial reporting purposes, with obvious effects on the volatility of the consolidated statement results and of the regulatory capital requirements.

10.3.3   IAS-IFRS and their effects on regulatory capital

The application of IAS–IFRS affects regulatory capital measurement, both due to the different calculation of eligibles provisioning and with respect to the creation of new items flowing into the reserves, based on the new accounting standards.

With reference to the calculation of eligibles provisioning, it is well known that measuring the optimal provision is the task of the account-ing body, but its definition has precise effects with respect to regulatory capital. The June 2004 version of the Basel Agreement, in fact, clari-fied how the regulatory capital to be held must be used exclusively to cover unexpected losses. In contrast, expected losses must be covered by ad hoc provisions. When the amount of expected losses exceeds the provisions, the difference must be taken from the regulatory capital in the measure of 50 per cent from Tier 1 and 50 per cent from Tier 2 (*shortfall*). However, when the provisions exceed the expected losses[15] the bank can use the excess amount to increase Tier 2 up to no more than 0.6 per cent of the weighted assets for the risk (*overprovisioning*).[16] From this perspective the role played by provisioning accounting is fundamental, because the capital requirement depends on both the risks being incurred and the provisions allocated to cover the expected losses, which arise directly from the valuation rationale imposed by the accounting standards.

In order to implement the amortized cost method with respect to the credit valuation, it is necessary to create a dataset to build the loss data over a long-term timeframe and to implement a uniform portfolio depreciation system based on the credit risk, data that are not always possessed by a small bank, as a cooperative credit bank might be.

Having regard to the creation of new items flowing in to reserve, the transition to IAS–IFRS raises various issues that have recently been the objects of regulation, with respect to:

- the treatment of fair value reserves measured in connection with cash flow hedges;
- the treatment of reserves generated in connection with the valuation of assets available for sale; and
- the distinction between equity instruments and debt instruments under IAS 32.

According to the Community directives, the net equity of a bank, like that of a company, can change as a result of management following the creation of an operating profit, which, at December 31, is recorded as a portion of the net equity and, at the first shareholders' meeting, is generally partly allocated to the reserves and partly distributed among the shareholders. Operating losses to may be viewed as movements of the net equity generated by management events. All other net equity movements are the result of extraordinary events, such as the increase or decrease of the share capital or of mandatory events imposed by the law in connection with losses exceeding a certain threshold.

In contrast, under the IAS–IFRS standards certain net equity items may be created not as a result of extraordinary events, but in connection with ordinary company operations. In particular, assets available for sale, which, at 31/12, feature a fair value in excess of the value recorded in the financial statements, will generate a valuation item in the net equity that will be subject to movement on an annual basis and which will recognized in the income statement only when the assets are sold. The same accounting method is used for cash-flow hedge techniques: the variations of the derivative's fair value are charged to a special net equity reserve that will be extinguished once the operation has been completed.

The admissibility of these reserves for regulatory purposes is doubtful: both the Bank of International Settlement (BIS) and the Committee of European Banking Supervision (CEBS) have intervened on the matter through the introduction of 'prudential filters' aimed at restoring to the regulatory capital its original stable risk-covering function.[17] The Committee, with reference to the 'available for sale' instruments, has provided the prudential filters on the following lines:

(1) in the case of 'equity' investments, any unrealized losses shall be deducted, after taxes, from Tier 1;
(2) any profits from equity investments may be recognized for the purpose of establishing Tier 2, for up to 45 per cent thereof; and
(3) the national authorities are free to regulate any loans and receivables designated in the available for sale category, according to the treatments provided for in paragraphs (1) and (2).

Having regard to the distinction between equity and liabilities, the CEBS encourages the national authorities to maintain the current distinction between equity and debt instruments for supervisory purposes. The CEBS also encourages the maintenance for supervisory purposes of the pre-IAS notion of trading book, with a view to defining the portfolio subject to market risks.

10.4   Share cooperatives under IAS 32

As highlighted above, the IAS–IFRS may have a more or less significant bearing on financial reporting, based on the approach of the previous accounting system. As regards cooperative entities in general and cooperative banks in particular, one of the greatest concerns arose in the wake of the approval of IAS 32 (2003 version). In particular, a literal interpretation of the principles it contains would require the classifying of the shares subscribed to by members not in the equity section of liabilities but among the company's liabilities, with obvious negative effects in terms of external reputation, ratings, funding costs and the regulatory capital to be held, both with respect to the 1988 Basel Agreement still in force and, above all, with respect to the more stringent rules introduced by the Basel 2 Agreement.[18]

The issue concerns the rules imposed by IAS 32 for separating that which can be defined as equity and that which can be defined as liability. IAS 32[19] (IAS 32, § 11 and Application Guidance (AG) 3–24, 2004), in fact, defines a financial liability as 'a contractual obligation' or 'a contract that will or may be settled in the entity's own equity instruments'. With reference to 'contractual obligations', IAS 32 stipulates that these can consist of either (a) the delivery of cash or another financial asset to another entity, or (b) an exchange of financial assets or financial liabilities with another entity under conditions that are potentially unfavourable to the entity (IAS 32, § 11, 2004). In IAS 32, an equity instrument is defined not directly but residually, as 'any contract that evidences a residual interest in the assets of an entity after deducting all of its liabilities'.

The rules for separating equity and debt instruments become more stringent in the following part of (Porzio, Squeo, 2005). Without prejudice to the obligation above all to investigate the substance of the instrument rather than its legal form, IAS 32 sets out two guidelines for differentiating financial liabilities from equity instruments, as follows:

> [A] critical feature in differentiating a financial liability from an equity instrument is the existence of a contractual obligation of one party to the financial instrument (the issuer) either to deliver cash or another financial asset to the other party (the holder) or to exchange financial assets or financial liabilities with the holder under conditions that are potentially unfavourable to the issuer.
>
> (IAS 32, § 17, 2004)

> [I]f an entity does not have an unconditional right to avoid delivering cash or another financial asset to settle a contractual obligation, the obligation meets the definition of a financial liability.
>
> (IAS 32, § 19, 2004)

Based on the definitions set out in IAS 32, it follows that if a financial instrument issued by an entity is redeemable – that is, it may be redeemed at the request of the beneficiaries – it must be classified as liability, not as an equity instrument. This interpretation would entail for most European cooperative banks the reclassification of members' shares among the debt instruments, an exponential increase in leverage, and obvious effects in terms of funding costs. There are innumerable examples at the European level: the Finnish Co-operative Act of 1901 allows the redemption of the shares subscribed to by a member who no longer wishes to use a cooperative's services; the Italian Civil Code contains a similar provision, although it allows the cooperative's governing charter to establish provisions relating to the assignment of shares; the general law on cooperatives in France allows members to request the redemption of their shares when they have made no use of the cooperative's services for a period of five years. In the case of Bulgaria, a country about to enter the EU (2007), although legislation on the matter is rather lacking, article 2 of the Cooperatives Act stipulates that a cooperative is 'a voluntary association of natural persons with variable capital and a variable number of members engaging in commercial activity along the lines of mutual assistance'.

The cooperative sector's reaction to the introduction of IAS 32 was rather harsh. In particular, the European Association of Co-operative Banks in October 2003 drafted a document clearly opposing the 2003 version of IAS 32 and claiming that most cooperative banks in Europe would have been deprived of their own capital under IAS 32 (European Association of Co-operative Banks, 2004). The arguments used were mostly based on the concept of the variability of a cooperative bank's capital and the link existing with the turnover. In fact,

> [I]n co-operatives, the variability of capital represents the logical extension of the dual nature of being both user and shareholder-member. The capital subscribed by a shareholder member is closely correlated with his/her status as user. This means that the volume of capital is proportional to the co-operative's activity; hence the need for equity in one sense as much as in the other.[20]

There was a great deal of opposition from non-banking cooperative entities, too, which sent the Board many letters protesting against such an interpretation of IAS 32.

The strong opposition from the cooperative sector persuaded the IASB to reconsider its policy, but through the International Financial Reporting Interpretations Committee (IFRIC) rather than by amending IAS 32. In January 2005, in fact, the IASB published IFRIC 2 'Members Shares in Co-operative Entities and Similar Instruments', which contains some important provisions relating to cooperative shares. In detail, and with a view to determining whether a financial instrument belongs to the equity or the liability component, IFRIC 2 lays down that cooperative shares may be considered equity if either of the following conditions applies:

(1) if the entity has an unconditional right to refuse redemption of the members' shares;
(2) if redemption is unconditionally prohibited by local law, regulation or the entity's governing charter, members' shares are equity. However, provisions in local law, regulation or the entity's governing charter that prohibit redemption only if conditions – such as liquidity constraints – are met (or are not met) do not result in members' shares being equity.[21]

Thus, cooperative shares may be classified as equity components if the cooperative bank has a right to unconditionally refuse redemption of the shares or if redemption is prohibited by local law, regulation or the entity's governing charter. If the limitation on redemption is exclusively subordinate to a condition precedent (such as, for example, the achievement of a certain percentage of liquidity) imposed by local law or by the entity's governing charter, then cooperative shares should be classified as liabilities, unless the cooperative enjoys an unconditional right to refusal.

The approval of IFRIC 2, however, has only partially solved the problem of cooperative shares: although the introduction of a provision in the entity's governing charter will allow them to be classified as equity components, this goes against one of the key principles of European cooperative banks, that is, capital variability. This condition could partially impair the cooperative banking market because share redemption will no longer be automatic – in the case of systems in which it is provided for – but will be subject to the entity's consent, which, for obvious reasons, will provide in its charter the possibility of unconditionally refusing the redemption, under the penalty of classifying the member shares as debt components.

10.5   Conclusions

The management complexity arising from the application of IAS–IFRS, especially for the smaller banks, requires, and will continue to require, a great deal of financial resources in terms of adapting information systems, re-engineering processes and general reorganization. Such high compliance costs will not be justified, at least in the short term, by any significant advantages in terms of financial reporting. Despite this, cooperative banks will benefit from an unquestionable twofold advantage over commercial banks:

- the fact that customers and member-shareholders coincide, with the possibility of positive effects on the core business, as a result of more efficient financial reporting; and
- the benefit of economies of scope and of range in case where networked banks define a common project providing for the pooling of specialized and dedicated resources.

The introduction of the IAS–IFRS standards entails the loss of one of the cornerstones of cooperative banking, that is, capital variability (only in a reductive capacity). The introduction of IFRIC 2 has avoided the risk of member shares having to be classified as debt components, at least in part; cooperative entities must now introduce provisions in their charters relating to 'the unconditional right to refuse redemption of a member's shares', under penalty of member shares being classified as debt components.

Notes

1. The Fourth Council Directive 78/660/EEC of 25 July 1978 and the Seventh Council Directive 83/349/EEC of 13 June 1983.
2. Communication No. 508 from the European Commission of 14 November 1995, 'Accounting Harmonisation: A New Strategy *vis-à-vis* International Harmonisation'.
3. A total of 39 provisions had been issued by 2008. Several important fields of financial intermediation have not yet been covered, first and foremost the approval of the Capital Adequacy Directive, CAD 3, relating to the introduction of the Basel 2 Agreement. See Gualandri and Grasso (2006).
4. The EU Commission itself has clarified that the word 'company', as used in Articles 4 and 5, should be construed in accordance with Article 48 of the Treaty of Rome, as follows:
   Article 48(2): 'Companies or firms' means companies or firms constituted under civil or commercial law, including cooperative societies, and other legal persons governed by public or private law, save for those which are non-profit making.'
5. For a broad-ranging review of the issue of culture in banking, see Carretta (2002).
6. On the organizational aspects of cooperative credit banks, see Chapter 3. To further investigate internal control-related issues, see Chapter 9.
7. To mention but a few, see Gray (1988); Hamid, Craig and Clarke (1993); Doupnik and Salter (1995).
8. The approach followed here is based on C. Nobes (1998).
9. See Munari (2003).
10. See IASB (2001).
11. In actual fact, § 45 of IAS 39 classifies financial assets into four portfolios, not including the FVTPL portfolio. IAS 32 §§ 60a and 94e require exposure for a further category for financial assets or liabilities that have made use of the fair value option.
12. See IASB (2004b), IAS 39 § 9.
13. For example, lacking the designation of fair value recognized in the income statement, a financial asset is classified as available for sale (with most fair value variations recognized directly in equity), while a liability that the entity considers to be related is, in contrast, valued according to the amortized cost method (with the unrecognized fair value variations). See OJEC (EC) Regulations No. 1864/2005.
14. In this section we do not consider the hedging of net investments in a foreign operation, as regulated by IAS 21.
15. However, this inclusion must first be authorized by the supervisory authority, which will be required to assess whether the Expected Losses (EL) fully

reflect the market conditions in which the bank operates. Basel Committee on Banking Supervision (2004), § 385.

16. See Basel Committee on Banking Supervision (2004), § 43. This applies in the event that the bank decides to adopt the IRB method. If the bank decides to apply the standardized approach, instead of the internal rating approach, in respect of certain types of exposure, it will be necessary to determine the proportion of general appropriations to be allocated to the two sections of the credit portfolio. Removing the portion of EL not covered by appropriations from the regulatory capital means increasing the equity requirements.

17. See CEBS (2004); Basel Committee on Banking Supervision, 2004.

18. With regard to the classification rules of equity instruments and liability instruments for supervisory purposes, reference should be made to the regulations recommended by the CEBS and by the BIS, as mentioned above. See CEBS (2004); BIS (2004).

19. In this chapter paper reference is made to the latest available version of IAS 32 at the time of writing, introduced by Reg. No. 2237/2004, as amended by Reg. Nos. 2086/2004, 2236/2004, 211/2005, 1864/2005 and 108/2006 published in the Official Journal of the European Community (OJEC).

20. See EACB (2003).

21. See IASB, 2005, no. 8 (2004).

References

Basel Committee on Banking Supervision (2004), *Capital Treatment of Certain Items Under IFRS*.

Carretta A. (ed.) (2002), *Il governo del cambiamento culturale in banca. Modelli di analisi, strumenti operativi, valori individuali*. Bancaria Editrice, Rome.

CEBS (Committee of European Banking Supervision) (2004), *Guideline on Prudential Filters for Regulatory Capital*, December.

Doupnik T. S. and S. B. Salter, 1995, 'External Environment, Culture, and Accounting Practice: A Preliminary Test of a General Model of International Accounting Development', *International Journal of Accounting*, vol. 3.

ECB (European Central Bank). (2003), The integration of Europe's financial markets, Monthly Bulletin, October.

European Association of Co-operative Banks (2004b), IAS 32 and Co-operative Shares: IASB Publishes, December.

European Association of Co-operative Banks (2003), What are Shares in the Capital of a Co-operative, October.

Gray S. J. (1988), 'Towards a Theory of Cultural Influence on the Development of Accounting Systems Internationally', *Abacus*, March.

Gualandri E. and Grasso A. G. (2006), 'Towards a New Approach to Regulation and Supervision in the EU: Post-FSAP and Comitology', *Revue Bancaire et Rinancière*, Forum Financier, no. 3.

Hamid S. R., Craig R. and Clarke F. L. (1993), 'Religion: A Confounding Cultural Element in the International Harmonization of Accounting?', *Abacus*, September.

IASB (International Accounting Standard Board) (2001), Framework for the Preparation and Presentation of Financial Statements.

IASB (2004a), IAS 32 – Financial Instruments: Disclosure and Presentation.
International Accounting Standard Board (2004b), IAS 39 – Financial Instruments: Recognition and Measurement.
IASB (2005), IFRIC 2 – Members Shares in Co-operative Entities and Similar Instruments.
Maspero D. (2005), 'L'impatto degli IAS-IFRS sull'attività in derivati delle banche', in Mazzeo R., Palombini E. and Zorzoli S. (eds), *IAS–IFRS e imprese bancarie*, Edibank, Milano.
Munari L. (ed.) (2003), *Schemi e logiche di implementazione del marketing strategico nel corporate e nel retail banking: il Customer Relationship Management*, Newfin Ricerche, Università Bocconi, Milano.
Nobes C. (1998), 'Towards a General Model of the Reasons for International Differences in Financial Reporting', *Abacus*, vol. 34, no. 2.
Porzio C. and Squeo G. (2005), 'IAS 32 e riforma societaria: come classificare gli strumenti finanziari', in Mazzeo R., Palombini, E. and Zorzoli, S. (eds), *IAS-IFRS e imprese bancarie*, Edibank, Milano.
Vezzani P. (2004), 'Implicazioni gestionali derivanti dall'introduzione degli Ias nelle banche italiane', *Cooperazione di Credito*, vol. 186.
Vitali F. R. and Vinzia M. A. (2004), 'Fair Value. Rappresentazione contabile e valutazioni finanziarie secondo gli' IAS', *Il Sole 24 Ore*, Milano.
Zysman J. (1983), *Government, Markets and Growth: Financial Systems and the Politics of Industrial Change*, Cornell University Press, New York.

11
Concluding Remarks

V. Boscia, A. Carretta and P. Schwizer

Since the late 1980s international events, such as globalization, innovation, deregulation, disintermediation, consolidation, and the new emphasis on shareholder value have deeply modified financial and banking markets. Other events have affected European banking markets in particular, such as the completion of the EU single market programme and its extension to eastern European countries, and the creation of the euro area. These events have rapidly brought about dramatic changes in the level of competition, influencing the quality and the price of financial services and banks' performance by squeezing profitability. In response to these changes, banks have initiated a deep restructuring and reorganization process at all levels, strategic, operational, and organizational. Yet, even in this increasingly competitive environment, cooperative banks remain successful and healthy, and are gaining market share at the expense of their competitors.

The main aim of this book has been to assess the reasons for the success of cooperative banking. It has investigated the 'modernity' of the traditional features of cooperative banking and the evolution and the invention of specific features of cooperative banking. Thus, this book represents a comprehensive analysis on cooperative banking, starting from the traditional concepts of cooperation and proceeding to a detailed analysis of the main innovations and developments.

Broadly, this book is divided into two parts. Part One begins by describing the current role and rationale of cooperation in the economy and in the banking industry, and deals with certain specific feature like governance, consolidation, outsourcing, shareholder value and rating evaluation. The literature on the economic role and rationale of cooperative banks is quite substantial, and overall it confirms its fundamental importance of cooperative banking even in the new environment and its fundamental role in the developing of the economy, especially in providing monetary services and lending to lower-quality customers (Chapter 2). In a competitive environment where dimension, efficiency, safety and soundness, and shareholder value are vital characteristics of banks, the central role of cooperation in the banking industry emerges. Specific features like mutuality, democracy, solidarity, and localism are useful for managing the traditional weaknesses of financial inter-mediation (such as adverse selection, information asymmetries, and monitoring costs). Cooperative banks are important for industrialized countries, not only by supporting and integrating the offer of financial services in order to promote economic development, but also by ensur-ing the stability of the financial system through their strong perfor-mance in terms of capitalization, profitability and soundness. Particularly for less developed transitional or emerging economies, cooperative banks play a crucial role by financing a large segment of the marginal population. Among the key features of cooperative banks, corporate governance is subjected to a special analysis since it is considered crucial to ensuring the healthy and conservative management of banks in the new environment (Chapter 3). The analysis produces several interest-ing results from both individual bank and system perspectives. In particular, from an individual cooperative bank perspective, agency problems may arise from the high degree of fragmentation of share-holders and the consequent inertial management, without an ade-quate control mechanism. Other problems may arise from the so-called captured decisions, as when decisions are taken on the basis of the interests of specific categories of economic actors in the cooperative banks – administrator-member, employee-member, customer-member, financial-member – without consideration of the global interest. Moreover, an increase in the number or in the territorial composition of share-holders may weaken traditional peer monitoring. At the system level, the analysis finds that the presence of a central organism, with strate-gic and organizational support functions and with a hierarchical con-trol function, may decrease possible conflicts between management and members.

Furthermore, cooperative banks have adopted two strategies in order to deal with the higher level of competition in the new environment. In particular, the causes and effects of consolidation are analysed in order to assess whether it could be considered a strategic choice com-patible with the traditional characteristics and competitive advantages of cooperative banks (Chapter 4). The analysis gives an account of the reorganization of the cooperative banking sector in Europe and points out the possible advantages and disadvantages of concentration, in light of the distinctive characters of the cooperative model. Moreover, it considers legislative modifications at the European level. The result of the analysis is quite clear: consolidation does not seem to provide significant advantages, since it may compromise the advantages of cooperative banks in terms of autonomy and proximity to their customers. Instead, benefits flow from other forms of concentration: formal or informal networks, centralised systems of operational and advisory services, or banking groups which leave cooperative banks as autonomous entities, providing them with genuine advantages that allow them to overcome their disadvantages in terms of limited dimension, operativity, geography and culture. The other strategy quite widely adopted by cooperative banks is outsourcing (Chapter 5). It emerges that outsourcing is a strategic choice consistent with present trends in banking industry experienced by cooperative banks to overcome their disadvantages in terms of limited dimension, operativity, geography, and culture. But outsourcing is a suitable strategy also to develop new businesses. But the recourse to outsourcing strategies should be adequately organized, managed and controlled like any internal activity, process or procedure. Moreover, in the case of cooperative banks, it could also be interpreted with the neologism 'co-sourcing', in the sense that it should provide, and not just externalize, resources and culture. For this purpose, cooperative banking may adopt a special form of outsourcing, namely, 'outsourcing by category', which can strengthen rather than disperse the distinctive expertise and culture of cooperative banks.

Performance evaluation is examined with two kinds of methodology. The first examines the shareholder value and the cost efficiency of cooperative banks, focusing on a large sample from four European countries, distinguishing cooperative banks from other institutional forms (Chapter 6). The results of this theoretical methodology show certain trends, even if not definitively. With regard to profitability and shareholder value created, mean levels of Economic Value Added (EVA) show that these are usually negative in every year and for all bank categories with a few exceptions, such as commercial banks. This may be justified by commercial banks' goal of profit maximization, which distinguishes them from cooperative banks. With regard to cost efficiency levels, which is an endogenous channel for creating shareholder value, results show that cooperative banks achieve higher mean levels of cost X-efficiency than do savings banks and commercial banks. Cooperative bank performance is also analysed with the methodology applied by rating agencies to cooperative banks (Chapter 7). The results show that rating agencies consider cooperative banks more risky in terms of information disclosure, but that they perform better in terms of stability of profits and riskiness of assets, and consequently in terms of their capitalization. Thus, the traditional distinctive features of cooperation influence their evaluation. Moreover, it is found that issuers' risk profiles are improved where there is a legally binding support mechanism among cooperative banks. Overall, the results show that rating agencies are more rigorous in evaluating cooperative banks than the market. Indeed, there is a mismatch between their ratings and the spreads paid by the market in issuing operations.

Part Two of the book examines the contents of certain provisions issued and implemented at the European level in order analyse the likely impact on the strategic, organizational and operational model of cooperative banks. Certainly, the new capital requirements introduced by the Accord named Basel 2 represent a challenge for banking systems as a whole and certainly for cooperative banking. Chapter 8 provides an analysis of the possible effects of the implementation of the New Capital Accord and of EU Directives 2006/48/EC and 2006/49/EC on cooperative banking. The analysis proceeds by comparing the viewpoints expressed by bank associations and the evidence provided by certain theoretical and empirical analyses. This makes it possible to infer the expected effects of the Accord on cooperative banking in relation to legal or institutional structure and the typical size of the sector. Overall, the Basel 2 Accord seems to penalize groups featuring a decentralized network structure. The medium-to-small size of cooperative banks, of groups operating at an international level, and in particular of decentralized local banks, makes it possible to extend to cooperative banking the considerations expressed in the literature about the effects of regulatory reform on the traditional equilibrium between larger and smaller banks, given that smaller banks will likely adopt the standardised approach to credit risks. The EC directive concerning capital requirements seems to lessen the impact of Basel 2 on the cooperative banking system if certain specific features of the sector are duly taken into account; but it does not solve all the problems connected with fair conditions of competition between institutions characterised by different legal or institutional structures. Also, the analysis of the supervisory provisions of internal controls yields interesting results for cooperative banking (Chapter 9). It emerges that cooperative banks have made many efforts to complete the transition to the international standards, at both individual and network levels. At the individual level, the implementation process has represented an occasion fore the banks to assess the adequacy of their organizational structure and to plan suitable changes which could lead to a culture of control in the work methods. Cooperative banks often outsource internal control to specialised entities that belong to cooperative networks. The cooperative system has experienced some improvements even at the network level, since the soundness of each cooperative bank or of each component of a cooperative group reinforces the entire cooperative system. Thus, central organisms have imposed new forms of internal control on their members. Moreover, in this case this is even legally recognized, for example when each bank takes part in networks, as it is in guarantee schemes.

The analysis of regulations deals with the introduction of the new IAS–IFRS accounting system in cooperative banking (Chapter 10). Apart from the administrative sphere the analysis encompasses the consequent cultural change in management. More precisely, the results show that the IAS–IFRS accounting standards that have most strongly affected cooperative banks are IAS 39 (concerning the valuation methods associated with each financial instrument), IAS 32 (concerning the classification of financial instruments and outlining other supplementary information) and IFRS 7 (which completes IAS 32). In terms of costs and benefits, the analysis emphasizes that, for cooperative banking, significant compliance costs would arise from the application of IAS–IFRS to the adaptation of information systems, re-engineering processes and reformulating organizational arrangements. Probably some benefits will flow from greater efficiency and transparency vis-à-vis their member-shareholders-customers, with the possibility of positive effects on the core business. Another source of benefits is economies of scope and of range, as when networked banks frame a common project providing for the pooling of specialized and dedicated resources.

In conclusion, the general results of this book show that the unique feature of the cooperative banking movement that makes it vital and strong is probably the 'cooperation' within each individual bank. Thus, it might become important to enforce, evolve and update the idea of cooperation between the cooperative banks of each country and between cooperative banking systems at the international level.

Index